The Kids' World Almanac of Baseball

THOMAS G. AYLESWORTH

Introduction by Cal Ripken, Jr.

WORLD ALMANAC BOOKS
An Imprint of Funk & Wagnalls Corporation
A K-III Communications Company

Major League Baseball trademarks and copyrights used with permission from Major League Baseball Properties, Inc.

Photos used for illustrations on pages 57 through 91: Babe Ruth, Rollie Fingers, Ken Griffey, Jr., Tris Speaker, and Walter Johnson by permission of the National Baseball Library & Archive, Cooperstown, N.Y.; Roger Maris, Mickey Mantle, and Joe DiMaggio courtesy New York Yankees; Frank Robinson courtesy Baltimore Orioles; Roberto Clemente courtesy Pittsburgh Pirates; Ted Williams and Carl Yastrzemski courtesy Boston Red Sox; Barry Bonds and Juan Marichal courtesy San Francisco Giants; Stan Musial courtesy St. Louis Cardinals; Sandy Koufax by permission of Los Angeles Dodgers; Kirby Puckett courtesy Minnesota Twins; Greg Maddux courtesy Atlanta Braves; Tony Gwynn courtesy San Diego Padres; Nolan Ryan courtesy Texas Rangers; Frank Thomas courtesy Chicago White Sox; Luis Aparicio and Johnny Bench, AP/Wide World; and from NEA/Acme Hank Aaron, Luke Appling, Lou Boudreau, Mordecai Brown, Roy Campanella, Ty Cobb, Dizzy Dean, Bob Feller, Lou Gehrig, Ferguson Jenkins, Harmon Killebrew, Connie Mack, Willie Mays, Satchel Paige, Cal Ripken, Jr., Jackie Robinson, Tom Seaver, Warren Spahn, Casey Stengel, and Cy Young.

Published by Funk & Wagnalls Corporation
A K-III Communications Company

First published in 1990.

Library of Congress Catalog Card Number: 95-62358

ISBN: 0-88687-788-1 (hardcover)
ISBN: 0-88687-787-3 (softcover)

Printed in the United States of America

Cover design: Bill Smith Studio
Interior illustrations: John Lane
Editor, 1996 Edition: Jacqueline Laks Gorman

World Almanac® Books
An Imprint of Funk & Wagnalls Corporation
One International Boulevard
Mahwah, NJ 07495-0017

10 9 8 7 6 5 4 3 2 1

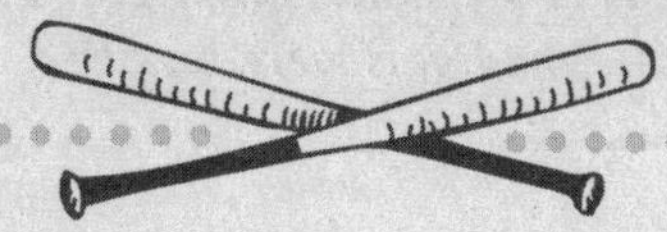

Contents

This book is dedicated to Wrigley Field before the lights were installed.

Thomas G. Aylesworth, who died in 1995, was the author of 87 books. During his tenure as senior editor and editor-in-chief of two major publishing houses, he edited numerous sports books. In addition, he wrote and edited many sports articles, beginning with his role as sports editor of his high school newspaper and his hometown daily newspaper, the Rochester (Indiana) *Sentinel*. Dr. Aylesworth collaborated on autobiographies with Pete Rose, Alex Karras, and Bruce Jenner, was coauthor of *Ivy League Football* and *The Encyclopedia of Baseball Managers*, and was the author of *Science at the Ball Game*, *The Cubs*, and *World Series Baseball*.

Dr. Aylesworth did his undergraduate and masters work at Indiana University, and took his Ph.D. at The Ohio State University. In addition to his career as an author and editor, he was a professor of science, writing, and education.

Dr. Aylesworth wished to gratefully acknowledge the invaluable assistance of Howard Blank, a baseball guru, who kept a sharp eye on the manuscript, and Carolyn Ashe of the National Association of Professional Baseball Leagues in St. Petersburg, Florida, not only the most patient person on the telephone, but surely the most knowledgeable human being on the subject of the minor leagues.

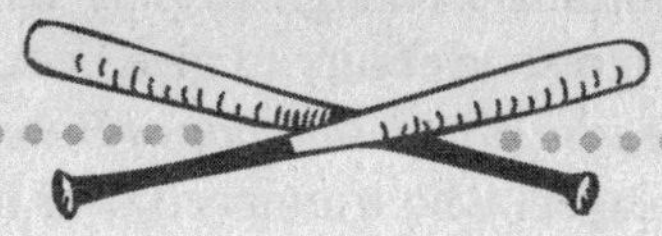

Introduction

Hi! I'm Cal Ripken, Jr. For the past 15 years I have played shortstop for the Baltimore Orioles. Being on a baseball team, at any level, is a great experience. In Little League and in high school I played at neighborhood parks with friends and family. I would often practice with my brother, Bill, who was also on the Orioles, and father, Cal, Sr., who was on the Orioles for many years. Baseball has been, and still is, a lot of fun to play. But along the way I learned a lot about the game and a lot about myself.

There were times when I really struggled with hitting and fielding. Occasionally, I got frustrated. However, I learned that giving up was not the answer. I had to work harder. After practice and games, I would stay and work on my skills. As I began to improve, I realized that hard work and dedication pay off. When my team won, I was happy, but I also learned how to be a gracious loser and compliment my opponents in defeat.

These lessons have helped me off of the baseball diamond as well. When it comes to education, hard work and setting goals are the best ways to improve your skills in reading, writing, and math. With this in mind, my wife, Kelly, and I established in Baltimore the Cal Ripken, Jr., Learning Center to help people learn to read. These people learn to meet challenges and to use their new skills to succeed in life. Kelly and I also donate time and money to other causes; I was proud to receive baseball's Bart Giamatti Caring Award and the Roberto Clemente Award in recognition of community service. I believe that because I am fortunate enough to play baseball and entertain many people, I have a responsibility to give back to the community.

Included in *The Kids' World Almanac of Baseball* are many heart-warming stories of players who triumphed over handicaps, and anecdotes on what made the MVPs and Hall of Famers so great. The sections on records, quotations, and trivia are fun to read aloud. I know how much you will enjoy this book. Read it . . . and allow yourself a chance to laugh, cry, dream, and learn.

—Cal Ripken, Jr.

Calvin "Cal" E. Ripken, Jr., was born in Havre de Grace, Maryland, on August 24, 1960. He made his major league debut for the Orioles in 1981. One year after earning the American League's Rookie of the Year honors, Cal was named the 1983 American League Most Valuable Player while leading the Baltimore Orioles to the World Series championship. In 1989 he won the Bart Giamatti Caring Award for his contributions to the community of Baltimore for his work with disadvantaged children and adults. Cal had arguably his best season in 1991 when he hit .323 with 34 home runs and 114 RBIs, while maintaining a .986 fielding percentage en route to his second American League Most Valuable Player Award. In 1991, Cal became the first player named The Sporting News *Major League Player of the Year while playing on a losing club. He also won it in 1983. At the end of the 1995 season, his career batting average was .276. He has won 2 Gold Gloves at shortstop and has an astonishing consecutive games streak. At the end of the 1995 season, he had played in 2,153 consecutive games, placing him first in major league history, ahead of Lou Gehrig's 2,130. (He broke Gehrig's record on September 6, 1995.) Cal's achievements have received fan recognition by his being chosen for the American League All-Star starting team 12 straight times.*

A Bit of History

The Beginning of Baseball

ABNER DOUBLEDAY DID NOT INVENT BASEBALL

In spite of all the American folklore on the subject, Abner Doubleday did not invent baseball in Cooperstown, New York, in 1839. The National Baseball Hall of Fame and Museum, Inc., is located in that charming little upstate New York town, and the annual Hall of Fame Baseball Game is played at Doubleday Field in Cooperstown, but Doubleday deserves no credit for our national pastime. General Doubleday, a West Pointer who became a Union hero in the Civil War, did live in Cooperstown, but his claim as the inventor of baseball was promoted by a relative. Doubleday neither played baseball nor did he write a single word about it during his long literary career.

EGYPTIANS PLAYED FIRST GAMES WITH BATS AND BALLS

The first recorded instance of batting contests goes back more than 5,000 years, when Egyptian priests engaged in mock contests with bats. The idea was to promote the fertility of crops and of people. After a while balls were introduced into the ceremonies. The balls represented springtime fertility and stood for either the sun or the mummified head of the god Osiris. By 2000 B.C., pictures of women playing ball were included in the carvings on the tomb of Beni Hasan.

In the eighth century A.D., these ball games were brought to Europe by the conquering Moors. The ball games were an immediate hit from Austria to France, where they were turned into Christian ceremonies. At the cathedral of Rheims, France, during the Middle Ages, Easter services ended with a game in which opposing teams either kicked a ball or batted it with a stick.

THE BRITISH CALLED IT STOOLBALL

The English developed the French game into one called stoolball. In this game, the pitcher tried to hit an inverted stool with a ball before the batter could bat the ball away with a stick. Later the game moved out of the churchyard into the countryside. More stools, or bases, were added, and these had to be circled after the ball was hit. The English children's game of rounders was born when a rule was added that a base runner could be put out by being hit by a thrown ball. As early as 1700, posts called "goals" or "bases" were driven into the ground, and the game was named "goal ball" or "base ball." In 1744 a picture book titled *A Pretty Little Pocketbook* was published by John Newbery (for whom the Newbery Medal was named) in London. It contained a rhymed description of the game and a picture captioned "Base-Ball." The book was also published in America several times between 1762 and 1787.

"PLAY AT BASE" IS A HIT IN AMERICA

The new game became popular in America. It was reported that boys "playing at base" in the Wall Street area of Manhattan left their game to join in one of the riots that preceded the American Revolution. And the journal of an American soldier at Valley Forge in 1778 told of the soldiers "playing at base."

In the 19th century, baseball in the United States developed from a children's game into a game for adult men. A how-to book called *The Book of Sports* was published in 1834, and it included illustrations and directions on how to play "base ball."

CARTWRIGHT: THE FATHER OF BASEBALL

Alexander J. Cartwright may well be the man who deserves the credit for creating the game of baseball as we know it. He was a surveyor who played with wealthy New Yorkers, and he was selected to head a committee to form a "base ball" club. On September 23, 1845, the Knickerbocker Base Ball Club was organized, and on September 29 the team adopted the 20 rules that Cartwright suggested to standardize the game.

Up to that time, the most popular form of the game had been "town ball" or "the Massachusetts game," and runners were called out when they were hit by a thrown ball. Cartwright's new rules stated that a man could be tagged out or forced out, but not thrown at. He also ruled that there were to be three strikes to a batter, three outs to end a half-inning, and equal distances between bases. An umpire was to be used, and teams were to wear uniforms.

NEW YORK NINE VS. KNICKERBOCKERS

Most historians think that on June 19, 1846, the first official game under the Cartwright rules was played between the New York Nine and the Knickerbockers at Elysian Fields in Hoboken, New Jersey.

Cartwright was the umpire, and the Knickerbockers were badly beaten by the New York Nine, 23–1. The ball was pitched underhand, and the dimensions of the diamond were still to face important changes. But the game marked the real beginning of organized baseball. Perhaps the first rhubarb in the new age of baseball occurred during the game when J. W. Davis of the Knickerbockers was fined 6¢ for swearing at umpire Cartwright.

On June 3, 1851, the first game between teams from far-apart cities was played at Red House Grounds in New York between the Knickerbockers and the Washington Base Ball Club. By 1858 there were more than 100 amateur (unpaid) clubs in the northern states. On March 10, 1858, the first baseball league was formed, an amateur league called the National Association of Base Ball Players. The first game charging admission was played between the Brooklyn All-Stars and the New York All-Stars on July 20, 1858. It was held at the Fashion Race Course on Long Island, and 1,500 people paid 50¢ apiece. On June 30, 1860, the Brooklyn Excelsiors began the first baseball tour, starting in Albany, New York.

CIVIL WAR HELPS SPREAD THE NEW GAME

As the Civil War began, enthusiasm in the North for the game seemed to have died down a bit, and many clubs folded. But the war helped spread the game to other parts of the country. On Christmas Day in 1862, 40,000 Union troops watched a baseball game between teams from the 165th New York Volunteer Infantry and Duryea's Zouaves, another Union Army unit. This was probably the largest crowd at any sporting event in the 19th century.

The year 1862 was also the year the first stadium designed for baseball was opened. It was the Union Grounds in Brooklyn. But the most significant event of that year was the invention of the curveball by a 14-year-old boy, William Arthur "Candy" Cummings, of Ware,

Massachusetts. He had tossed a clamshell into the ocean and noted its curve. He later duplicated the effect by holding a baseball in a "death grip" and twisting his wrist as he threw an underhand pitch. But he didn't use the curveball until 1867, when he was pitching for the Brooklyn Excelsiors against Harvard College and curved the Harvard players to death.

BASEBALL TURNS PRO

Professionalism had been sneaking into baseball for several years. As early as 1860, James P. Creighton was paid under the table to play for the Excelsiors. In 1862 players for the New York Mutuals were splitting the money received after expenses from their 10¢ admission at the Union Grounds, and the Brooklyn Atlantics were doing the same at their Capitoline Grounds. In 1864, Al Roach of the Philadelphia Athletics was signed as the first openly professional baseball player.

In 1858, Harry Wright, a British-born jeweler's apprentice, was invited to join the Knickerbockers, largely to help the team defeat their archrivals, the Atlantics. In 1869, Wright, who became known as "The Father of Professional Baseball," was asked to head up a professional team in Cincinnati. The Cincinnati Red Stockings became America's first fully professional baseball team. George Wright, Harry's brother, was professional baseball's first star. He batted .519 and hit 59 home runs in 66 games that year and was paid $1,400 for the whole season.

After winning their first game against Great Western, 45–9, the Red Stockings traveled almost 12,000 miles by boat and rail from Massachusetts to California and took on all comers. They played before more than 200,000 people and lost not a game—winning 56 and tying one. Their tour transformed baseball in the United States by taking the game to the hinterlands and proving that professional teams could succeed. In 1870 their winning streak ended at 84 games.

THE FIRST PRO LEAGUE IS FORMED

On March 17, 1871, ten men met at Collier's Cafe on the corner of Broadway and 13th Street in New York City to establish the first professional baseball league. Called the National Association of Professional Base-Ball Players, it included the Philadelphia Athletics, the Chicago White Stockings, the Boston Red Stockings, the Cleveland Forest Citys, the New York Mutuals, the Rockford Forest Citys, the Washington Olympics, the Troy Haymakers, and the Fort Wayne Kekiongas. The president was James N. Kerns, who was the representative of the Athletics. The Kekiongas folded in August and were replaced by the Brooklyn Eckfords, who had stayed out of the league because they didn't like the $10 fee required to join.

The league lasted only five years. The Athletics took the first championship, but the next four were won by the Boston club, which was staffed by Harry Wright and his former Cincinnati stars. The public got bored with Boston's dominance. There was also no way of preventing many players from jumping from team to team. And poor scheduling led to the Red Stockings playing 79 games in 1875 while the new team in Keokuk, Iowa, played only 13. Finally, by 1875, the clubs were riddled with heavy gambling, drunkenness, game throwing, player desertion, contract jumping, and plain rowdiness.

INVENTION OF GLOVE CHANGES THE GAME

In 1875 came an invention that changed the nature of baseball. In the barehanded days of early baseball, the catcher required the nerves of a test pilot. A team might carry only one or two pitchers, but it took a lot of catchers to finish a game. In a game against Harvard in 1875, catcher Bill "Gunner" McGunnigle of the Fall River, Massachusetts, team wore a pair of bricklayer's gloves. Soon, heavily padded gloves for catchers were on the market. An 1890 ad for Spalding Gloves listed four different models priced from $2 to $5. The ad pointed out, "No player subject to sore hands should be without a pair."

THE NATIONAL LEAGUE IS BORN

A Chicago businessman, William Ambrose Hulbert, who also owned the Chicago White Stockings (later the Cubs), was disgusted with the situation in the National Association of Professional Base-Ball Players and decided to do something about it. At a secret meeting in Louisville, Kentucky, in 1876, he convinced representatives from the St. Louis, Cincinnati, and Louisville clubs that his scheme for a new league was sound. On February 2, 1876, he met with representatives of Boston, Hartford, Philadelphia, and New York in a room at the Grand Central Hotel in New York. It is said that Hulbert locked the door while he read the proposed constitution and player contract he had prepared with the aid of Albert Spalding (a star pitcher for Boston who was to become a member of the White Stockings). The Easterners agreed to the formation of a new league, and the National League was born.

The constitution forbade gambling and the sale of alcohol on the grounds, made each team play a full schedule, and required each franchise to represent a city with a population of at least 75,000. Each club paid an entry fee and annual dues of $100 and was required to play 70 games, meeting each opponent ten times, five at home and five away. Admission was set at 50¢ (considered rather high for the time), and the team winning the most games would receive a pennant costing not less than $100.

On April 22, 1876, the first National League game was played in Philadelphia, with Boston winning, 6–5. The final standings in that first year were Chicago, St. Louis, Hartford, Boston, Louisville, New York, Philadelphia, and Cincinnati. Hulbert expelled New York and Philadelphia after the first season for refusing to complete their schedules and fired four Louisville players for gambling. Teams from 23 cities came and went until 1900, when the National League settled into the eight franchises it would maintain until 1962.

ALL-OUT WAR AS A NEW LEAGUE IS FORMED

In 1882 another new league was formed around the nucleus of the Cincinnati club that had been expelled at the end of the 1880 season from the National League for permitting Sunday games and liquor on the grounds. It was the American Association of Base Ball Clubs. The new league played Sunday games and allowed liquor in the stands. More important, the games cost only 25¢. It was all-out war, and in 1883, National League President A. G. Mills brought about a National Agreement, a sort of peace treaty, between the National League and American Association. It granted mutual protection on player contracts and even suggested postseason playoffs between league champions.

In 1884 both major leagues faced a challenge from St. Louis millionaire Henry V. Lucas, whose Union Association lured away many players. But the National League and the American Association raided so many of the Union's players that the new league was reduced from 12 to five franchises by the end of the year, and it folded after a single season.

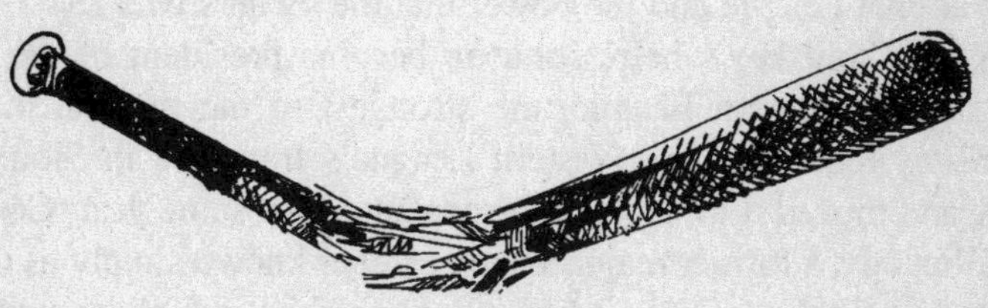

1890: A DISASTER YEAR

In 1890 came a more serious threat by the National Brotherhood of Professional Players, an organization that had been formed in 1885. The players resented such things as salary ceilings, arbitrary fines, and other abuses by the club owners. Eighty percent of the National League's players, including the entire Washington team, left to join the Brotherhood's newly formed Players' League in 1890.

The 1890 season was a disaster for all three leagues. Over the winter the debt-ridden Players' League, represented by former New York Giant John Montgomery Ward, was outmaneuvered and dissolved by the National League. The crippled American Association barely made it through the 1891 season. Then it folded and the National League acquired its Baltimore, St. Louis, Washington, and Louisville clubs, bringing its roster to 12 teams. With only one league in the business, peace had come back to professional baseball.

From 1894 to 1897, the first- and second-place teams in the National League battled for a gaudy trophy called the Temple Cup. No one seemed too interested in the outcome, and, after Baltimore beat Boston, four games to one, in 1897, the whole idea was dropped.

FINALLY, A STRONG RIVAL LEAGUE IS FORMED

In 1900 the American League was formed, an occurrence that led to the two major leagues we know today. Ban Johnson and Charles A. Comiskey, both of whom had played baseball in college (Comiskey also played professionally), had met in 1892 in Cincinnati, where Johnson was a sportswriter for the *Commercial Gazette* and Comiskey was managing the Reds. They soon found out that they both disliked the National League and the power that the owners wielded.

With Comiskey's help, Johnson became president of the newly reorganized Western League, the strongest of the minors, in 1893. Comiskey took over the Western League's franchise in Sioux City, Iowa, and moved it to St. Paul, Minnesota. That same year, Cornelius McGilicuddy, a former major league catcher known simply as Connie Mack, bought the league's Milwaukee franchise, which he eventually moved to Philadelphia.

The league got the financial backing of coal magnate Charles Somers, and in October 1899, Johnson renamed his league the American League. It was still a minor league operation. But in 1900 the National League cut its roster to eight clubs (from 12 in 1895), and Johnson picked up the Cleveland franchise.

THE AMERICAN LEAGUE GOES MAJOR

Johnson announced that the American League would be a major league in 1901 and withdrew from the minor league National Agreement. Johnson placed franchises in three National League cities—Chicago, Philadelphia, and Boston—plus the American League franchises in Detroit, Cleveland, Baltimore, Washington, and Milwaukee. In 1902, Milwaukee was replaced by St. Louis (because St. Louis was the largest Midwestern city other than Chicago that didn't ban Sunday baseball), and in 1903, Baltimore was replaced by New York.

The order of finish in the American League in 1901, its first major league year, was Chicago, Boston, Detroit, Philadelphia, Baltimore, Washington, Cleveland, and Milwaukee. In 1902 the National League was trying its best to ignore the upstarts, but that year the Americans actually outdrew the Nationals in attendance, by 2,200,000 to 1,682,000. Even more embarrassing was the fact that the American

League teams outdrew the National League teams in the four cities to have teams in both leagues—Boston, Chicago, Philadelphia, and St. Louis.

Early in 1903 a National Commission was formed to oversee major league baseball. The commission consisted of Harry C. Pulliam and Ban Johnson, the presidents of the National and American leagues, respectively; commissioner-at-large August Herrmann, the owner of the Cincinnati ball club; and a nonvoting secretary. The American League was recognized as a major league, the way was clear for a World Series between the two leagues, and professional baseball entered the modern era.

The Longest, Shortest, and Most Memorable

Baseball has always been a game of statistics. It seems that true baseball fans are never without a pencil and a piece of paper to keep score, figure out batting averages, or write down trivia. They keep track of all kinds of records, and when a batter breaks Hank Aaron's top performance of 2,297 career RBIs, it will go into the record books. Here are some of the many records that have been set by the men who have made a living playing a kid's game.

The Oldest and the Youngest

Oldest Rookie Manager: On June 18, 1960, the San Francisco Giants fired manager Billy Rigney and hired Tom Sheehan to pilot the club. Sheehan was born March 31, 1894, in Grand Ridge, Illinois, and had been a right-handed pitcher for six years (1915–1916, 1921, 1924–1926) in the major leagues. At 66 years, two months, and 18 days, he was the oldest man to be named a first-time manager.

Oldest Home Run Hitter: In the first Old-timers' All-Star Classic, played on July 19, 1982, at Washington's RFK Stadium before 29,000 fans, the American League Old-timers beat the National League Old-timers, 7–2. Luke Appling, the Hall of Fame shortstop for the Chicago White Sox (1930–1950), hit a home run over the left field fence off pitcher Warren Spahn. Appling was 73 years old.

Oldest Regular Season Hitter: Saturnino Orestes Armas Arrieta "Minnie" Minoso, who played the outfield for various clubs (1949, 1951–1964, 1976, 1980), got his last major league hit as the designated hitter for the Chicago White Sox on September 12, 1976. The hit was a single, and he was 53 years old.

Oldest Shutout Pitcher: On August 6, 1952, Hall of Fame pitcher Leroy Robert "Satchel" Paige, at the age of 46, pitched a complete game shutout for the St. Louis Browns, beating the Detroit Tigers, 1–0, in 12 innings.

Oldest Major League Player: On September 25, 1965, the same Satchel Paige, aged 59, took the mound for the Kansas City Athletics and pitched three scoreless innings against the Red Sox. He gave up only one hit—to Carl Yastrzemski.

Oldest Batting Leader: Ted Williams played his whole career in the outfield for the Boston Red Sox (1939–1942, 1946–1960) before being elected to the Hall of Fame. In 1958, at age 40, he won the American League batting title with a .328 average.

Youngest Rookie Manager: Roger Peckinpaugh played shortstop in the major leagues for four teams for 17 years. On September 16, 1914, at the tender age of 23, he was appointed manager of the New York Yankees.

Youngest Major League Player: On June 10, 1944, Joe Nuxhall found himself on the mound for the Cincinnati Reds in a game against the St. Louis Cardinals. He was 15 years, ten months, and 11 days old that day. Nuxhall had been signed by the Reds during World War II, when baseball talent was hard to find since so many players were in the service. A left-hander, Nuxhall pitched two-thirds of an inning, gave up five runs, and was part of an 18–0 shellacking by the Cards. He came back from the military and the minors in 1952 and pitched for 15 successful years for the Reds and Kansas City Athletics.

Youngest Home Run Hitter: Tommy "Buckshot" Brown played primarily shortstop for the Brooklyn Dodgers (1944–1945, 1947– 1951), Philadelphia Phillies (1951–1952), and Chicago Cubs (1952–1953). On August 20, 1945, at the age of 17 years, eight months, and 14 days, he hit a home run in Ebbets Field in Brooklyn against Preacher Roe of the Pittsburgh Pirates.

Youngest World Series Player: In his first year with the New York Giants, Hall of Fame third baseman/outfielder Freddie Lindstrom appeared in the 1924 World Series at the age of 18 years, ten months, and 13 days. He did amazingly well, batting .333 with ten hits and went on to a fine 13-year career, retiring to coach the Northwestern University baseball team.

Youngest Cy Young Winner: In 1985, Dwight Gooden of the New York Mets, at age 20, became the youngest winner of the Cy Young Award.

The Longest and the Shortest

Longest Consecutive Game Playing Streak: Shortstop Cal Ripken, Jr., who has played for the Baltimore Orioles since 1981, had played in 2,153 consecutive games through the end of the 1995 season—a streak that began in 1982. Until September 6, 1995, when Ripken played in his 2,131st consecutive game, the record had belonged to New York Yankees superstar and Hall of Famer Lou Gehrig, who played first base for the club for 17 years (1923–1939) and from 1925 to 1939 played in 2,130 consecutive games.

Longest Career: Nolan Ryan, who pitched for four teams in 27 years—the Mets (1966, 1968–1971), Angels (1972–1979), Astros (1980–1988), and Rangers (1989–1993)—had the longest career in baseball history.

Longest Home Run: The longest measured major league home run was hit by New York Yankees outfielder Mickey Mantle on September 10, 1960. It was a 643-foot shot in Detroit's Briggs Stadium. On April 17, 1953, Mantle cleared the bleachers at Griffith Stadium in Washington with a 565-foot blast off Chuck Stobbs of the Senators in the fifth inning of the Yankees' 7–3 victory. Other stellar homers were hit by Dick Allen, the Philadelphia Phillies third baseman (529 feet in Philadelphia's Connie Mack Stadium on May 29, 1965) and Frank Robinson, the Baltimore Orioles outfielder (the only player to hit a ball out of Baltimore's Memorial Stadium—541 feet—on May 8, 1966).

Longest Scoreless Game: On July 16, 1909, pitcher Ed Summers of the Detroit Tigers allowed seven hits and pitched all 18 innings of a 0–0 tie with the Washington Senators, the longest scoreless game in American League history.

Longest Game: On May 1, 1920, the Boston Braves tied the Brooklyn Dodgers, 1–1, in the sixth inning. There were 20½ scoreless innings until the game was called after 26. The longest game that ended in a decision, and the longest in elapsed time, was played on May 9, 1984, when the Chicago White Sox and Milwaukee Brewers played eight hours and six minutes before the White Sox won, 7–6, in the 25th inning.

Longest Doubleheader of Two Nine-Inning Games: On May 24, 1995, the Chicago White Sox and Texas Rangers played two nine-inning games that lasted a total of seven hours and 39 minutes. There was a combined total of 37 runs, 49 hits, 32 walks, 45 men left on base, eight wild pitches, and 739 pitches (including 321 called balls).

Shortest Major League Player: Eddie Gaedel, a 3'7", 65-pound midget, appeared at the plate one time for the St. Louis Browns on August 19, 1951. He walked.

Shortest Major League Game: On September 28, 1919, the New York Giants beat the Philadelphia Phillies 6–1, in a game that lasted only 51 minutes.

Shortest American League Game: On August 21, 1926, Ted Lyons of the Chicago White Sox pitched a no-hitter against the Boston Red Sox in Boston. The score was 6–0, and the game took only one hour and seven minutes.

Team Efforts

Most Runs Scored in a Season: The Boston Beaneaters (later the Braves) scored 1,222 runs in 132 games in 1894.

Most Runs Scored in the First Inning: In the modern era in the National League, the Brooklyn Dodgers scored 15 runs against the Cincinnati Reds in the first inning on May 21, 1952, going on to win, 19–1. In the American League, the Cleveland Indians scored 14 runs in the first inning against the Philadelphia Athletics on September 21, 1950, and went on to win, 21–2.

Most Runs Scored in an Inning: On September 6, 1883, the Chicago White Stockings (later the Cubs) scored 18 runs in one inning. The modern record is 17, set by the Red Sox on June 18, 1953.

Most Runs Scored Before the First Out: On May 3, 1911, the New York Giants scored ten runs against the St. Louis Cardinals before the first man was out.

Most Runs Scored by One Team in a Game: On June 29, 1897, the Chicago Cubs scored 36 runs in one game.

Most Runs Scored in a Doubleheader: On August 14, 1937, the Detroit Tigers scored 36 runs against the St. Louis Browns in the two games of a doubleheader.

Most Runs Scored in a Doubleheader Shutout: The Detroit Tigers scored 26 runs and swept the St. Louis Browns, 12–0 and 14–0, on September 22, 1936.

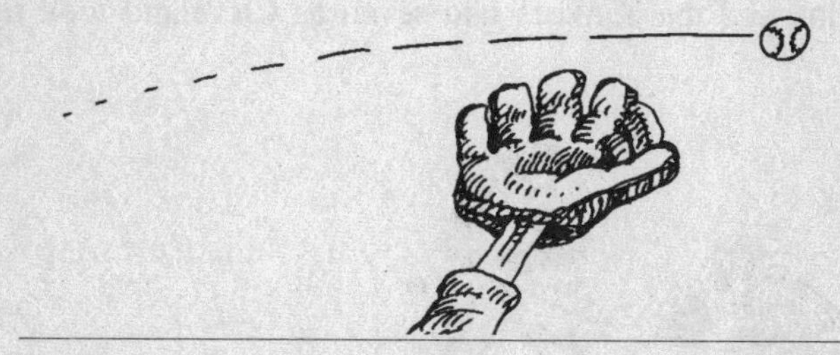

Most Runs Scored by Two Teams on Opening Day: On April 19, 1900, the Philadelphia Phillies beat the Boston Beaneaters (later the Braves), 19–17, in ten innings. Boston had scored nine runs in the ninth inning to tie the score.

Most Runs Scored by a Losing Team: The Philadelphia Phillies scored 23 runs on August 25, 1922, but lost to the Chicago Cubs, who scored 26.

Most Home Runs in a Season: The New York Yankees hit 240 home runs in 1961.

Most Home Runs in a Game: The Milwaukee Braves hit eight home runs in the first game of a doubleheader on August 30, 1953. They beat the Pittsburgh Pirates, 19–4.

Most Home Runs by Two Teams in a Game: On May 28, 1995, the Chicago White Sox beat the Detroit Tigers, 14–12, as the two teams combined for 12 home runs. The Tigers had seven and the Sox had five.

Most Home Runs in an Inning: The Philadelphia Phillies hit five homers off the Cincinnati Reds in the eighth inning of a game on June 2, 1949.

Most Long Hits in a Game: On June 8, 1950, the Boston Red Sox had 17 extra-base hits against the St. Louis Browns—nine doubles, one triple, and seven home runs. The Sox won the game, 29–4, and also set a record for most total bases with 60.

Most Doubles Hit by Two Teams: The Cleveland Indians and the New York Yankees combined to hit 16 doubles on July 21, 1921. The Indians had nine and the Yankees had seven as Cleveland took the game, 17–8.

Most Hits in a Game: The Philadelphia Phillies set the National League record of 36 hits on August 17, 1894. In the modern era, the Cleveland Indians collected 33 hits against the Philadelphia Athletics on July 10, 1932, to take the major league record.

Most Singles Given Up: On April 28, 1901, Cleveland Indians pitchers gave up 23 singles as the Chicago White Sox beat them, 13–1.

Highest Team Batting Average: In the 1894 season, the Philadelphia Phillies had a team batting average of .349.

Fewest Shutouts in a Season: In 1932 the New York Yankees became the only team not to be shut out during a single season.

Earliest Date of Clinching a Pennant: In 1942 the New York Yankees clinched the American League pennant on September 4.

Largest Winning Margin: The Cleveland Indians ended the 1995 season 30 games ahead of second-place Kansas City in the American League's Central Division.

Most Batters Used by Two Teams in a Game: On September 11, 1974, the St. Louis Cardinals beat the New York Mets in a 25-inning game that lasted seven hours and four minutes. A record 202 at bats were recorded. Mets Felix Millan and John Milner had 12 appearances apiece.

Most Pinch Hitters by Two Teams in a Game: On May 2, 1956, the New York Giants and Chicago Cubs each used seven pinch hitters in a 17-inning game for a total of 14.

Most Pinch Hitters Used by One Team in an Inning: The San Francisco Giants sent six pinch hitters to the plate in one inning in a game played on May 5, 1958.

Most Shutouts in a Season: The Chicago Cubs and Chicago White Sox share the record of 32 shutouts pitched in a single season. The Sox did it in 1906 and the Cubs did it in 1909.

Biggest Shutout Score in a Night Game: On the night of August 3, 1961, the Pittsburgh Pirates beat the St. Louis Cardinals, 19–0.

Best Season Winning Record: The 1906 Chicago Cubs won 116 games and lost only 36.

Longest Winning Streak: In 1916 the New York Giants won 26 games in a row—a streak that began on September 7, when they beat the Brooklyn Dodgers, 4–1.

Longest Losing Streak: In 1961 the Philadelphia Phillies lost 23 games in a row—a streak that ended when they beat the Milwaukee Braves, 7–4, on August 20. The only bright spot in the streak for the Phillies was when they beat the Minnesota Twins in an exhibition game that didn't count.

Longest Losing Streak at the Beginning of the Season: The 1988 Baltimore Orioles lost the first 21 games of the season, finally beating the Chicago White Sox, 9–0, on April 28.

Most Doubleheaders in Succession: On September 4, 1928, the Boston Braves were forced to play a string of nine straight doubleheaders.

Most Doubleheader Sweeps in a Row: On September 4, 1906, the New York Highlanders (later the Yankees) beat the Boston Red Sox twice, 7–0 and 1–0. In doing so, they set a record by winning five straight doubleheaders.

Largest Crowd at a Day Doubleheader: On September 12, 1954, 84,587 fans saw the Cleveland Indians play a doubleheader with the New York Yankees in Cleveland.

Largest Crowd at a Night Game: On August 20, 1948, 78,382 fans saw the Cleveland Indians play the Chicago White Sox in Cleveland.

Smallest Major League Crowd: On the last day of the 1881 season in Troy, New York, only 12 die-hard fans showed up to see their Haymakers play the Chicago White Stockings (later the Cubs).

Largest World Series Crowd: At the fifth game of the 1959 World Series in the Los Angeles Memorial Coliseum on October 6, 92,706 fans watched the Chicago White Sox beat the Los Angeles Dodgers, 1–0.

Most Strikeouts in a Season: Houston Astros pitchers struck out 1,221 opponents in 1969.

Most Double Plays in a Season: The 1949 Philadelphia Athletics turned in 217 double plays.

Most Double Plays in a World Series: The 1955 World Series winners, the Brooklyn Dodgers, pulled off 12 double plays against the New York Yankees in seven games.

Fewest Errors in a Season: The 1964 Baltimore Orioles committed only 95 errors in 162 games.

Most Errorless Games in a Season: The 1964 New York Yankees played 91 games without committing an error.

Fewest Errors in a World Series: The 1937 New York Yankees committed no errors in a five-game Series. The 1966 Baltimore Orioles went errorless in a four-game Series.

Most Errors in a Game: The Detroit Tigers committed 12 errors in a 1901 game against the Chicago White Sox. The White Sox did the same in a 1903 game against the Tigers.

Most Errors by Two Teams in a Game: The Chicago White Sox and the Detroit Tigers combined for 18 errors in a 1903 game.

Most Walks in an Inning: In 1949 an assortment of New York Yankees pitchers gave up 11 walks in a single inning.

Most Men Left on Base by One Team: On September 8, 1905, the Pittsburgh Pirates stranded 18 runners in an 8–3 nine-inning loss to the Cincinnati Reds.

Most Men Left on Base by Two Teams: In 1988 the Cardinals and Phillies stranded 38 men in a 14-inning game. St. Louis, which won the game, 3–2, left 20 men on and Philadelphia left 18.

Heavy Hitters

Longest Consecutive Game Hitting Streak: On May 15, 1941, Joe DiMaggio, who played the outfield for the New York Yankees (1936–1942, 1946–1951), got a hit. Starting that day, he hit safely in 56 consecutive games until July 17, when Cleveland Indians pitchers Al Smith and Jim Bagby shut him out. In the National League, Pete Rose, who played several positions for the Cincinnati Reds (1963–1978), Philadelphia Phillies (1979–1983), Montreal Expos (1984), and Reds again (1984–1986), got at least one hit in 44 straight games before going 0 for 4 on August 1, 1978, against Atlanta pitchers Larry McWilliams and Gene Garber. (Baltimore's Wee Willie Keeler also hit in 44 straight games in 1897.)

Longest Rookie Consecutive Game Hitting Streak: San Diego Padres catcher Benito Santiago had at least one hit in 34 consecutive games in his rookie year—1987.

Highest Lifetime Batting Average: Ty Cobb, outfielder for the Detroit Tigers (1905–1926) and Philadelphia Athletics (1927–1928), had 4,191 hits in 11,429 at bats for a .367 lifetime batting average.

Highest Single Season Batting Average: In 1894 outfielder Hugh Duffy of the Boston Beaneaters (later the Braves) had 236 hits in 539 at bats for a .438 batting average. In the modern era, second baseman Rogers Hornsby of the St. Louis Cardinals had 227 hits in 536 at bats for a .424 average in 1924.

Most Career Hits: Pete Rose had a career hit production of 4,256 in regular-season games, plus 80 more in postseason play.

Most Career Singles: Pete Rose had 3,215 singles in his playing career.

Most Hits in a Season: In 1920, St. Louis Browns first baseman George Sisler had 257 hits. This included 49 doubles, 18 triples, and 19 home runs.

Most Career Runs Scored: Ty Cobb scored 2,245 runs in his 24-year career.

Most Career Runs Batted In: Hank Aaron, who played the outfield for the Braves in Milwaukee and Atlanta (1954–1974) and the Milwaukee Brewers (1975–1976), batted in 2,297 runs in his 23-year career.

Most Hits in Succession: San Francisco Giants infielder Mike Benjamin had 14 successive hits in three games in 1995.

Most Hits in a Game: Pittsburgh Pirates second baseman Rennie Stennett had seven hits in a game played on September 16, 1975.

Most Sacrifice Hits in a Game: Brooklyn Dodgers first baseman Jake Daubert had four sacrifice hits in one game on August 15, 1914.

Most Consecutive Pinch Hits: Dave Philley, the Philadelphia Phillies outfielder, had eight consecutive pinch hits in 1958 and stretched his record to nine by getting another hit in his first time pinch-hitting in the 1959 season.

Most Hits in the World Series: New York Yankees catcher Yogi Berra had 71 World Series hits in his career, including ten doubles and 12 home runs.

Highest Batting Average in a Single World Series: Billy Hatcher of the Cincinnati Reds batted .750 in the 1990 World Series against the Oakland A's, with nine hits in 12 at bats.

Highest Career Batting Average in the World Series: Two players are tied with .418—Pepper Martin of the St. Louis Cardinals (in 1928, 1931, and 1934), and Paul Molitor of the Milwaukee Brewers (1982) and Toronto Blue Jays (1993).

Most World Series Pinch Hits: The record for most Series pinch hits is three. Seven men are tied for this mark:

Ken Boswell (second base, Mets), 3 for 3 in 1969, 1973
Bobby Brown (third base, Yankees), 3 for 6 in 1947, 1949–1951
Bob Cerv (outfield, Yankees), 3 for 3 in 1955–1956, 1960
Carl Furillo (outfield, Dodgers), 3 for 7 in 1947, 1949, 1952–1953, 1955–1956, 1959
Gonzalo Marquez (first base, A's), 3 for 5 in 1972
Johnny Mize (first base, Yankees), 3 for 8 in 1949–1953
Ken O'Dea (catcher, Cubs and Cardinals), 3 for 8 in 1935, 1938, 1942–1944

Highest Career Slugging Average: Babe Ruth of the Yankees had a slugging average of .690 in his 22-year career.

Highest Slugging Average in a Season: Babe Ruth had a slugging percentage of .847 in the 1920 season.

Highest World Series Slugging Average: Reggie Jackson, who played the outfield for the Kansas City and Oakland Athletics (1967–1975), Baltimore Orioles (1976), New York Yankees (1977–1981), California Angels (1982–1986), and A's again (1987), had a .755 slugging average in five World Series.

Home Run Hitters

Most Career Home Runs: Hank Aaron of the Milwaukee/Atlanta Braves and Milwaukee Brewers hit 755 home runs in his career. He tied Babe Ruth's total of 714 on April 4, 1974, and broke it four days later off Dodgers pitcher Al Downing in Atlanta.

Most Home Runs in a Season: Outfielder Roger Maris of the New York Yankees hit 61 home runs in the 1961 season. He hit another homer in the World Series against the Cincinnati Reds that same year.

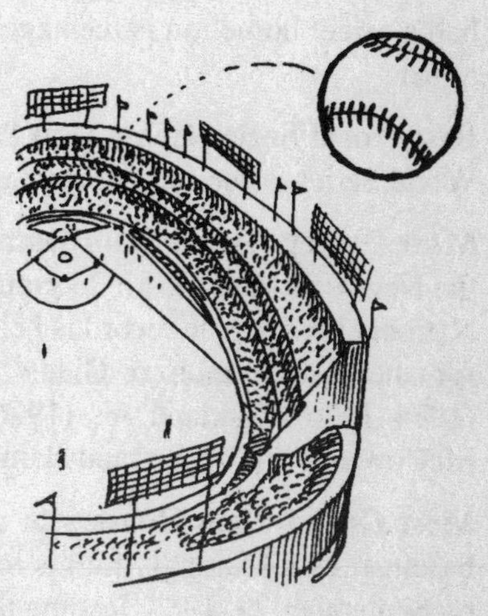

Most Home Runs by a Rookie: Mark McGwire, the first baseman for the Oakland A's, hit 49 home runs in 1987—his first full year in the majors.

Most Career Pinch Hit Home Runs: On August 5, 1984, designated hitter Cliff Johnson of the Toronto Blue Jays hit his 19th career pinch hit homer as Toronto beat the Orioles, 4–3, at Baltimore's Memorial Stadium.

Most Pinch Hit Home Runs in a Season: Outfielder Johnny Frederick of the Brooklyn Dodgers hit six pinch hit homers in the 1932 season. His sixth homer was hit September 12 in the ninth inning to give Brooklyn a 4–3 triumph over the Chicago Cubs at Ebbets Field.

Most Home Runs in a Season by a Pitcher: On September 5, 1955, right-handed pitcher Don Newcombe of the Brooklyn Dodgers hit his seventh home run of the season as he beat the Philadelphia Phillies, 11–4.

Most Career Home Runs by a Pitcher: Right-hander Wes Ferrell, who pitched for the Indians (1927–1933), Red Sox (1934–1937),

Senators (1937–1938), Yankees (1938–1939), Dodgers (1940), and Braves (1941), hit 38 homers in his 15-year career.

Most Home Runs in Four Consecutive Games: Ralph Kiner, the Pittsburgh Pirates outfielder (1947), and Don Mattingly, the New York Yankees first baseman (1987), are tied with eight round-trippers in four straight games.

Best Home Run Percentage: Babe Ruth of the New York Yankees had a career home run percentage of 8.5, or 8.5 homers per 100 times at bat.

Best World Series Home Run Percentage: Babe Ruth had an 11.6 World Series home run percentage.

Most Career Grand Slam Homers: First baseman Lou Gehrig of the New York Yankees hit 23 grand slams in his 17-year career. In the National League, the record is held by Willie McCovey, first baseman for the San Francisco Giants (1959–1973), San Diego Padres (1974–1976), Oakland A's (1976), and Giants again (1977–1980). McCovey hit his 18th grand slam homer on August 1, 1977.

Most Grand Slam Homers in a Season: New York Yankees first baseman Don Mattingly hit his record sixth grand slam of the season on September 29, 1987, leading the Yankees to a 6–0 victory over the Boston Red Sox.

Most World Series Home Runs: Mickey Mantle of the New York Yankees hit 18 homers in 12 World Series.

Total, Extra, and Stolen Bases

Most Career Total Bases: Hank Aaron of the Milwaukee/Atlanta Braves and Milwaukee Brewers had 6,856 total bases in his 23-year career.

Most Total Bases in a Game: First baseman Joe Adcock, who played for the Cincinnati Reds (1950–1952), Milwaukee Braves (1953–1962), Cleveland Indians (1963), and Los Angeles/California Angels (1964–1966), hit for 18 total bases on July 31, 1954. He had four home runs and one double.

Most Career Extra-Base Hits: Hank Aaron had 1,477 extra-base hits in his career.

Most Extra-Base Hits in a Season: Babe Ruth had 119 extra-base hits in 1921.

Most Career Stolen Bases: Rickey Henderson, who has played the outfield for the Oakland A's (1979–1984), New York Yankees (1985–1989), A's again (1990–1992), Toronto Blue Jays (1993), and A's yet again (1994–), had accumulated 1,149 regular-season stolen bases at the end of the 1995 season.

Most Stolen Bases in a Season: Rickey Henderson stole 130 bases for the A's in 1982.

Most World Series Stolen Bases: Two players are tied for this record with 14. Eddie Collins, the second baseman for the Philadelphia Athletics (1906–1914), Chicago White Sox (1915–1926), and Athletics again (1927–1930), in six Series, and Lou Brock, the outfielder for the Chicago Cubs (1961–1964) and St. Louis Cardinals (1964–1979), in three Series.

Most Stolen Bases by One Team in an Inning: The 1915 Washington Senators and the 1919 Philadelphia Phillies had eight steals in one inning.

Most Stolen Bases in a Game: The modern-day record is six, set by Eddie Collins of the Philadelphia Athletics in 1912 and Otis Nixon of the Atlanta Braves in 1991.

Most Consecutive Successful Steals: Outfielder Vince Coleman of the St. Louis Cardinals stole 50 straight bases without being caught in 1989–1990.

RBIs, Doubles, and Triples

Most Runs Batted In in a Game: Cardinals first baseman Jim Bottomley had six hits—including two home runs—in six plate appearances on September 16, 1924. He drove in a record 12 runs as the Cardinals beat the Dodgers, 17–3. Mark Whiten of the Cardinals tied the record on September 7, 1993.

Most Runs Batted In in a Season: In 1930, Hack Wilson, the Chicago Cubs outfielder, drove in 190 runs.

Most Career RBIs: Hank Aaron of the Milwaukee/Atlanta Braves and Milwaukee Brewers knocked in 2,297 runs in his 23-year career.

Most Consecutive Runs Batted In: The record is eight, recorded on two straight grand slam home runs, and is held by two players. Jim Gentile, the Baltimore Orioles first baseman, did it on May 9, 1961, and on June 24, 1968, Jim Northrup, the Detroit Tigers outfielder, did the same.

Most Consecutive Doubles: Ernie Lombardi, the Cincinnati Reds catcher, hit four consecutive doubles in four consecutive innings off four consecutive Philadelphia Phillies pitchers on May 8, 1935.

Most Career Doubles: Tris Speaker, who played the outfield for the Boston Red Sox (1907–1915), Cleveland Indians (1916–1926), Washington Senators (1927), and Philadelphia Athletics (1928), hit 793 doubles in his 22-year career.

Most Doubles in a Season: Outfielder Earl Webb of the Boston Red Sox recorded 67 doubles in 1931.

Most World Series Doubles: New York Yankees catcher Yogi Berra had ten doubles in 14 World Series. Frankie Frisch, who played second base for the New York Giants (1919–1926) and St. Louis Cardinals (1927–1937), had ten doubles in eight World Series.

Most Doubles in a Doubleheader: On August 27, 1948, Philadelphia Athletics third baseman Hank Majeski hit six doubles in a doubleheader.

Most Career Triples: Sam Crawford, who played the outfield for the Cincinnati Reds (1899–1902) and Detroit Tigers (1903–1917), had 312 triples in his 19-year career.

Most Triples in a Season: Outfielder Owen Wilson of the Pittsburgh Pirates recorded 36 triples in 1912.

Most World Series Triples: Tris Speaker hit four triples in three World Series.

The Pitchers

Most Games Won: Cy Young, the right-handed pitcher for the Cleveland Spiders (1890–1898), St. Louis Cardinals (1899–1900), Boston Red Sox (1901–1908), Cleveland Naps (later the Indians,

1909–1911), and Boston Pilgrims (later the Braves, 1911), won 511 games in his 22-year career.

Most Games Lost: While winning those 511 games, Cy Young also lost 316 games in his career.

Most Innings Pitched: Cy Young pitched 7,356 innings in his career.

Most Complete Games: Cy Young pitched 750 complete games in his career.

Most Games Pitched: Hoyt Wilhelm, the right-handed pitcher for the New York Giants (1952–1956), St. Louis Cardinals (1957), Cleveland Indians (1957–1958), Baltimore Orioles (1958–1962), Chicago White Sox (1963–1968), California Angels (1969), Atlanta Braves (1969–1970), Chicago Cubs (1970), Braves again (1971), and Los Angeles Dodgers (1971–1972), pitched in 1,070 games in his 21-year career.

Most Pitching Appearances in a Season: Right-hander Mike Marshall, a relief pitcher for the Los Angeles Dodgers, appeared in 106 games in 1974.

Most Complete Games in a Season: Right-hander Will White of the Cincinnati Reds started 76 games in 1879 and completed 75 of them. The modern-day record is 48, set by Jack Chesbro of the New York Yankees in 1904.

Most Games Won in a Season: Charles "Old Hoss" Radbourn, a right-hander, won 60 games for the Providence Grays in 1884. In the modern era, Jack Chesbro of the Yankees won 41 games in 1904.

Most Consecutive Games Won: New York Giants left-hander Carl Hubbell won 24 straight games—16 in 1936 followed by eight in 1937.

Most Consecutive Games Lost: Mets pitcher Anthony Young lost 27 straight games from April 1992 to July 1993.

Most Consecutive Rookie Games Won: On July 25, 1939, right-hander Atley Donald of the New York Yankees beat the St. Louis Browns, 5–1, for his 12th consecutive win in his first full year of play.

Most Career Shutouts: Walter Johnson of the Washington Senators (1907–1927) pitched 110 shutouts in his 21-year career.

Most Shutouts in a Season: George Bradley of St. Louis pitched 16 shutouts in 1876. Grover Cleveland Alexander of the Philadelphia Phillies did the same in 1916.

Most Consecutive Shutouts: Don Drysdale, the Los Angeles Dodgers right-hander, pitched six straight shutouts in 1968.

Most Consecutive Scoreless Innings: Right-hander Orel Hershiser of the Dodgers pitched 59 straight scoreless innings in 1988, and he extended his streak to 67 in the League Championship Series against the Mets.

Most Dependable Pitcher: On August 13, 1906, Chicago Cubs right-hander Jack Taylor was knocked out in the third inning by the Brooklyn Superbas (later the Dodgers), ending a streak of 187 complete games and 15 relief games that Taylor had finished without relief help.

Most Career Strikeouts: Right-hander Nolan Ryan, who played for the New York Mets (1966, 1968–1971), California Angels (1972–1979), Houston Astros (1980–1988), and Texas Rangers (1989–1993), struck out 5,714 opposing batters in his 27-year career.

Most Strikeouts in a Season: The record is 513 by left-hander Matt Kilroy of the Baltimore Orioles in 1886, but that was at a time when the pitcher's mound was only 50 feet from the plate. The modern record is 383, set by Nolan Ryan in 1973 when he was with the Angels.

Most Strikeouts in a Nine-Inning Game: On April 29, 1986, right-handed pitcher Roger Clemens of the Boston Red Sox struck out 20 Seattle Mariners as the Sox won the game, 3–1.

Most Strikeouts in an Extra-Inning Game: Right-hander Tom Cheney of the Washington Senators fanned 21 Baltimore Orioles in a 16-inning game on September 12, 1962, which he won, 2–1.

Most Rookie Strikeouts in a Game: Montreal Expos right-hander Bill Gullickson struck out 18 batters, September 10, 1980, in a 4-2 victory over the Chicago Cubs.

Most Consecutive Strikeouts: Tom Seaver of the New York Mets struck out ten men in a row on April 22, 1970.

Most Career Bases on Balls: Nolan Ryan holds the record of allowing 2,795 walks.

Most Bases on Balls in a Season: Amos Rusie of the New York Giants walked 218 in 1893. The modern record is 208, set by Bob Feller of the Cleveland Indians in 1938.

Most Bases on Balls in a Shutout: Yankees pitcher Lefty Gomez walked 11 St. Louis Browns batters on August 1, 1941, in a 9–0 victory.

Most Career Home Runs Allowed: Right-hander Robin Roberts, who pitched for 19 years for the Phillies (1948–1961), Orioles (1962–1965), Astros (1965–1966), and Cubs (1966), gave up 505 home runs.

Lowest Earned Run Average in a Season: In 1914, Boston Red Sox left-hander Hubert "Dutch" Leonard registered a 1.01 ERA in 36 games.

Fewest Pitches in a Nine-Inning Game: Right-hander Charles "Red" Barrett of the Boston Braves threw only 58 pitches on August 10, 1944, to beat the Cincinnati Reds, 2–0.

Most Home Runs Allowed in a Season: Minnesota Twins right-hander Bert Blyleven allowed 50 round-trippers in 1986.

Most Career Saves: As of the end of the 1995 season, right-handed relief pitcher Lee Smith, who has pitched for the Chicago Cubs

(1980–1987), Boston Red Sox (1988–1990), St. Louis Cardinals (1990–1993), New York Yankees (1993), Baltimore Orioles (1994), and California Angels (1995–), had registered 471 regular-season saves.

Most Saves in a Season: Bobby Thigpen, the White Sox right-hander, had 57 in 1990.

Most Saves in a Season by a Single Pitching Staff: The Chicago White Sox bullpen registered 68 saves in 1990.

Most Hits Given Up by a Winning Pitcher: On July 10, 1932, the Philadelphia Athletics defeated the Cleveland Indians, 18–17, in an 18-inning game. Right-hander Eddie Rommel of the Athletics pitched the last 17 innings, and, although he gave up 29 hits and 14 runs, he won the game.

Most Relief Pitchers Used in an Inning: On July 22, 1967, the Atlanta Braves used five pitchers in one inning against the Cardinals.

Longest Relief Appearance: On June 17, 1915, Chicago Cubs right-hander Zip Zabel was called into a game against the Brooklyn Dodgers with two out in the first inning. He won, 4–3, in the 19th after 18$^1/_3$ innings of relief.

Best Relief Appearance: On June 23, 1917, right-hander Ernie Shore of the Boston Red Sox relieved lefty Babe Ruth in the first inning of a game against the Washington Senators. No one was out and there was a man on first. The base runner was cut down stealing and Shore threw a perfect game, retiring all 26 batters he faced. He won the game, 4–0.

Most Career Relief Wins: Right-hander Hoyt Wilhelm, who pitched for the New York Giants (1952–1956), St. Louis Cardinals (1957), Cleveland Indians (1957–1958), Baltimore Orioles (1958–1962),

Chicago White Sox (1963–1968), California Angels (1969), Atlanta Braves (1969–1970), Chicago Cubs (1970), Braves again (1971), and Los Angeles Dodgers (1971–1972), won 123 games in relief in his 21-year career.

Most Pitchers Used by a Club in a Nine-Inning Game: The St. Louis Cardinals used nine pitchers against the Chicago Cubs on October 2, 1949.

Most No-Hit Games: The record is seven, recorded by Nolan Ryan. He threw four when he was with the Angels (two in 1973, one in 1974, and one in 1975), one with the Astros (in 1981), and two with the Rangers (in 1990 and 1991).

The Only Double No-Hit Game: Right-hander Fred Toney of the Cincinnati Reds and left-hander Jim "Hippo" Vaughn of the Chicago Cubs each pitched a no-hitter for nine innings against each other on May 2, 1917. Each pitcher issued only two walks in the first nine innings. Then, in the tenth, the Reds scored to win the game, 1–0, handing Vaughn the loss.

The Longest No-Hitter: Lefty Harvey Haddix of the Pittsburgh Pirates threw 12 innings of no-hit ball on May 26, 1959, but he lost the game, 1–0, on a hit in the 13th.

Most Consecutive No-Hit Games: Johnny Vander Meer, a left-hander for the Cincinnati Reds, threw two straight no-hitters in 1938. In the first, on June 11, he beat the Boston Braves, 3–0; in the second, on June 15, he triumphed over the Brooklyn Dodgers, 6–0.

Most World Series Wins: Left-hander Whitey Ford of the New York Yankees collected ten wins in 11 World Series in 1950, 1953, 1955–1958, and 1960–1964.

Most World Series Losses: Whitey Ford also lost eight games in his 11 World Series.

Most World Series Games Pitched: Whitey Ford appeared in 22 World Series games.

Most World Series Games Started: Whitey Ford started all 22 of those World Series games.

Most World Series Innings Pitched: Whitey Ford pitched 146 innings.

Most Innings Pitched in a Single World Series: Deacon Phillippe, a right-hander for the Pittsburgh Pirates, pitched 44 innings in the eight-game 1903 World Series in which the Boston Red Sox beat the Pirates, five games to three.

Most World Series Hits Allowed: Whitey Ford gave up 132 hits in 22 World Series games.

Most Bases on Balls Given Up in the World Series: Whitey Ford walked 34 men in 22 World Series games.

Most World Series Strikeouts: Whitey Ford struck out 94 men in 11 World Series.

Most Strikeouts in a Single World Series: Right-hander Bob Gibson of the St. Louis Cardinals struck out 35 batters in the 1968 Series. But St. Louis lost the Series to the Detroit Tigers, three games to four.

Most Strikeouts in a Single World Series Game: Bob Gibson of the Cardinals struck out 17 Tigers in the first game of the 1968 Series.

Most World Series Complete Games: Right-hander Christy Mathewson of the New York Giants pitched ten complete games in four World Series (1905, 1911–1913).

Most World Series Shutouts: Christy Mathewson threw four shutouts in the World Series—three in 1905 and one in 1913.

Most World Series Saves: Right-handed reliever Rollie Fingers saved six games for the Oakland A's in three World Series (1972–1974).

Most World Series Wins in Relief: Rosy Ryan, a right-hander for the New York Giants, won three in relief in 1922, 1923, and 1924.

The Only Perfect World Series Game: Yankees right-hander Don Larsen threw a perfect game (no runs, no hits, no walks) against the Dodgers in the fifth game of the 1956 World Series on October 8. He retired the minimum number of 27 Brooklyn Dodgers and won the game, 2–0, throwing only 97 pitches.

Best World Series Winning Percentages: Thirteen pitchers are tied with a perfect 1.000 record in World Series play:

- Babe Adams (Pirates), 3–0 in 1909, 1925
- Jesse Barnes (New York Giants), 2–0 in 1921–1922
- Jack Coombs (Philadelphia Athletics and Brooklyn Dodgers), 5–0 in 1910–1911, 1916
- Lefty Gomez (Yankees), 6–0 in 1932, 1936–1939
- Jerry Koosman (Mets), 3–0 in 1969, 1973
- Mickey Lolich (Tigers), 3–0 in 1968
- Monte Pearson (Yankees), 4–0 in 1936–1939
- Herb Pennock (Philadelphia Athletics and Yankees), 5–0 in 1914, 1923, 1926–1927, 1932
- George Pipgras (Yankees), 3–0 in 1927–1928, 1932
- Ed Reulbach (Cubs), 2–0 in 1906–1908, 1910
- Babe Ruth (Red Sox), 3–0 in 1916, 1918
- Luis Tiant (Red Sox), 2–0 in 1975
- Tom Zachary (Senators and Yankees), 3–0 in 1924–1925, 1928

Most Hits Given Up in a Game: Three pitchers are tied with 26: right-hander Harley "Idol" Parker of Cincinnati in 1901, right-hander Allan Travers of Detroit in 1912 (in his only major league game), and Philadelphia Athletics right-hander Hod Lisenbee in 1936.

Most Losses in a Season: In 1883 right-hander John Coleman of the Philadelphia Phillies suffered 48 losses.

Most Runs Given Up in a Game: In his only major league game, on May 18, 1912, right-hander Allan Travers of the Detroit Tigers gave up 24 runs.

Most Walks Given Up in a Game: In 1915 left-hander Bruno Haas of the Philadelphia Athletics yielded 16 bases on balls in one game.

The Managers

Most Consecutive Games Won by a New Manager: Joe Morgan of the Boston Red Sox won his first 12 games in 1988.

Most Times Fired by the Same Team: Billy Martin was fired five times from his position as manager of the New York Yankees by majority owner George Steinbrenner.

Best Winning Percentage: Joe McCarthy, who managed the Cubs (1926–1930), Yankees (1931–1946), and Red Sox (1948–1950), won 2,126 regular-season games while losing 1,335 for a winning percentage of .614.

Best World Series Winning Percentage: Managing the Cubs and Yankees, Joe McCarthy won 30 World Series games while losing 13 for a .698 percentage.

Most Games Managed: Connie Mack, who skippered the Pittsburgh Pirates (1894–1896) and Philadelphia Athletics (1901–1950), managed 7,878 games in 53 seasons.

Most World Series Managed: Casey Stengel, who managed the Brooklyn Dodgers (1934–1936), Boston Braves (1938–1943), New York Yankees (1949–1960), and New York Mets (1962–1965), managed in ten World Series—all with the Yankees.

Most World Series Games Managed: Casey Stengel piloted the Yankees through 63 World Series games.

Most World Series Wins: Casey Stengel led the Yankees to 37 wins in ten years.

Most World Series Losses: John McGraw, who managed in Baltimore (1899, 1901–1902) and with the New York Giants (1902–1932), lost 28 games with the Giants in nine World Series appearances.

Most League Championship Series Games: Bobby Cox, who managed the Atlanta Braves (1978–1981), Toronto Blue Jays (1982–1985), and Braves again (1990–), managed 31 games in the LCS.

Most League Championship Series Wins: Sparky Anderson, who managed the Cincinnati Reds (1970–1978) and Detroit Tigers (1979–1995), won 18 League Championship Series (LCS) games—14 with the Reds and four with the Tigers.

Most League Championship Series Losses: Bobby Cox, Whitey Herzog, who managed the Texas Rangers (1973), Kansas City Royals (1975–1979), and St. Louis Cardinals (1980–1990), and Tommy Lasorda, manager of the Los Angeles Dodgers (1976–), are tied with 14 LCS losses.

Best League Championship Series Percentage: Earl Weaver, who managed the Baltimore Orioles (1968–1982, 1985–1986), won 15 LCS games while losing seven for a .682 record.

Other Records

Most Career Bases on Balls: Babe Ruth drew 2,056 walks during his 22-year career.

Most Career Strikeouts: Outfielder Reggie Jackson had 2,597 strikeouts in his 21-year career with the Kansas City and Oakland Athletics (1967–1975), Orioles (1976), Yankees (1977–1981), Angels (1982–1986), and A's again (1987).

Most Strikeouts in a Season: San Francisco Giants outfielder Bobby Bonds struck out 189 times in 1970.

Most Passed Balls in an Inning: Catcher Ray Katt of the New York Giants was charged with four passed balls in one inning in 1954.

Most Runs Scored in a Season: Outfielder "Sliding Billy" Hamilton of the Philadelphia Phillies scored 196 runs in 131 games in 1894. In the modern era, Babe Ruth scored 177 in 152 games in 1921.

Most Successive Double Plays Hit Into: Outfielder Goose Goslin of the Detroit Tigers hit into four consecutive double plays in 1934.

Most Triple Plays Hit Into: Orioles third baseman Brooks Robinson hit into four triple plays during his 23-year career (1955–1977).

Longest Catch: Joe Sprinz, a catcher for the Cleveland Indians, caught a baseball dropped from an airship at a height of 800 feet in 1931. The force of catching the ball broke his jaw.

Most Valuable Players

In 1931 the Baseball Writers Association of America began to name a Most Valuable Player in each league. The person named was considered to be the best and most inspirational player in the league. Here are the MVPs, their positions and teams, and the final league or division standings of their clubs.

NATIONAL LEAGUE

1931—Frankie Frisch, 2B, St. Louis Cardinals (first)

1932—Chuck Klein, RF, Philadelphia Phillies (fourth)

1933—Carl Hubbell, P, New York Giants (first)

1934—Dizzy Dean, P, St. Louis Cardinals (first)

1935—Gabby Hartnett, C, Chicago Cubs (first)

1936—Carl Hubbell, P, New York Giants (first)

1937—Joe Medwick, LF, St. Louis Cardinals (fourth)

1938—Ernie Lombardi, C, Cincinnati Reds (fourth)

1939—Bucky Walters, P, Cincinnati Reds (first)

1940—Frank McCormick, 1B, Cincinnati Reds (first)
1941—Dolf Camilli, 1B, Brooklyn Dodgers (first)
1942—Mort Cooper, P, St. Louis Cardinals (first)
1943—Stan Musial, RF, St. Louis Cardinals (first)
1944—Marty Marion, SS, St. Louis Cardinals (first)
1945—Phil Cavarretta, 1B, Chicago Cubs (first)
1946—Stan Musial, 1B/OF, St. Louis Cardinals (first)
1947—Bob Elliott, 3B, Boston Braves (third)
1948—Stan Musial, LF, St. Louis Cardinals (second)
1949—Jackie Robinson, 2B, Brooklyn Dodgers (first)

1950—Jim Konstanty, P, Philadelphia Phillies (first)
1951—Roy Campanella, C, Brooklyn Dodgers (second)
1952—Hank Sauer, LF, Chicago Cubs (fifth)
1953—Roy Campanella, C, Brooklyn Dodgers (first)
1954—Willie Mays, CF, New York Giants (first)
1955—Roy Campanella, C, Brooklyn Dodgers (first)

1956—Don Newcombe, P, Brooklyn Dodgers (first)
1957—Henry Aaron, RF, Milwaukee Braves (first)
1958—Ernie Banks, SS, Chicago Cubs (fifth)
1959—Ernie Banks, SS, Chicago Cubs (fifth)
1960—Dick Groat, SS, Pittsburgh Pirates (first)
1961—Frank Robinson, RF, Cincinnati Reds (first)
1962—Maury Wills, SS, Los Angeles Dodgers (second)
1963—Sandy Koufax, P, Los Angeles Dodgers (first)

1964—Ken Boyer, 3B, St. Louis Cardinals (first)

1965—Willie Mays, CF, San Francisco Giants (second)

1966—Roberto Clemente, RF, Pittsburgh Pirates (third)

1967—Orlando Cepeda, 1B, St. Louis Cardinals (first)

1968—Bob Gibson, P, St. Louis Cardinals (first)

1969—Willie McCovey, 1B, San Francisco Giants (second)

1970—Johnny Bench, C, Cincinnati Reds (first)

1971—Joe Torre, 3B, St. Louis Cardinals (second)

1972—Johnny Bench, C, Cincinnati Reds (first)

1973—Pete Rose, LF, Cincinnati Reds (first)

1974—Steve Garvey, 1B, Los Angeles Dodgers (first)

1975—Joe Morgan, 2B, Cincinnati Reds (first)

1976—Joe Morgan, 2B, Cincinnati Reds (first)

1977—George Foster, LF, Cincinnati Reds (second)

1978—Dave Parker, RF, Pittsburgh Pirates (second)

1979—(tie) Willie Stargell, 1B, Pittsburgh Pirates (first); **Keith Hernandez,** 1B, St. Louis Cardinals (third)

1980—Mike Schmidt, 3B, Philadelphia Phillies (first)

1981—Mike Schmidt, 3B, Philadelphia Phillies (third)

1982—Dale Murphy, CF, Atlanta Braves (first)

1983—Dale Murphy, CF, Atlanta Braves (second)

1984—Ryne Sandberg, 2B, Chicago Cubs (first)

1985—Willie McGee, CF, St. Louis Cardinals (first)

1986—Mike Schmidt, 3B, Philadelphia Phillies (second)

1987—**Andre Dawson**, RF, Chicago Cubs (sixth)

1988—Kirk Gibson, LF, Los Angeles Dodgers (first)

1989—Kevin Mitchell, OF, San Francisco Giants (first)

1990—Barry Bonds, LF, Pittsburgh Pirates (first)

1991—Terry Pendleton, 3B, Atlanta Braves (first)

1992—Barry Bonds, LF, Pittsburgh Pirates (first)

1993—Barry Bonds, LF, San Francisco Giants (second)

1994—Jeff Bagwell, 1B, Houston Astros (second)

1995—Barry Larkin, SS, Cincinnati Reds (first)

AMERICAN LEAGUE

1931—Lefty Grove, P, Philadelphia Athletics (first)

1932—Jimmie Foxx, 1B, Philadelphia Athletics (second)

1933—Jimmie Foxx, 1B, Philadelphia Athletics (third)

1934—Mickey Cochrane, C/Mgr, Detroit Tigers (first)

1935—Hank Greenberg, 1B, Detroit Tigers (first)

1936—Lou Gehrig, 1B, New York Yankees (first)

1937—Charlie Gehringer, 2B, Detroit Tigers (second)

1938—Jimmie Foxx, 1B, Boston Red Sox (second)

1939—Joe DiMaggio, CF, New York Yankees (first)

1940—Hank Greenberg, LF, Detroit Tigers (first)

1941—Joe DiMaggio, CF, New York Yankees (first)

1942—Joe Gordon, 2B, New York Yankees (first)

1943—Spud Chandler, P, New York Yankees (first)

1944—Hal Newhouser, P, Detroit Tigers (second)

1945—Hal Newhouser, P, Detroit Tigers (first)

1946—Ted Williams, LF, Boston Red Sox (first)

1947—Joe DiMaggio, CF, New York Yankees (first)

1948—Lou Boudreau, SS/Mgr, Cleveland Indians (first)

1949—Ted Williams, LF, Boston Red Sox (second)

1950—Phil Rizzuto, SS, New York Yankees (first)
1951—Yogi Berra, C, New York Yankees (first)
1952—Bobby Shantz, P, Philadelphia Athletics (fourth)
1953—Al Rosen, 3B, Cleveland Indians (second)
1954—Yogi Berra, C, New York Yankees (second)
1955—Yogi Berra, C, New York Yankees (first)
1956—Mickey Mantle, CF, New York Yankees (first)

1957—Mickey Mantle, CF, New York Yankees (first)
1958—Jackie Jensen, RF, Boston Red Sox (third)
1959—Nellie Fox, 2B, Chicago White Sox (first)
1960—Roger Maris, RF, New York Yankees (first)
1961—Roger Maris, RF, New York Yankees (first)
1962—Mickey Mantle, CF, New York Yankees (first)
1963—Elston Howard, C, New York Yankees (first)
1964—Brooks Robinson, 3B, Baltimore Orioles (third)
1965—Zoilo Versalles, SS, Minnesota Twins (first)
1966—Frank Robinson, RF, Baltimore Orioles (first)
1967—Carl Yastrzemski, LF, Boston Red Sox (first)
1968—Denny McLain, P, Detroit Tigers (first)
1969—Harmon Killebrew, 3B/1B, Minnesota Twins (first)
1970—Boog Powell, 1B, Baltimore Orioles (first)
1971—Vida Blue, P, Oakland A's (first)
1972—Dick Allen, 1B, Chicago White Sox (second)
1973—Reggie Jackson, RF, Oakland A's (first)
1974—Jeff Burroughs, RF, Texas Rangers (second)

1975—Fred Lynn, CF, Boston Red Sox (first)

1976—Thurman Munson, C, New York Yankees (first)

1977—Rod Carew, 1B, Minnesota Twins (fourth)

1978—Jim Rice, LF/DH, Boston Red Sox (second)

1979—Don Baylor, LF/DH, California Angels (first)

1980—George Brett, 3B, Kansas City Royals (first)

1981—Rollie Fingers, P, Milwaukee Brewers (first)

1982—Robin Yount, SS, Milwaukee Brewers (first)

1983—Cal Ripken, Jr., SS, Baltimore Orioles (first)

1984—Willie Hernandez, P, Detroit Tigers (first)

1985—Don Mattingly, 1B, New York Yankees (second)

1986—Roger Clemens, P, Boston Red Sox (first)

1987—George Bell, LF, Toronto Blue Jays (second)

1988—José Canseco, RF, Oakland A's (first)

1989—Robin Yount, LF/CF, Milwaukee Brewers (fourth)

1990—Rickey Henderson, LF, Oakland A's (fourth)

1991—Cal Ripken, Jr., SS, Baltimore Orioles (sixth)

1992—Dennis Eckersley, P, Oakland A's (first)

1993—Frank Thomas, 1B, Chicago White Sox (first)

1994—Frank Thomas, 1B, Chicago White Sox (first)

1995—Mo Vaughn, 1B, Boston Red Sox (first)

Cy Young Award Winners

The Cy Young Award, given annually by the Baseball Writers Association of America, goes to the most successful pitcher or pitchers of the year. From 1956 to 1966, the award went to the single pitcher considered the best in major league baseball. Beginning in 1967, separate awards have been given in each league. Here are the winners, their teams, their won-lost records, and the final league or division standing of their teams.

1956—Don Newcombe, Brooklyn Dodgers, 27–7 (first)

1957—Warren Spahn, Milwaukee Braves, 21–11 (first)

1958—Bob Turley, New York Yankees, 21–7 (first)

1959—Early Wynn, Chicago White Sox, 22–10 (first)

1960—Vernon Law, Pittsburgh Pirates, 20–9 (first)

1961—Whitey Ford, New York Yankees, 25–4 (first)

1962—Don Drysdale, Los Angeles Dodgers, 25–9 (second)

1963—Sandy Koufax, Los Angeles Dodgers, 25–5 (first)

1964—Dean Chance, Los Angeles Angels, 20–9 (fifth)

1965—Sandy Koufax, Los Angeles Dodgers, 26–8 (first)

1966—Sandy Koufax, Los Angeles Dodgers, 27–9 (first)

NATIONAL LEAGUE

1967—Mike McCormick, San Francisco Giants, 22–10 (second)

1968—Bob Gibson, St. Louis Cardinals, 22–9 (first)

1969—Tom Seaver, New York Mets, 25–7 (first)

1970—Bob Gibson, St. Louis Cardinals, 23–7 (fourth)

1971—Ferguson Jenkins, Chicago Cubs, 24–13 (third)

1972—Steve Carlton, Philadelphia Phillies, 27–10 (sixth)

1973—Tom Seaver, New York Mets, 19–10 (first)

1974—Mike Marshall, Los Angeles Dodgers, 15–12 with 21 saves (first)

1975—Tom Seaver, New York Mets, 22–9 (third)
1976—Randy Jones, San Diego Padres, 22–14 (fifth)
1977—Steve Carlton, Philadelphia Phillies, 23–10 (first)
1978—Gaylord Perry, San Diego Padres, 21–6 (fourth)
1979—Bruce Sutter, Chicago Cubs, 6–6 with 37 saves (fifth)
1980—Steve Carlton, Philadelphia Phillies, 24–9 (first)
1981—Fernando Valenzuela, Los Angeles Dodgers, 13–7 (second)
1982—Steve Carlton, Philadelphia Phillies, 23–11 (second)
1983—John Denny, Philadelphia Phillies, 19–6 (first)
1984—Rick Sutcliffe, Chicago Cubs, 16–1 (first)
1985—Dwight Gooden, New York Mets, 24–4 (second)
1986—Mike Scott, Houston Astros, 18–10 (first)
1987—Steve Bedrosian, Philadelphia Phillies, 5–3 with 40 saves (fourth)
1988—Orel Hershiser, Los Angeles Dodgers, 23–8 (first)
1989—Mark Davis, San Diego Padres, 4–3 with 44 saves (second)
1990—Doug Drabek, Pittsburgh Pirates, 22–6 (first)
1991—Tom Glavine, Atlanta Braves, 20–11 (first)
1992—Greg Maddux, Chicago Cubs, 20–11 (fourth)
1993—Greg Maddux, Atlanta Braves, 20–10 (first)
1994—Greg Maddux, Atlanta Braves, 16–6 (second)
1995—Greg Maddux, Atlanta Braves, 19–2 (first)

AMERICAN LEAGUE

1967—Jim Lonborg, Boston Red Sox, 22–9 (first)
1968—Denny McLain, Detroit Tigers, 31–6 (first)
1969—(tie) Denny McLain, Detroit Tigers, 24–9 (second);
Mike Cuellar, Baltimore Orioles, 23–11 (first)
1970—Jim Perry, Minnesota Twins, 24–12 (first)
1971—Vida Blue, Oakland A's, 24–8 (first)
1972—Gaylord Perry, Cleveland Indians, 24–16 (fifth)

1973—Jim Palmer, Baltimore Orioles, 22–9 (first)

1974—Catfish Hunter, Oakland A's, 25–12 (first)

1975—Jim Palmer, Baltimore Orioles, 23–11 (second)

1976—Jim Palmer, Baltimore Orioles, 22–13 (second)

1977—Sparky Lyle, New York Yankees, 13–5 with 26 saves (first)

1978—Ron Guidry, New York Yankees, 25–3 (first)

1979—Mike Flanagan, Baltimore Orioles, 23–9 (first)

1980—Steve Stone, Baltimore Orioles, 25–7 (second)

1981—Rollie Fingers, Milwaukee Brewers, 6–3 with 28 saves (first)

1982—Pete Vuckovich, Milwaukee Brewers, 18–6 (first)

1983—LaMarr Hoyt, Chicago White Sox, 24–10 (first)

1984—Willie Hernandez, Detroit Tigers, 9–3 with 32 saves (first)

1985—Bret Saberhagen, Kansas City Royals, 20–6 (first)

1986—Roger Clemens, Boston Red Sox, 24–4 (first)

1987—Roger Clemens, Boston Red Sox, 20–9 (fifth)

1988—Frank Viola, Minnesota Twins, 24–7 (second)

1989—Bret Saberhagen, Kansas City Royals, 23–6 (second)

1990—Bob Welch, Oakland A's, 27–6 (first)

1991—Roger Clemens, Boston Red Sox, 18–10 (second)

1992—Dennis Eckersley, Oakland A's, 7–1 with 51 saves (first)

1993—Jack McDowell, Chicago White Sox, 22–10 (first)

1994—David Cone, Kansas City Royals, 16–5 (third)

1995—Randy Johson, Seattle Mariners, 18–2 (first)

Rookie of the Year Winners

Since 1947 the Baseball Writers Association of America has given an award to the Rookie of the Year. For the first two years, only one award was given—for the single best first-year player in the majors. In 1949 the Association began giving the prize to a player in each league. Here are the players, their positions and clubs, and the final league or division standings of their teams.

1947—Jackie Robinson, 1B, Brooklyn Dodgers (first)

1948—Alvin Dark, SS, Boston Braves (first)

NATIONAL LEAGUE

1949—Don Newcombe, P, Brooklyn Dodgers (first)

1950—Sam Jethroe, CF, Boston Braves (fourth)

1951—Willie Mays, CF, New York Giants (first)

1952—Joe Black, P, Brooklyn Dodgers (first)

1953—Jim Gilliam, 2B, Brooklyn Dodgers (first)

1954—Wally Moon, CF, St. Louis Cardinals (sixth)

1955—Bill Virdon, CF, St. Louis Cardinals (seventh)

1956—Frank Robinson, LF, Cincinnati Reds (third)

1957—Jack Sanford, P, Philadelphia Phillies (fifth)

1958—Orlando Cepeda, 1B, San Francisco Giants (third)

1959—Willie McCovey, 1B, San Francisco Giants (third)

1960—Frank Howard, RF, Los Angeles Dodgers (fourth)

1961—Billy Williams, LF, Chicago Cubs (seventh)

1962—Ken Hubbs, 2B, Chicago Cubs (ninth)

1963—Pete Rose, 2B, Cincinnati Reds (fifth)

1964—Richie Allen, 3B, Philadelphia Phillies (third)

1965—Jim Lefebvre, 2B, Los Angeles Dodgers (first)

1966—Tommy Helms, 3B, Cincinnati Reds (seventh)

1967—Tom Seaver, P, New York Mets (tenth)

1968—Johnny Bench, C, Cincinnati Reds (fourth)

1969—Ted Sizemore, 2B, Los Angeles Dodgers (fourth)

1970—Carl Morton, P, Montreal Expos (sixth)

1971—Earl Williams, C, Atlanta Braves (third)

1972—Jon Matlack, P, New York Mets (third)

1973—Gary Matthews, LF, San Francisco Giants (third)

1974—Bake McBride, CF, St. Louis Cardinals (second)

1975—John Montefusco, P, San Francisco Giants (third)

1976—(tie) Butch Metzger, P, San Diego Padres (fifth); **Pat Zachry,** P, Cincinnati Reds (first)

1977—Andre Dawson, CF, Montreal Expos (fifth)

1978—Bob Horner, 3B, Atlanta Braves (sixth)

1979—Rick Sutcliffe, P, Los Angeles Dodgers (third)

1980—Steve Howe, P, Los Angeles Dodgers (second)

1981—Fernando Valenzuela, P, Los Angeles Dodgers (second)

1982—Steve Sax, 2B, Los Angeles Dodgers (second)

1983—Darryl Strawberry, RF, New York Mets (sixth)

1984—Dwight Gooden, P, New York Mets (second)

1985—Vince Coleman, LF, St. Louis Cardinals (first)

1986—Todd Worrell, P, St. Louis Cardinals (third)

1987—Benito Santiago, C, San Diego Padres (sixth)

1988—Chris Sabo, 3B, Cincinnati Reds (second)

1989—Jerome Walton, CF, Chicago Cubs (first)

1990—David Justice, RF, Atlanta Braves (sixth)

1991—Jeff Bagwell, 1B, Houston Astros (sixth)

1992—Eric Karros, 1B, Los Angeles Dodgers (sixth)

1993—Mike Piazza, C, Los Angeles Dodgers (fourth)

1994—Raul Mondesi, OF, Los Angeles Dodgers (first)

1995—Hideo Nomo, P, Los Angeles Dodgers, (first)

AMERICAN LEAGUE

1949—Roy Sievers, LF, St. Louis Browns (seventh)

1950—Walt Dropo, 1B, Boston Red Sox (third)

1951—Gil McDougald, 3B, New York Yankees (first)

1952—Harry Bird, P, Philadelphia Athletics (fourth)

1953—Harvey Kuenn, SS, Detroit Tigers (sixth)

1954—Bob Grim, P, New York Yankees (second)

1955—Herb Score, P, Cleveland Indians (second)

1956—Luis Aparicio, SS, Chicago White Sox (third)

1957—Tony Kubek, SS/OF, New York Yankees (first)

1958—Albie Pearson, CF, Washington Senators (eighth)

1959—Bob Allison, CF, Washington Senators (eighth)

1960—Ron Hansen, SS, Baltimore Orioles (second)

1961—Don Schwall, P, Boston Red Sox (sixth)

1962—Tom Tresh, SS, New York Yankees (first)

1963—Gary Peters, P, Chicago White Sox (second)

1964—Tony Oliva, RF, Minnesota Twins (seventh)

1965—Curt Blefary, LF, Baltimore Orioles (third)

1966—Tommie Agee, CF, Chicago White Sox (fourth)

1967—Rod Carew, 2B, Minnesota Twins (third)

1968—Stan Bahnsen, P, New York Yankees (fifth)

1969—Lou Piniella, LF, Kansas City Royals (fourth)

1970—Thurman Munson, C, New York Yankees (second)

1971—Chris Chambliss, 1B, Cleveland Indians (sixth)

1972—Carlton Fisk, C, Boston Red Sox (second)

1973—Al Bumbry, OF, Baltimore Orioles (first)

1974—Mike Hargrove, 1B, Texas Rangers (second)

1975—Fred Lynn, CF, Boston Red Sox (first)

1976—Mark Fidrych, P, Detroit Tigers (fifth)

1977—Eddie Murray, DH, Baltimore Orioles (second)

1978—Lou Whitaker, 2B, Detroit Tigers (fifth)

1979—(tie) John Castino, 3B, Minnesota Twins (fourth);
Alfredo Griffin, SS, Toronto Blue Jays (seventh)

1980—Joe Charboneau, OF/DH, Cleveland Indians (sixth)

1981—Dave Righetti, P, New York Yankees (third)

1982—Cal Ripken, Jr., SS/3B, Baltimore Orioles (second)

1983—Ron Kittle, LF, Chicago White Sox (first)

1984—Alvin Davis, 1B, Seattle Mariners (sixth)

1985—Ozzie Guillen, SS, Chicago White Sox (third)

1986—José Canseco, LF, Oakland A's (fourth)

1987—Mark McGwire, 1B, Oakland A's (third)

1988—Walt Weiss, SS, Oakland A's (first)

1989—Greg Olson, P, Baltimore Orioles (second)

1990—Sandy Alomar, Jr., C, Cleveland Indians (seventh)

1991—Chuck Knoblauch, 2B, Minnesota Twins (first)

1992—Pat Listach, SS, Milwaukee Brewers (second)

1993—Tim Salmon, OF, California Angels (fifth)

1994—Bob Hamelin, DH, Kansas City Royals (third)

1995—Marty Cordova, OF, Minnesota Twins (fifth)

World Series Most Valuable Players

Since 1955 an award has been given to the Most Valuable Player in the World Series. The only time the award has been given to a member of the losing team was in 1960, when the Pirates beat the Yankees in the World Series, four games to three. That year, Yankee Bobby Richardson was selected as World Series MVP. Here are the MVPs and their positions, teams, and leagues.

1955—Johnny Podres, P, Brooklyn Dodgers (NL)

1956—Don Larsen, P, New York Yankees (AL)

1957—Lew Burdette, P, Milwaukee Braves (NL)
1958—Bob Turley, P, New York Yankees (AL)
1959—Larry Sherry, P, Los Angeles Dodgers (NL)
1960—Bobby Richardson, 2B, New York Yankees (AL)
1961—Whitey Ford, P, New York Yankees (AL)
1962—Ralph Terry, P, New York Yankees (AL)
1963—Sandy Koufax, P, Los Angeles Dodgers (NL)
1964—Bob Gibson, P, St. Louis Cardinals (NL)
1965—Sandy Koufax, P, Los Angeles Dodgers (NL)
1966—Frank Robinson, RF, Baltimore Orioles (AL)
1967—Bob Gibson, P, St. Louis Cardinals (NL)
1968—Mickey Lolich, P, Detroit Tigers (AL)
1969—Donn Clendenon, 1B, New York Mets (NL)
1970—Brooks Robinson, 3B, Baltimore Orioles (AL)
1971—Roberto Clemente, RF, Pittsburgh Pirates (NL)
1972—Gene Tenace, C, Oakland A's (AL)
1973—Reggie Jackson, RF, Oakland A's (AL)
1974—Rollie Fingers, P, Oakland A's (AL)
1975—Pete Rose, 3B, Cincinnati Reds (NL)
1976—Johnny Bench, C, Cincinnati Reds (NL)
1977—Reggie Jackson, RF, New York Yankees (AL)
1978—Bucky Dent, SS, New York Yankees (AL)
1979—Willie Stargell, 1B, Pittsburgh Pirates (NL)
1980—Mike Schmidt, 3B, Philadelphia Phillies (NL)
1981—(tie) Ron Cey, 3B, Los Angeles Dodgers (NL); **Steve Yeager,** C, Los Angeles Dodgers (NL); **Pedro Guerrero,** RF, Los Angeles Dodgers (NL)
1982—Darrell Porter, C, St. Louis Cardinals (NL)

1983—Rick Dempsey, C, Baltimore Orioles (AL)
1984—Alan Trammell, SS, Detroit Tigers (AL)
1985—Bret Saberhagen, P, Kansas City Royals (AL)

1986—Ray Knight, 3B, New York Mets (NL)
1987—Frank Viola, P, Minnesota Twins (AL)
1988—Orel Hershiser, P, Los Angeles Dodgers (NL)
1989—Dave Stewart, P, Oakland A's (AL)
1990—José Rijo, P, Cincinnati Reds (NL)
1991—Jack Morris, P, Minnesota Twins (AL)
1992—Pat Borders, C, Toronto Blue Jays (AL)
1993—Paul Molitor, DH, Toronto Blue Jays (AL)
1994—No World Series
1995—Tom Glavine, P, Atlanta Braves (NL)

The Superstars

What does it take to be a baseball superstar? These men don't have to be handsome, or Yogi Berra wouldn't qualify. They don't have to be well educated, or no one would like Babe Ruth. They don't have to look like Rambo, or nobody would admire Cal Ripken, Jr. They don't even have to be pleasant, or we would never remember Ty Cobb. What they have to be is good, hardworking, and an inspiration to their teams. Here are some of them.

HANK AARON

Most Career Home Runs
Born: *February 5, 1934, Mobile, AL*
Hall of Fame: *1982*

Henry Louis "Hank" Aaron played with intensity throughout his career, even though his teams were rarely pennant contenders. Aaron was an outfielder for the Braves in Milwaukee (1954–1965) and in Atlanta (1966–1974), and he returned to

Milwaukee to become the designated hitter for the Brewers (1975–1976). His records include the most career home runs (755), the most career runs batted in (2,297), the most total bases (6,856), and the most extra-base hits (1,477).

LUIS APARICIO

Expert Thief

Born: *April 29, 1934, Maracaibo, Venezuela*

Hall of Fame: *1984*

Luis Ernesto Montiel "Little Looie" Aparicio was a slick-fielding shortstop who was one of the first of many Venezuelan players who were to contribute so much to the national pastime. He played for the White Sox (1956–1962), Orioles (1963–1967), White Sox again (1968–1970), and Red Sox (1971–1973). He led the league in stolen bases for nine straight years (1956–1964).

LUKE APPLING

Master of the Foul Ball

Born: *April 2, 1909, High Point, NC*

Died: *January 3, 1991, Cumming, GA*

Hall of Fame: *1964*

Lucius Benjamin "Luke" "Old Aches and Pains" Appling seemed to be able to foul off any number of pitches until he got the one he wanted. A hero in Chicago, he played shortstop for the White Sox for 20 years (1930–1943, 1945–1950) and finished his career with a .310 batting average.

ERNIE BANKS

Cubs Hero

Born: *January 31, 1931, Dallas, TX*

Hall of Fame: *1977*

Ernest "Mr. Cub" Banks was the most enthusiastic baseball player of his time. Primarily a first baseman/shortstop, he played for the Cubs for 19 years (1953–1971) and was twice named Most Valuable Player in the National League (1958 and 1959)—the first player to be named in two straight years—although the Cubs finished fifth in both those years.

JOHNNY BENCH

Golden Glover

Born: *December 7, 1947, Oklahoma City, OK*

Hall of Fame: *1989*

Johnny Lee Bench, an All-Star playing with All-Stars, was the backbone of the Cincinnati Reds' "Big Red Machine." In his 17 years as a catcher with the Reds (1967–1983), Bench was twice named National League Most Valuable Player (1970 and 1972), won ten Gold Gloves for fielding excellence, and set the home run record for catchers with 389.

YOGI BERRA

Star Catcher and Manager

Born: *May 12, 1925, St. Louis, MO*

Hall of Fame: *1972*

Lawrence Peter "Yogi" Berra, the ever-cheerful, was as well known for his humorous misuse of words as he was for his brilliant career as a catcher. His friend, former player and sportscaster Joe Garagiola, once said, "Yogi doesn't say funny things. He says things funny." Berra played for the Yankees (1946–1963) and Mets (1965), setting the records for most World Series games played (75), most World Series at bats (259), most World Series hits (71), and most World Series doubles (ten). He managed the Yankees (1964), Mets (1972–1975), and Yankees again (1984–1985), winning pennants in 1964 and 1973.

BARRY BONDS

Famous Son

Born: *July 24, 1964, Riverside, CA*

Barry Lamar Bonds is the son of Bobby Bonds, the slugging outfielder. Barry has played the outfield for the Pirates (1986–1992) and Giants (1993–   ). A three-time MVP (1990, 1992, and 1993), he led the league in slugging average in those years, and in 1993 he also had the most home runs (46) and runs batted in (123). In 1995 he led the league in walks (120) and on-base percentage (.431).

LOU BOUDREAU

Super Shortstop and Manager

Born: *July 17, 1917, Harvey, IL*

Hall of Fame: *1970*

Louis Boudreau was a slick-fielding shortstop, and as a player/manager he was an inspiration to his team. He played for the Indians (1938–1950) and Red Sox (1951–1952), hitting over .300 four times, including a .355 average in 1948. As a manager, he skippered the Indians (1942–1950, winning the World Series in 1948), Red Sox (1952–1954), Kansas City Athletics (1955–1957), and Cubs (1960).

GEORGE BRETT

Power at Third Base

Born: *May 15, 1953, Glen Dale, WV*

George Howard Brett was a great power hitter and quite capable of displays of righteous indignation—for example, when he was called for putting pine tar too far up his bat. A third baseman, Brett played his entire major league career with the Royals (1973–1993). He won the American League Most Valuable Player Award in 1980 and led the league in batting three times—1976, 1980 (when he hit .390), and 1990.

LOU BROCK

The Fleet of Foot

Born: *June 18, 1939, El Dorado, AR*

Hall of Fame: *1985*

Louis Clark Brock could bat, field, and steal. He played the outfield for the Cubs (1961–1964) and Cardinals (1964–1979). For 12 years he owned the career record for most stolen bases with 938, until Rickey Henderson broke it, and he led the league in steals in eight separate years.

THREE FINGER BROWN

Pro at Fooling Batters

Born: *October 19, 1876, Nyesville, IN*

Died: *February 14, 1948, Terre Haute, IN*

Hall of Fame: *1949*

Mordecai Peter Centennial "Three Finger" "Miner" Brown was the victim of a childhood accident that left him with only three fingers on his pitching hand. But his unusual three-fingered grip proved successful. He pitched for the Cardinals (1903), Cubs (1904–1912), Reds (1913), three teams in the Federal League (1914–1915), and Cubs again (1916), and he had a career earned run average of 2.06, the third best in baseball history.

ROY CAMPANELLA

Legendary Catcher
Born: *November 19, 1921, Philadelphia, PA*
Died: *June 26, 1993, Woodland Hills, CA*
Hall of Fame: *1969*

Roy Campanella, a three-time MVP winner (1951, 1953, and 1955), was 26 years old before he played major league baseball because the sport was segregated at that time. He played in the Negro Leagues until after Jackie Robinson broke the color barrier in 1947. Campanella came to the Brooklyn Dodgers in 1948 and played with them until after the 1957 season, when he suffered an automobile accident that left him a paraplegic.

JOSÉ CANSECO

Speed and Power
Born: *July 2, 1964, Havana, Cuba*

José Canseco began his career in 1985 as the outfielder of the Oakland A's. He was voted the Most Valuable Player in the American League in 1988, after being the first and only man ever to hit 40 or more home runs and steal 40 or more bases in one season. In 1992 he was traded to the Texas Rangers and in 1995 went to the Boston Red Sox.

ROD CAREW

The Man With the Golden Bat

Born: *October 1, 1945,*
Gaton, Panama
Hall of Fame: *1991*

Rodney Cline Scott Carew was one of the best natural hitters ever to play baseball. He played first and second base for the Twins (1967–1978) and Angels (1979–1985), and he had a career batting average of .328—seven times leading the league in hitting and hitting over .300 15 times. He won the Most Valuable Player Award in the American League in 1977.

GARY CARTER

The Human Backstop

Born: *April 8, 1954,*
Culver City, CA

Gary Edmund "The Kid" Carter is one of the few baseball players to turn a whole franchise around. This catcher first played for the Expos (1974–1984), but when he went to the Mets in 1985, he immediately became the team leader and helped the Mets win the World Series in 1986. He later played for the Giants (1990), Dodgers (1991), and Expos again (1992) before retiring.

ROGER CLEMENS

The Man With the Golden Arm

Born: *August 4, 1962, Dayton, OH*

William Roger "Rocket" Clemens is one of the few pitchers ever truly to dominate a league in one year. This right-hander came up to the Red Sox in 1984, and in 1986 he led the league in wins (24), winning percentage (.857), and earned run average (2.48). That year he was named the American League's MVP and winner of the Cy Young Award, which he won again in 1987 and 1991. He holds the record for most strikeouts in a game, with 20.

ROBERTO CLEMENTE

Baseball Star and Hero

Born: *August 18, 1934, Carolina, PR*

Died: *December 31, 1972, San Juan, PR*

Hall of Fame: *1973*

Roberto Walker "Bob" Clemente was one of the shining stars of baseball. He was an outstanding outfielder for the Pirates (1955–1972) with a career batting average of .317. He led the league in batting in four separate years and hit over .300 13 times, amassing exactly 3,000 hits and winning the National League Most Valuable Player Award in 1966. He died in a plane crash while taking relief supplies to victims of an earthquake in Nicaragua. The election committee of the Hall of Fame waived the five-year waiting requirement for naming a player to the Hall, electing Clemente early in 1973.

TY COBB

The Georgia Peach

Born: *December 18, 1886, Narrows, GA*

Died: *July 17, 1961, Atlanta, GA*

Hall of Fame: *1936*

Tyrus Raymond "The Georgia Peach" Cobb, one of the best baseball players of all time, was also one of the most unpleasant. He was known for sharpening his spikes to injure opposing players, but he was also known for his hitting. He holds the major league record career batting average of .367. He also holds the record for runs scored (2,245) and is second in hits (4,191). Cobb played the outfield for the Tigers (1905–1926) and Philadelphia Athletics (1927–1928).

ANDRE DAWSON

Excellence in the Outfield

Born: *July 10, 1954, Miami, FL*

Andre Fernando "Hawk" Dawson, the slugger and outfielder par excellence, began his career with the Expos in 1976. He joined the Cubs in 1987 and immediately won the National League Most Valuable Player Award (with 49 homers and 137 RBIs), even though the Cubs finished in last place in the National League East. Dawson later played for the Red Sox (1993–1994) and went to the Marlins in 1995.

DIZZY DEAN

The Country Boy

Born: *January 16, 1911, Lucas, AR*
Died: *July 17, 1974, Reno, NV*
Hall of Fame: *1953*

Jay Hanna "Dizzy" Dean, the right-handed pitcher, was one of the zaniest of the Gashouse Gang in St. Louis. He pitched for the Cardinals (1930, 1932–1937), Cubs (1938–1941), and St. Louis Browns (1947). During his 12-year career he twice led the league in wins, three times in innings pitched, and four times in complete games. He was also the strikeout leader four times, and he even led the league in saves in 1936 with 11.

JOE DIMAGGIO

The Yankee Clipper

Born: *November 25, 1914, Martinez, CA*
Hall of Fame: *1955*

Joseph Paul "Joltin' Joe" "The Yankee Clipper" DiMaggio's middle name should have been "Dignity." Seldom has there been a player so universally admired. He played the outfield for the Yankees (1936–1942, 1946–1951), ending with a career .325 batting average after hitting over .300 in 11 of his 13 seasons. DiMaggio's greatest feat was his 1941 string of 56 consecutive games in which he had at least one hit—a record that may never be broken. He was a three-time MVP (1939, 1941, and 1947).

BOB FELLER

Rapid Robert

Born: *November 3, 1918, Van Meter, IA*

Hall of Fame: *1962*

Robert William Andrew "Rapid Robert" Feller was a teenage right-handed fireball thrower when he started his career with the Indians in 1936. He stayed with the team until 1941 and returned after service in World War II to pitch from 1945 to 1956. Feller led the league in strikeouts seven times, in wins six times, in innings pitched five times, and in games started five times. He also threw three no-hitters.

ROLLIE FINGERS

Mustachioed Fireman

Born: *August 25, 1946, Steubenville, OH*

Hall of Fame: *1992*

Roland Glen Fingers was a star right-handed relief pitcher for the A's (1968–1976), Padres (1977–1980), and Brewers (1981–1982, 1984–1985). His 341 career saves total is the third highest in history, and he also racked up 114 wins. That made him one of only four relief pitchers who both won at least 100 games in relief and saved more than 100 games. Fingers won both the American League MVP and Cy Young awards in 1981.

WHITEY FORD

The Yankee Meal Ticket

Born: *October 21, 1926, New York, NY*

Hall of Fame: *1974*

Edward Charles "Whitey" "The Chairman of the Board" Ford was a dependable left-handed pitcher for the Yankees (1950, 1953–1967). His .690 winning percentage is the third best in baseball history, and he led the league in wins three times. He also led the league twice in lowest earned run average, games started, innings pitched, and shutouts. Ford was in 11 World Series and set the records for most wins (ten), most losses (eight), most games (22), most games started (22), most innings pitched (146), most hits given up (132), most walks (34), and most strikeouts (94).

LOU GEHRIG

Pride of the Yankees

Born: *June 19, 1903, New York, NY*

Died: *June 2, 1941, Riverdale, NY*

Hall of Fame: *1939*

Henry Louis "The Iron Horse" "Columbia Lou" Gehrig was a great player and a gentleman. He played first base for the Yankees (1923–1939) and batted .340. In his seven World Series appearances he batted .361. Gehrig also led the league in RBIs five times and in homers three times. But his most splendid achievement was that he played in 2,130 consecutive regular-season games. In 1939 he learned that he was suffering from an incurable disease, amyotrophic lateral sclerosis—now often referred to as Lou Gehrig's disease. He was the first man to be elected to the Hall of Fame before the usual five-year waiting period was over.

KEN GRIFFEY, JR.

Another Famous Son

Born: *November 21, 1969, Donora, PA*

George Kenneth "Junior" "Kid" Griffey, Jr., is the son of Ken Griffey, Sr., who batted .299 in his 15-year career. The younger Griffey broke in with the Seattle Mariners in 1989. A hard-hitting center fielder, he had a league-leading 40 home runs and a chance to break Roger Maris's record 61 in 1994 when the baseball strike ended his season.

TONY GWYNN

Batting Champion

Born: *May 9, 1960, Los Angeles, CA*

Anthony Keith Gwynn broke in with the San Diego Padres in 1982 as an outfielder. Since then he has led the league in batting average six times and had the most total hits six times, having hit over .300 12 times. When the strike ended the season in 1994, Gwynn was hitting .394. He ended the 1995 season with a lifetime average of .336.

OREL HERSHISER

The Comeback Kid

Born: *September 16, 1958, Buffalo, NY*

Orel Leonard Quinton "O" Hershiser began his right-handed pitching career with the Dodgers in 1983, going 0–0 and pitching only eight innings. But by 1988 he was a star. That year he went 23–8 with a 2.26 ERA. He won the Cy Young Award and World Series MVP, was named *Sports Illustrated*'s Sportsman of the Year, and ended the regular season with a record 59 consecutive scoreless innings. He joined the Indians in 1995 and that year was the MVP of the American League Championship Series.

CATFISH HUNTER

The Old Reliable

Born: *April 18, 1946, Hertford, NC*

Hall of Fame: *1987*

James Augustus "Catfish" Hunter was a steady, talented right-handed pitcher. He played for the A's, both in Kansas City and Oakland (1965–1974), and Yankees (1975–1979). In his career, he won 224 regular-season games and lost 166. He twice led the league in wins, threw a perfect game in 1968, and won the Cy Young Award in 1974. In his six World Series, Hunter won five games and lost three.

REGGIE JACKSON

Mr. October
Born: *May 18, 1946, Wyncote, PA*
Hall of Fame: *1993*

Reginald Martinez "Mr. October" Jackson was the consummate player, and the world knew it. This outfielder played for the A's in Kansas City and Oakland (1967–1975), Orioles (1976), Yankees (1977–1981), Angels (1982–1986), and A's again (1987). He led the league four times in home runs, but he also set the career record for most strikeouts (2,597). In 1973 he was voted the Most Valuable Player in the American League. In the 1977 World Series he led the Yankees to victory by hitting three successive homers, each on the first pitch, in the sixth game.

FERGUSON JENKINS

The Cubs Reliable
Born: *December 13, 1943, Chatham, Ontario, Canada*
Hall of Fame: *1991*

Ferguson Arthur "Fergie" Jenkins was a right-handed pitcher for the Phillies (1965–1966), Cubs (1966–1973), Rangers (1974–1975), Red Sox (1976–1977), Rangers again (1978–1981), and Cubs again (1982–1983). He was the pitcher with the most wins in 1971 and 1974 and led in strikeouts in 1969. Along the way he won the Cy Young Award in 1971.

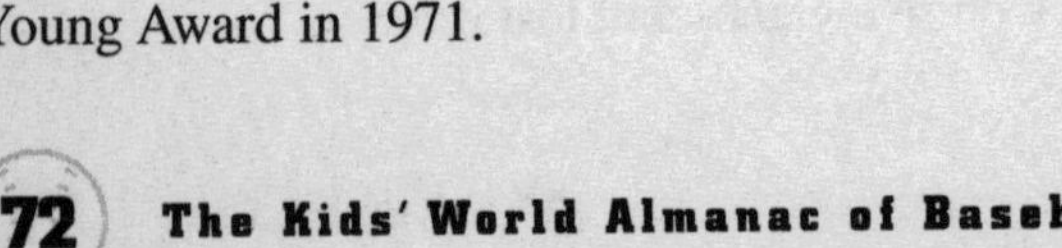

WALTER JOHNSON

The Pitcher's Pitcher
Born: *November 6, 1887, Humboldt, KS*
Died: *December 10, 1946, Washington, DC*
Hall of Fame: *1936*

Walter Perry "The Big Train" "Barney" Johnson was the ace right-handed pitcher for the Washington Senators for 21 years (1907–1927). His 416 wins rank him second in baseball history. Johnson led the league in wins six times and in ERA five times (his lifetime ERA was 2.17). His 3,508 strikeouts were the result of 12 league-leading seasons. Along the way he pitched a record 110 shutouts.

AL KALINE

Tigers Great
Born: *December 19, 1934, Baltimore, MD*
Hall of Fame: *1980*

Albert William Kaline was the most dependable Tigers player of his time. He played his entire career in the outfield for the Tigers (1953–1974). Kaline's lifetime batting average was .297, and, of his 3,007 hits, 972 were for extra bases. In 1955, when he hit .340, he was only 20—the youngest player to win a batting title. He was also a ten-time Gold Glover.

HARMON KILLEBREW

Killer Slugger

Born: *June 29, 1936, Payette, ID*

Hall of Fame: *1984*

Harmon Clayton "Killer" Killebrew was a legendary power hitter who played first base, third base, and the outfield for the Washington Senators (1954–1960), Twins (1961–1974), and Royals (1975). A slugger, he connected for extra-base hits 887 times out of his career 2,086 hits, and his home run percentage of 7.0 ranks third in baseball history. In 1969 he was named the American League's Most Valuable Player.

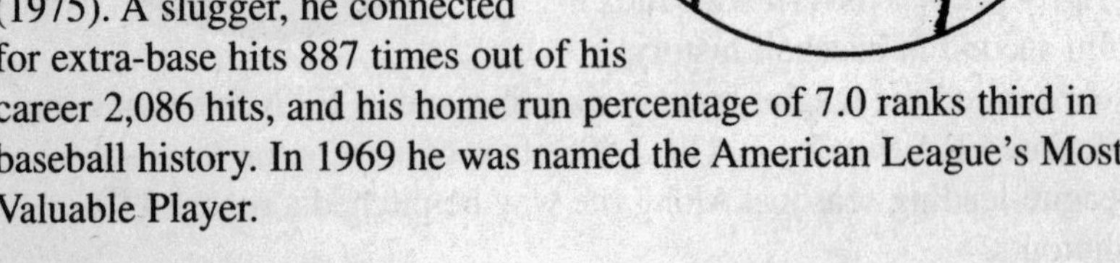

SANDY KOUFAX

Southpaw Ace

Born: *December 30, 1935, Brooklyn, NY*

Hall of Fame: *1972*

Sanford Koufax had magic in his left arm. He hurled for the Dodgers in Brooklyn and Los Angeles (1955–1966). During his 12-year career, he led the league in wins three times, in earned run average five times, in shutouts three times, and in strikeouts four times. In his four World Series, he registered an incredible 0.95 ERA, pitched two shutouts in eight games, and struck out 61 in 57 innings. He won the Cy Young Award three times (1963, 1965, and 1966) and in 1963 was the National League's Most Valuable Player. He also pitched a perfect game in 1965 and three other no-hitters.

CONNIE MACK

Legendary Manager

Born: *February 22, 1862, Brookfield, MA*

Died: *February 8, 1956, Germantown, PA*

Hall of Fame: *1937*

Cornelius Alexander "The Tall Tactician" McGilicuddy, better known as Connie Mack, set a record that will certainly never be broken—he was a baseball manager for 53 years. As a player, he caught for the Washington Senators in the National League (1886–1889), Buffalo in the Players' League (1890), and the Pirates in the National League (1891–1896). Mack was the manager of the Pirates (1894–1896) and Philadelphia Athletics (1901–1950). He won more regular-season games than any manager (3,731) and also lost more (3,948). He also won nine pennants and five World Series.

GREG MADDUX

Cy Young Winner

Born: *April 14, 1966, San Angelo, TX*

Gregory Alan Maddux, the amazing right-handed pitcher, joined the Chicago Cubs in 1986 and went to the Atlanta Braves in 1993. He has led the National League in ERA three times and in games started three times. In 1995 he became the first pitcher ever to win the Cy Young Award in four consecutive years. In 1995 he also won his sixth straight Gold Glove Award.

MICKEY MANTLE

Oklahoma Boy Makes Good

Born: *October 20, 1931, Spavinaw, OK*
Died: *August 13, 1995, Dallas, TX*
Hall of Fame: *1974*

Mickey Charles "The Commerce Comet" Mantle was "Mr. Reliable" during the 1950s and 1960s—he could always be counted on to come up with the big play or the big hit. He played the outfield and first base for the Yankees (1951–1968) and carried a lifetime batting average of .298, hitting 536 home runs in those 18 years. He led the league in homers four times and in runs scored six times. In 12 World Series, he set the record for most home runs (18), runs scored (42), runs batted in (40), and bases on balls (43). Mantle was a three-time MVP (1956, 1957, 1962) and won the Triple Crown (for best batting average, most homers, and most RBIs) in 1956.

JUAN MARICHAL

The Pitchin' Magician

Born: *October 20, 1937, Laguna Verde, Dominican Republic*
Hall of Fame: *1983*

Juan Antonio Sanchez "Manito" "The Dominican Dandy" Marichal was one of the most feared right-handed pitchers of all time. He threw for the Giants (1960–1973), Red Sox (1974), and Dodgers (1975). In his 16 years, he twice led the league in wins and in shutouts. Marichal's lifetime won-lost record was 243–142.

ROGER MARIS

Home Run Hammerer

Born: *September 10, 1934, Hibbing, MN*

Died: *December 14, 1985, Houston, TX*

Roger Eugene Maris was a quiet man who let his bat speak for him. He broke Babe Ruth's single-season home run record by hitting 61 in 1961. Maris played the outfield for the Indians (1957–1958), Kansas City Athletics (1958–1959), Yankees (1960–1966), and Cardinals (1967–1968). In those 12 years, he hit 275 regular-season home runs. He was the AL MVP in 1960 and 1961.

BILLY MARTIN

The Brat

Born: *May 16, 1928, Berkeley, CA*

Died: *December 25, 1989, Johnson City, NY*

Alfred Manuel Pesano, better known as Billy Martin, was always a fighter—both on and off the field. As a slick-fielding second baseman, he played for the Yankees (1950–1957), Kansas City Athletics (1957), Tigers (1958), Indians (1959), Reds (1960), Milwaukee Braves (1961), and Twins (1961). He turned to managing and skippered the Twins (1969), Tigers (1971–1973), Rangers (1974–1975), Yankees (1975–1979), A's (1980–1982), and Yankees again (1983, 1985, 1988). He won the World Series with New York in 1977.

DON MATTINGLY

Donnie Baseball

Born: *April 21, 1961, Evansville, IN*

Donald Arthur Mattingly was one of the purest hitters of his generation. This first baseman broke in with the Yankees in 1982, and within two years he led the league in hitting with a .343 batting average. Mattingly, a nine-time Gold Glove fielder, also led the league in runs batted in with 145 in 1985 (the year he won the American League Most Valuable Player Award) and in hits in 1984 and 1986.

WILLIE MAYS

A Giant Among Giants

Born: *May 6, 1931, Westfield, AL*

Hall of Fame: *1979*

Willie Howard "Say Hey" Mays was one of the most enthusiastic players of all time—always ready to work his fielding and hitting magic. A swift outfielder, he played for the Giants in New York and San Francisco (1951–1952, 1954–1972), as well as the Mets (1972–1973). Mays was Rookie of the Year in 1951 and National League Most Valuable Player in 1954 and 1965. A lifetime .302 hitter, he had a total of 3,283 hits in his 22-year career, 1,323 of them for extra bases, including 660 home runs (third all-time). He also won 12 Gold Gloves.

MARK McGWIRE

The Slugger

Born: *October 1, 1963, Pomona, CA*

Mark David McGwire was one of the youngest sluggers to make an impression on organized baseball. He came up to the A's in 1986 and the very next year led the league in home runs with 49, winning the American League Rookie of the Year Award. He has been a home run threat ever since and finished the 1995 season with 277 career home runs.

DALE MURPHY

The Pride of Atlanta

Born: *March 12, 1956, Portland, OR*

Dale Bryan Murphy was a superstar with the Braves for many years. This outfielder came up to Atlanta in 1976 and twice led the league in home runs (1984 and 1985). In 1982 and 1983 he won back-to-back National League Most Valuable Player Awards, leading the league in runs batted in both years. Murphy later played for the Phillies (1990–1992) and retired from the Rockies in May 1993.

EDDIE MURRAY

Quiet Consistency

Born: *February 24, 1956, Los Angeles, CA*

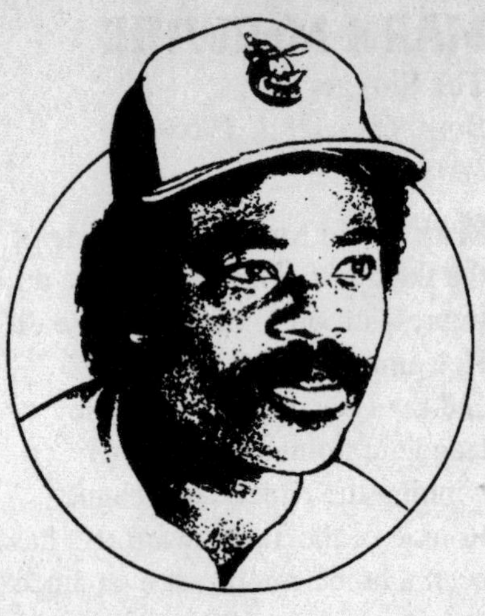

Eddie Clarence Murray hit the big leagues with a bang. He came up to the Orioles in 1977 and promptly won the American League Rookie of the Year Award, batting .283. In the strike-shortened 1981 season, this first baseman/designated hitter led the league in homers (22) and runs batted in (78). He played with the Dodgers (1989–1991) and Mets (1992–1993) and joined the Indians in 1994. Murray collected his 3,000th career hit during the 1995 season, and ended the year with 479 career home runs.

STAN MUSIAL

Everybody's Favorite

Born: *November 21, 1920, Donora, PA*

Hall of Fame: *1969*

Stanley Frank "Stan the Man" Musial is one of the few baseball players who is liked by everyone. What's more, he is universally admired. He played the outfield and first base for the Cardinals (1941–1944, 1946–1963), and of his 3,630 career hits, 1,377 were for extra bases. Musial led the league in hits six times, in doubles eight times, in triples five times, and in runs scored five times. He won seven batting titles, winding up with a lifetime batting average of .331. He was the National League's Most Valuable Player three times (1943, 1946, and 1948).

SATCHEL PAIGE

The Legend

Born: *July 7, 1906, Mobile, AL*
Died: *June 8, 1982, Kansas City, MO*
Hall of Fame: *1971*

Leroy Robert "Satchel" Paige was one of the most beloved baseball players of all time. He was a legendary pitcher in the Negro Leagues for more than 20 years and, when the color line was broken in baseball, finally made it to the majors at age 42. Paige, a right-hander, threw for the Indians (1948–1949), St. Louis Browns (1951–1953), and Kansas City Athletics (1965). His best year in the majors was 1952, when, as a relief pitcher, he was credited with ten saves and led the league in relief wins with eight.

KIRBY PUCKETT

The Twins' Hitting Star

Born: *March 14, 1961, Chicago, IL*

Kirby Puckett, the star outfielder for the Minnesota Twins since 1984, had a lifetime batting average of .318 as of the end of the 1995 season. Four times he led his league in hits, once in batting average, and once in runs batted in. In 1993 he was selected as the MVP of the All-Star Game and in 1991 as MVP of the American League Championship Series.

CAL RIPKEN, JR.

Orioles' Iron Man

Born: *August 24, 1960, Havre de Grace, MD*

Calvin Edwin Ripken, Jr., has been the main man at shortstop for the Baltimore Orioles since 1981. Along the way, he has been selected to start in 12 consecutive All-Star Games. Ripken was named Rookie of the Year in 1982 and won the American League's Most Valuable Player Award in 1983 and 1991. In 1995 he set a major league record for consecutive games played, beating Lou Gehrig's legendary 2,130 mark that had stood since 1939. Ripken finished the season having played 2,153 games in a row.

BROOKS ROBINSON

The Human Vacuum Cleaner

Born: *May 18, 1937, Little Rock, AR*

Hall of Fame: 1983

Brooks Calbert Robinson was arguably the best third baseman ever to play the game. He performed for the Orioles from 1955 to 1977, and of his 2,848 hits, 818 were for extra bases. A 16-time Gold Glover, he led the league in runs batted in with 118 in 1964, the year he was voted the American League's Most Valuable Player. He was also the World Series MVP in 1970.

FRANK ROBINSON

The First Black Manager

Born: *August 31, 1935, Beaumont, TX*

Hall of Fame: *1982*

Frank Robinson was always an inspiration to his teammates. An incredibly skilled ball player, he was the NL Rookie of the Year in 1956. As an outfielder, he starred for the Reds (1956–1965), Orioles (1966–1971), Dodgers (1972), Angels (1973–1974), and Indians (1974–1976). A .294 lifetime hitter, he accumulated 586 homers (fourth all-time) in his 21-year career and is the only player to have won the Most Valuable Player Award in both the National and American leagues (1961 and 1966). Robinson became the first black manager in the major leagues when he took over the Indians in 1975. He stayed with them until 1977 and then managed the Giants (1981–1984) and Orioles (1988–1991).

JACKIE ROBINSON

Breaking the Color Barrier

Born: *January 31, 1919, Cairo, GA*

Died: *October 24, 1971, Stamford, CT*

Hall of Fame: *1962*

Jack Roosevelt Robinson was probably the most courageous baseball player ever to grace the game. He played for the Kansas City Monarchs in the Negro American League in 1945 and then signed with the Dodgers organization. After an internship in the International League, he became the first black player in modern major league history. Primarily a second baseman, he starred for the Brooklyn Dodgers (1947–1956). He was Rookie of the Year in 1947 and National League Most Valuable Player in 1949, the year he led the league with a .342 batting average. He was also a daring baserunner and led the league in stolen bases in 1947 and 1949. Robinson finished his major league career with a .311 batting average. (For more on Jackie Robinson, see page 226.)

PETE ROSE

The Spirit of Cincinnati

Born: *April 14, 1941, Cincinnati, OH*

Peter Edward "Charlie Hustle" Rose was the most dedicated baseball player in the game. Rose played several positions in the infield and outfield for the Reds (1963–1978), Phillies (1979–1983), Expos (1984), and Reds again (1984–1986). He was National League Rookie of the Year in 1963, the Most Valuable Player in 1973, and the batting champion in 1968, 1969, and 1973, retiring with a .303 lifetime batting average. He is the all-time leader in hits (4,256), games (3,562), and at bats (14,053). Rose was a player/manager for the Reds from 1984 to 1986 and continued to manage the team until 1989, when he was banned from baseball for life for "acts detrimental" to the game involving gambling; he also served a prison sentence for tax evasion in 1990.

BABE RUTH

The Great Bambino

Born: *February 6, 1895, Baltimore, MD*
Died: *August 16, 1948, New York, NY*
Hall of Fame: *1936*

George Herman "Babe" "The Sultan of Swat" "The Bambino" Ruth was the most charismatic baseball player of all time. He began his career as a left-handed pitcher and won three World Series games in 1916 and 1918 while losing none. But he was soon sent to the outfield to take advantage of his hitting ability. Ruth played for the Red Sox (1914–1919), Yankees (1920–1934), and Boston Braves (1935). He led the league 12 times in home runs, ending up with 714 (second all-time), plus 15 in the World Series. He also scored a phenomenal 2,174 runs, batted in 2,211 runs, and drew 2,056 walks.

NOLAN RYAN

Strikeout King

Born: *January 31, 1947, Refugio, TX*

Lynn Nolan Ryan was the most awesome strikeout pitcher in history, having thrown 5,714 strikeouts. This right-hander, who hurled for the Mets (1966, 1968–1971), Angels (1972–1979), Astros (1980–1988), and Rangers (1989–1993), led his league in strikeouts 11 times. He has a record seven no-hitters to his credit, and in 1981 and 1987 led the NL in ERA (with 1.69 and 2.76, respectively).

BRET SABERHAGEN

Journeyman Stopper

Born: *April 11, 1964, Chicago Heights, IL*

Bret William Saberhagen was a star right-handed pitcher for the Royals and other clubs. He broke into the game with the Royals in 1984, and in 1985 he won the Cy Young Award by going 20–6. That year he was also named the World Series Most Valuable Player when he went 2–0 in the Fall Classic. Saberhagen won another Cy Young Award in 1989 (23–6). He joined the Mets in 1992 and the Rockies midway through the 1995 season.

RYNE SANDBERG

Sparkling Cub

Born: *September 18, 1959, Spokane, WA*

Ryne Dee "Ryno" Sandberg was a key factor in the renaissance of the Cubs. A second baseman, he began his career with the Phillies (1981) and was then traded to the Cubs in 1982. A fine hitter and team leader, he was named the Most Valuable Player in the National League in 1984, when he batted .314 with 114 runs scored. Sandberg retired unexpectedly in 1994, having appeared in ten All-Star Games and won nine Gold Gloves, but he announced his return to the Cubs following the end of the 1995 season.

MIKE SCHMIDT

Pride of the Phillies

Born: *September 27, 1949, Dayton, OH*

Hall of Fame: *1995*

Michael Jack Schmidt was long the star of the Philadelphia club. This third baseman joined the Phillies in 1972 and won National League Most Valuable Player Awards in 1980, 1981, and 1986. He was also voted the Most Valuable Player in the 1980 World Series, was the league home run leader eight times, and was the runs batted in leader four times. By the time he retired in 1989, he had amassed 548 homers and won ten Gold Gloves.

TOM SEAVER

The Franchise of the Mets

Born: *November 17, 1944, Fresno, CA*

Hall of Fame: *1992*

George Thomas "Tom Terrific" Seaver was a right-handed pitcher for the Mets (1967–1977), Reds (1977–1982), Mets again (1983), White Sox (1984–1986), and Red Sox (1986). During his career he won 311 games, struck out 3,640 batters, and threw 61 shutouts. He was the Rookie of the Year in 1967 and won the Cy Young Award three times—in 1969, 1973, and 1975. When he was elected to the Hall of Fame in his first year of eligibility, it was with the highest voting percentage ever achieved—98.84 percent.

WARREN SPAHN

The Heart of the Braves

Born: *April 23, 1921, Buffalo, NY*
Hall of Fame: *1973*

Warren Edward Spahn was the premier left-handed pitcher for the Braves, both in Boston and Milwaukee (1942, 1946–1964). He also pitched for the Mets (1965) and Giants (1965). In his 21-year career, he won 363 games (the most by a left-hander) while losing 245, and he pitched 63 shutouts. He led the league in wins eight times and in complete games nine times. Spahn, who won the Cy Young Award in 1957, also pitched two no-hitters in 1960 and 1961, when he was more than 39 years old.

TRIS SPEAKER

Extra-Base Hitter

Born: *April 14, 1888, Hubbard, TX*
Died: *December 8, 1958, Lake Whitney, TX*
Hall of Fame: *1937*

Tristram E. "The Grey Eagle," "Spoke" Speaker played the outfield for the Boston Red Sox (1907–1915), Cleveland Indians

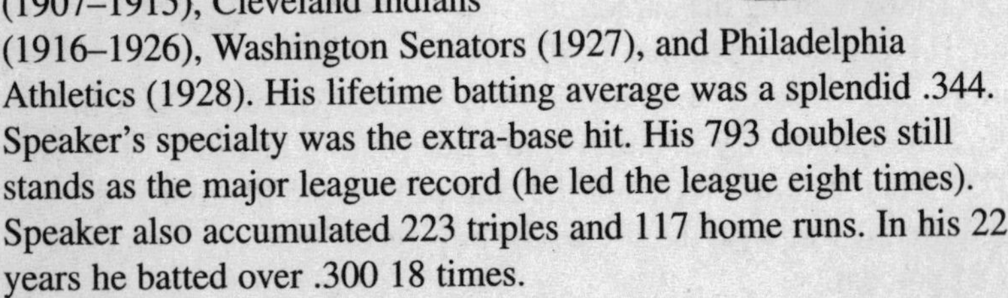

(1916–1926), Washington Senators (1927), and Philadelphia Athletics (1928). His lifetime batting average was a splendid .344. Speaker's specialty was the extra-base hit. His 793 doubles still stands as the major league record (he led the league eight times). Speaker also accumulated 223 triples and 117 home runs. In his 22 years he batted over .300 18 times.

CASEY STENGEL

Comedian and Baseball Genius
Born: *July 30, 1890, Kansas City, MO*
Died: *September 29, 1975, Glendale, CA*
Hall of Fame: *1966*

Charles Dillon "Casey" "The Old Professor" Stengel began as a joker and ended as one of the finest baseball minds in history. He played the outfield for the Brooklyn Dodgers (1912–1917), Pirates (1918–1919), Phillies (1920–1921), New York Giants (1921–1923), and Boston Braves (1924–1925), batting .284. But he made his mark as a manager. Stengel managed the Brooklyn Dodgers (1934–1936), Boston Braves (1938–1943), Yankees (1949–1960), and Mets (1962–1965). His greatest success came with the Yankees, with whom he won ten pennants and seven World Series in 12 years.

FRANK THOMAS

Sox Socker
Born: *May 27, 1968, Columbus, GA*

Frank "The Big Hurt" Thomas broke in with the Chicago White Sox in 1990. At the end of the 1995 season, this first baseman became the first player in baseball history to bat .300, hit 20 homers, have 100 RBIs, score 100 runs, and walk 100 times in five consecutive seasons. Opposing pitchers handed him the league lead in bases on balls in 1991, 1994, and 1995. Thomas was selected as the American League MVP in 1993 and 1994.

TED WILLIAMS

Boston Hero

Born: *August 30, 1918, San Diego, CA*

Hall of Fame: *1966*

Theodore Samuel "The Splendid Splinter" "The Thumper" Williams was arguably the best natural hitter of all time. He played the outfield for the Red Sox (1939–1942, 1946–1960) and had a lifetime .344 batting average. Williams led the league twice in doubles and four times in home runs. He also led the league six times in runs scored and four times in runs batted in. Plus he was a six-time batting champion, hitting .406 in 1941. Williams was voted the American League Most Valuable Player in 1946 and 1949. He managed the Washington Senators (1969–1971) and went with them when they became the Texas Rangers, managing them in 1972.

DAVE WINFIELD

Consistent Star Hitter

Born: *October 3, 1951, St. Paul, MN*

David Mark Winfield was a talented outfielder, making catches that most outfielders could never dream of making. He broke into the game with the Padres (1973–1980) and later played for the Yankees (1981–1990), Angels (1990–1991), Blue Jays (1992), Twins (1993–1994), and Indians (1995–). In 1979 he led the National League in runs batted in with 118, and he was a Gold Glover seven times. In 1992, Winfield became the first 40-year-old to knock in over 100 runs, when he had 108 RBIs. He finished the 1995 season with 3,110 career hits and 465 home runs.

CARL YASTRZEMSKI

Boston's All-Star

Born: *August 22, 1939, Southampton, NY*

Hall of Fame: *1989*

Carl Michael "Yaz" Yastrzemski was the pride of Boston for many years. Primarily an outfielder, he played for the Red Sox from 1961 to 1983. During his 23-year career, he played in 3,308 games, second in baseball history. A .285 lifetime hitter, he had 3,419 hits—sixth place in history—452 of which were home runs. Yastrzemski, the first alumnus of Little League Baseball to make the Hall of Fame, was the last player to win the Triple Crown, when he led the league in batting average (.326), home runs (44), and runs batted in (121) in 1967.

CY YOUNG

The Cyclone

Born: *March 29, 1867, Gilmore, OH*

Died: *November 4, 1955, Newcomerstown, OH*

Hall of Fame: *1937*

Denton True "Cy" Young was such a great pitcher that he had an award named after him. A right-hander, his nickname came from the word "cyclone." He threw for the Cleveland Spiders of the National League (1890–1898), Cardinals (1899–1900), Red Sox (1901–1908), Cleveland Naps (later the Indians, 1909–1911), and Boston Pilgrims (later the Braves, 1911). Young won 511 games in his career to place him first in baseball history. He also set the records for complete games (751) and innings pitched (7,356). He led the league four times in wins and seven times in shutouts.

Champions of the World

The World Series between the National and American league champions has been played since 1903. With the exception of 1904 and 1994, the Fall Classic, as it has come to be known, has been played annually. Here are facts on the World Series from 1903 on.

1903

Boston (AL) 5, Pittsburgh (NL) 3. The first World Series was a casual thing. It was decided in August that the games would be played, when it looked as though Boston and Pittsburgh were going to win their pennants. Then the presidents of the two clubs personally made plans to have a playoff. At the end of the season, the Boston Pilgrims (later the Red Sox) finished 14½ games ahead of the Philadelphia Athletics, and the Pirates won by 6½ games over the New York Giants. Then Boston defeated Pittsburgh in the best-of-nine game Series.

1904

No Series. The New York Giants owner, John T. Brush, and his manager, John McGraw, resented the new American League, which they thought was no more than a minor league. So the AL-leading Boston team and the Giants, who led the NL, did not meet that year.

1905

New York (NL) 4, Philadelphia (AL) 1. Brush changed his mind in 1905, and his Giants met the Philadelphia Athletics in the Series. The chief interest of this best-of-seven game Series was that it was a pitchers' battle all the way, and every game was a shutout.

1906

Chicago (AL) 4, Chicago (NL) 2. This year was an upset year, and the first time that teams from the same city met for the championship. The Chicago White Sox were called the "Hitless Wonders" because they had a team batting average of .230—the lowest in the American League—while the Chicago Cubs had won the pennant by 20 games over the Giants. Still, the Sox took the Series.

1907

Chicago (NL) 4, Detroit (AL) 0, 1 tie. After the first game ended in a 3–3 tie, called because of darkness, the Cubs went on to sweep the next four games.

1908

Chicago (NL) 4, Detroit (AL) 1. The Cubs had a bit of a problem when they ended the season in a tie with the New York Giants. This caused the first major league playoff game to decide a pennant, which the Cubs won, 4–2. And once again the Cubs took the Series. The people of Detroit seemed to sense the impending devastation. The last game was played in Detroit, and only 6,201 people showed up at Bennett Park—a record low for a World Series crowd.

1909

Pittsburgh (NL) 4, Detroit (AL) 3. For the first time in history, the World Series went the full seven games.

1910

Philadelphia (AL) 4, Chicago (NL) 1. Both teams had run away from the pack this year, the Cubs winning by 13 games and the Athletics by 14½. But Philadelphia humiliated the Chicagoans with their .316 batting average and by scoring an average of seven runs per game.

1911

Philadelphia (AL) 4, New York (NL) 2. This was a long Series—it spanned 13 days because rain forced a six-day postponement between the third and fourth games.

1912

Boston (AL) 4, New York (NL) 3, 1 tie. During the regular season, the Red Sox set an American League record by winning 105 games and finishing 14 games ahead of the Senators. The Giants also ran away from the rest of their league, finishing ten games ahead of the Pirates. The Series, not surprisingly, was a cliff-hanger.

1913

Philadelphia (AL) 4, New York (NL) 1. The Athletics and Giants met for the third time in nine years. The Athletics dominated the Series, their only loss being a ten-inning shutout by Christy Mathewson in the second game.

1914

Boston (NL) 4, Philadelphia (AL) 0. This was the year of the Boston "Miracle Braves." On July 19, the team was in last place. But after an incredible winning streak, they were in second place on August 10, moved into first on September 2, slipped a bit to third, and returned to first on September 8. Winning 60 of their last 76 games, they took the pennant by 10½ games over the Giants. The miracle continued into the Fall Classic as the Philadelphia Athletics became the first team in baseball history to be beaten in four straight games.

1915

Boston (AL) 4, Philadelphia (NL) 1. This was the year that another Philadelphia team—the Phillies—made it to the World Series with their .592 won-lost percentage, the lowest to capture the flag up to that time. A guest at the World Series was President Woodrow Wilson, who traveled all the way from Washington to Philadelphia to throw out the first ball of the second game.

1916

Boston (AL) 4, Brooklyn (NL) 1. In the second game, Babe Ruth made his first World Series start as a Red Sox pitcher and won the game, 2–1. This was the longest game played in World Series history in terms of innings played. It went 14 innings, and the Babe gave up only six hits.

1917

Chicago (AL) 4, New York (NL) 2. Two teams representing the nation's most populous cities met in this first World Series during wartime—beginning only six months after the United States had entered World War I.

1918

Boston (AL) 4, Chicago (NL) 2. The United States was still at war in 1918, and the major leagues were ordered to suspend the season by Labor Day. Only the last two championship clubs were allowed to extend their seasons in order to play the World Series. Babe Ruth, pitching for the Red Sox, ran his string of consecutive scoreless innings to a whopping 29⅔ innings—a record that was not broken until 1961.

1919

Cincinnati (NL) 5, Chicago (AL) 3. The White Sox finished 3½ games ahead of the Indians this year. They were one of the greatest teams of all time, with stars at every position. In the National League, it was the underdog Reds, who beat out the Giants by nine games. But the Reds won their first world championship—which was again a best-of-nine contest, as it would also be in 1920 and 1921. It was a tainted championship, however, since this was the year of the infamous Black Sox Scandal, in which several players on the Chicago team threw the World Series. (See page 196 for more information on the Black Sox Scandal.)

1920

Cleveland (AL) 5, Brooklyn (NL) 2. This Series was marked by two unusual events. In the fifth game, Bill Wambsganns, the Cleveland second baseman, made the only unassisted triple play in World Series history. And since Cleveland shortstop Ray Chapman had become the only major league player ever to have been killed during a game after having been hit by a pitch late in the season, the Indians were permitted to play Joe Sewell, who had been procured after the September 1 deadline.

1921

New York (NL) 5, New York (AL) 3. This was the first "Subway Series" between two New York teams. The Giants had won the pennant by four games over the Pirates, and the Yankees had beaten the Indians by 4½ games.

1922

New York (NL) 4, New York (AL) 0, 1 tie. After a three-year trial of the best-of-nine games, baseball went back to a World Series of a maximum seven games. The highlight of the Series was the second

game, which ended in a 3–3 tie. The game was called at the end of the tenth inning by the home plate umpire "on account of darkness." Since there was still about a half-hour of light remaining, many of the fans were understandably upset. Thinking that Baseball Commissioner Kenesaw Mountain Landis was responsible for the decision, some fans followed him with a chorus of boos as he made his way across the field after the game. Landis ordered that the receipts of the game be turned over to New York charities.

1923

New York (AL) 4, New York (NL) 2. It was the Yankees and the Giants once again. In the regular season, the Bronx Bombers, playing in the brand-new Yankee Stadium, finished 16 games over the Tigers. The Giants had ended the season 4½ games ahead of the Reds. This time, outfielder Babe Ruth was not to be denied. He hit .368 with three home runs (two in succession in the second game), a triple, a double, and two singles (and walked eight times).

1924

Washington (AL) 4, New York (NL) 3. This Series featured one of the most notable games in history—the final game. With the Giants leading in the eighth inning, 3–1, the Senators tied it up and then won the game, 4–3, in the 12th inning.

1925

Pittsburgh (NL) 4, Washington (AL) 3. For the first time, a team down three games to one went on to take three straight and win the Series. Some of this comeback was the fault of Roger Peckinpaugh, the Senators' shortstop, who was the American League MVP that year. He committed an astonishing eight errors in his 40 chances.

1926

St. Louis (NL) 4, New York (AL) 3. The Cardinals had just won their first National League pennant. The hero of the Series was their 39-year-old pitcher, Grover Cleveland Alexander. He won the second and sixth games and saved the last game after he was called in in the seventh inning with the bases loaded, but with his team leading, 3–2. He gave up no hits in his 2⅓ innings.

1927

New York (AL) 4, Pittsburgh (NL) 0. Many consider the 1927 Yankees to have been the best baseball team of all time. They didn't surrender first place all year, and with Ruth, Gehrig, et al., on the Yankees staff, the Series was no contest.

1928

New York (AL) 4, St. Louis (NL) 0. The Yankees came up with their second straight sweep of the National League champions. This was done despite many of the stars of the team being laid up—pitcher Herb Pennock, center fielder Earle Combs, second baseman Tony Lazzeri. Even outfielder Babe Ruth limped on his lame ankle throughout the Series. But the St. Louis pitchers still couldn't do better than a combined ERA of 6.09 against the Yankees' hitters.

1929

Philadelphia (AL) 4, Chicago (NL) 1. Once again the two participants won their pennants in a walkaway. The Cubs finished 10½ games in front and the Athletics 18. But the Series was settled by the pitchers, with Philadelphia's hurlers posting a 2.40 ERA, while Chicago came up with a less than mediocre 4.33.

1930

Philadelphia (AL) 4, St. Louis (NL) 2. Even though the Cards had been 12 games behind the Cubs in August, they came up with the National League pennant. St. Louis faded in the Series, however, and the pitchers made the difference, with Philadelphia's 1.73 ERA topping St. Louis's 3.35. The pitching had to be good, since the Athletics could come up with only a pitiful .197 batting average. The Cards weren't much better at .200.

1931

St. Louis (NL) 4, Philadelphia (AL) 3. This turned out to be Connie Mack's last pennant—his ninth. But the Cardinals had a secret weapon in John "Pepper" Martin, who stole five bases and batted .500 in the Series. With four doubles in 24 times at bat, he batted in five runs in a Series in which St. Louis scored only 19.

1932

New York (AL) 4, Chicago (NL) 0. This was the year of Joe McCarthy's revenge. He had been dismissed as the manager of the Cubs late in the 1930 season. Now he was manager of the Yankees, and he brought them in in first place. Revenge was sweet for McCarthy as the Yankees swept the Series.

1933

New York (NL) 4, Washington (AL) 1. Even though the Giants dominated the Senators, this was a Series of star hitters. For Washington, center fielder Fred Schulte hit .333 and shortstop Joe Cronin .318. On the New York side, right fielder Mel Ott turned in an astonishing .389 with two homers, and center fielder George "Kiddo" Davis batted .368.

1934

St. Louis (NL) 4, Detroit (AL) 3. The Detroit Tigers took their first pennant in 25 years. In the National League, the Cardinals beat out the Giants on the last day of the season, finishing two games ahead of New York. The first six games of the Series were well played, but the seventh game was a travesty, with the Cardinals winning in Detroit, 11–0, to take the Series. During that game, Commissioner Landis was forced to remove Cardinals left fielder Joe "Ducky" Medwick from the action after an incredible display by bottle- and vegetable-throwing Tigers fans. They were protesting Medwick's aggressive slide into Tigers third baseman Marv Owen.

1935

Detroit (AL) 4, Chicago (NL) 2. The Cubs were in the Series following a sensational 21-game September winning streak. But light hitting cost them the championship of the world.

1936

New York (AL) 4, New York (NL) 2. In this New York Subway Series, rookie Joe DiMaggio batted .346, and the Yankees' batters overwhelmed the Giants with an average of .302 against .246. The Giants pitchers did not help much, with their combined ERA of 6.79.

1937

New York (AL) 4, New York (NL) 1. The Yankees took the Series, and they turned it into a debacle. Of the Yanks' total of 42 hits, six were doubles, four were triples, and four were home runs.

1938

New York (AL) 4, Chicago (NL) 0. Once again, the Yankees whitewashed the Cubs in the Series.

1939

New York (AL) 4, Cincinnati (NL) 0. The Yankees took the World Series—their fourth straight world championship and the fifth time they had won a Series by sweeping all four games.

1940

Cincinnati (NL) 4, Detroit (AL) 3. The hero of this Series was a Cincinnati coach—Jimmie Wilson. The regular catcher, Ernie Lombardi, had an ankle injury, and Wilson came in to catch in six games. He hit .353 and stole the only base of the Fall Classic.

1941

New York (AL) 4, Brooklyn (NL) 1. It was the Yankees again on top of the heap in 1941, a season highlighted by center fielder Joe DiMaggio's record-breaking 56-game streak in which he had at least one hit in every contest. The Yankees clinched the pennant on September 4—the earliest date ever—in their 136th game, ending 17 games ahead of the Red Sox. The Dodgers were the winners in the National League after the lead had changed hands between Brooklyn and the Cardinals 27 times during the season, and they finished 2½ games ahead of the Redbirds.

1942

St. Louis (NL) 4, New York (AL) 1. After losing the first game, the Cardinals went on to a four-game sweep. This gave the Yankees as many World Series losses as they had accumulated in the eight Series they played from 1927 to 1941.

1943

New York (AL) 4, St. Louis (NL) 1. Both teams had left the rest of their leagues in the dust, with the Cardinals finishing 18 games in front and the Yanks 13½. This was the tenth World Series victory for the New Yorkers and the last for their legendary manager, Joe McCarthy.

1944

St. Louis (NL) 4, St. Louis (AL) 2. The year 1944 gave baseball fans a contest that will probably never be repeated—an all–St. Louis World Series. The perennial doormats, the Browns, finally won the American League pennant by one game over the Tigers. The Cardinals had no trouble, finishing 14½ games ahead of the Pirates. The Redbirds won the Series, and the key to the championship was the fielding. The Cardinals made no errors in the six games, while the Browns committed ten.

1945

Detroit (AL) 4, Chicago (NL) 3. Despite two pitching masterpieces—Hank Borowy's six-hit shutout in the first game and Claude Passeau's one-hitter in the third—the Cubs maintained their losing streak of seven straight World Series.

1946

St. Louis (NL) 4, Boston (AL) 3. With Ted Williams back from serving in World War II, the Red Sox won their first pennant since 1918, finishing 12 games ahead of the Tigers. In the National League, it was the Cardinals, but they did it the hard way. Finishing the season in a tie with the Dodgers, they played the first pennant-deciding playoff series in major league history and won the first two games of the best-of-three contest.

1947

New York (AL) 4, Brooklyn (NL) 3. This World Series was the first in which a black man participated—Dodgers first baseman Jackie Robinson. But the Yankees won again.

1948

Cleveland (AL) 4, Boston (NL) 2. The Indians ended the season in a tie for first place with the Boston Red Sox but beat them in a one-game playoff. The batting heroes in the Series were first baseman Earl Torgeson of the Braves, who hit .389, and the first black man to play in the American League, center fielder Larry Doby of the Indians, who hit .318.

1949

New York (AL) 4, Brooklyn (NL) 1. This was the first World Series in which lights were used. In the final game, when it was getting dark, Ebbets Field in Brooklyn had to be illuminated in the ninth inning.

1950

New York (AL) 4, Philadelphia (NL) 0. This was the Yankees' sixth World Series sweep and their 13th world championship.

1951

New York (AL) 4, New York (NL) 2. The Giants made the most historic run toward the pennant since the "Miracle Braves" of 1914. Starting on August 12, when they trailed Brooklyn by 13½ games, they won 16 consecutive games and were only 5½ behind the Dodgers on September 9. Then they won 16 of their last 20 to force a playoff series. The Giants and Dodgers split the first two games. In the final game, with the Dodgers ahead, 4–1, in the bottom of the ninth, the Giants scored a run. Then, with two men on, Giants third baseman Bobby Thomson hit a home run off Ralph Branca to win the pennant. The Yankees had less trouble, finishing five games in front of the Indians. The Giants' heroics gave out in the World Series, as the Yankees took yet another championship.

1952

New York (AL) 4, Brooklyn (NL) 3. The batting heroes in this grueling seven-game Series were left fielder Gene Woodling of the Yankees, who hit .348, and three other players who tied at .345: Yankees center fielder Mickey Mantle, Dodgers shortstop Peewee Reese, and Dodgers center fielder Duke Snider.

1953

New York (AL) 4, Brooklyn (NL) 2. The Yankees, under manager Casey Stengel, won their fifth straight world championship—a record. On the other hand, the Dodgers lost their seventh straight World Series. This Series also featured a startling raise in ticket prices—box seats were $10 (from the previous $8), grandstand seats were $7 (from $6), and bleacher seats were $2 (from $1).

1954

New York (NL) 4, Cleveland (AL) 0. The Giants swept the Series by hitting .254 against the Indians' .190. And add to that the New Yorkers' 1.46 ERA, compared with Cleveland's 4.84.

1955

Brooklyn (NL) 4, New York (AL) 3. The Dodgers took their first world championship in eight tries by becoming the first team to battle back after losing the first two games in a seven-game Series.

1956

New York (AL) 4, Brooklyn (NL) 3. The most spectacular event of this World Series came in the fifth game. Don Larsen, the Yankees' pitcher, was perfect that day. Not a single Dodger made it to first base. It was the one and only perfect game in Series history.

1957

Milwaukee (NL) 4, New York (AL) 3. The hero was Braves pitcher Lew Burdette, who posted three victories and hurled 24 consecutive scoreless innings. He also allowed but two runs in his 27 total innings for an ERA of 0.67.

1958

New York (AL) 4, Milwaukee (NL) 3. The Yankees were the first team since 1925 to win the Fall Classic after being down three games to one.

1959

Los Angeles (NL) 4, Chicago (AL) 2. For the first time, no complete game was pitched in a World Series. In the fifth game, for the first time in Series history, three pitchers combined to throw a shutout. They were Bob Shaw, Billy Pierce, and Dick Donovan of the White Sox, and the score was 1–0.

1960

Pittsburgh (NL) 4, New York (AL) 3. The teams split the first six games, and the final game was a free-for-all. Pittsburgh scored two runs in the first inning and two in the second. The Yankees scored one run in the fifth and four in the sixth. In the eighth, New York added two more runs, and the Pirates added five. The Yankees tied the ball game in the ninth with two more runs. But then came the bottom of the inning. Pirates second baseman Bill Mazeroski stepped up to the plate, took one pitch for a ball, and then hit the homer that made the Pirates the champions of the world. The Yanks had scored 55 runs to the Pirates' 27, but the Bucs triumphed in the Series.

1961

New York (AL) 4, Cincinnati (NL) 1. It was in the fourth game of the Series that Whitey Ford broke Babe Ruth's record of pitching $29^2/_3$ consecutive scoreless innings in World Series play. When Ford won the first game of the 1961 Series, he had gone 27 innings without giving up a run. In the fourth game, he went five scoreless innings before he injured his ankle in the sixth. But he had set a new World Series record of 32 innings without a run scored.

1962

New York (AL) 4, San Francisco (NL) 3. Even though the Yankees batted a miserable .199 against the Giants' .226 and were outscored 21–20, they made their moves when the chips were down and won their 20th world championship.

1963

Los Angeles (NL) 4, New York (AL) 0. This was the first time in history that the Yankees were swept in the World Series. The Dodgers outhit them, .214 to .171, and outpitched them, with a team ERA of 1.00 to 2.91 and with remarkable starting pitching from Sandy Koufax, Don Drysdale, and Johnny Podres.

1964

St. Louis (NL) 4, New York (AL) 3. Probably the strangest thing coming out of this year's Series happened to the managers. The day after the Series ended, manager Johnny Keane of the Cardinals resigned, and Yogi Berra, the rookie Yankees manager, was fired, although he had won a pennant in his first year of managing. Four days later, Keane was named as Yankees manager, and in November, Berra went to the Mets as a coach.

1965

Los Angeles (NL) 4, Minnesota (AL) 3. The Dodgers, who hit only 78 home runs during the season, turned things around at bat, hitting .274 against the Twins' .195. Plus, Sandy Koufax posted an ERA of 0.38 in three games.

1966

Baltimore (AL) 4, Los Angeles (NL) 0. This was a humiliating World Series for the Dodgers, who lost four straight. They managed to score only two runs in four games, going 33 innings without scoring. They committed six errors—all of them in the second game—while the Orioles went errorless.

1967

St. Louis (NL) 4, Boston (AL) 3. The Red Sox had finished in ninth place the year before, and their winning the American League pennant on the last day of the season was a minor miracle. But the impossible dream died in seven games in the Series.

1968

Detroit (AL) 4, St. Louis (NL) 3. The pitchers were the stars of this World Series. The Cardinals' Bob Gibson struck out 17 batters in the first game and ended up with two victories, while the Tigers' Mickey Lolich won three. Both posted ERAs of 1.67.

1969

New York (NL) 4, Baltimore (AL) 1. This Series went to the "Miracle Mets," who had been losers throughout their history. Before the 1969 season began, the two leagues had added expansion teams and had broken up into two separate divisions. The winners in the two divisions would face each other in a best-of-five playoff—called the LCS, or League Championship Series. Never higher than ninth since being awarded an expansion franchise in 1962, Gil Hodges's Mets surprised everybody by winning the Eastern Division and then by sweeping the Western Division leader, the Atlanta Braves, in the play-offs. The Orioles wiped out the American League's Western Division winners, the Minnesota Twins, also in three games. Then in the Series, the Mets outhit and outpitched Baltimore.

1970

Baltimore (AL) 4, Cincinnati (NL) 1. Baltimore made up for its collapse the year before by first sweeping the Twins in the playoffs while the Reds were also sweeping the Pirates, and then going on to take the Series. This was the first Series in which some games were played on artificial turf (in Cincinnati's Riverfront Stadium).

1971

Pittsburgh (NL) 4, Baltimore (AL) 3. The Pirates beat the Giants, three games to one, in the NL LCS, while the Orioles swept the A's in three straight games. In the Series, the fourth game, in Pittsburgh, was the first World Series night game. Pittsburgh right fielder Roberto Clemente was the batting star, hitting .414 with two doubles, one triple, and two homers in his 29 times at bat.

1972

Oakland (AL) 4, Cincinnati (NL) 3. The A's won the league crown by beating the Tigers in a five-game LCS, while the Reds knocked off the Pirates in a five-game series that wasn't decided until the last inning of the last game. Then the A's won their first world championship since 1930, when the team was in Philadelphia. Catcher Gene Tenace batted .348 with four homers and nine RBIs. Night World Series games were played the first and the last weekend.

1973

Oakland (AL) 4, New York (NL) 3. The "Amazin' Mets" pulled a repeat miracle. They were in last place on August 30, but they managed to win the NL Eastern Division by 1½ games over the Cardinals.

The Mets then took the Reds in the LCS, while the A's triumphed over the Orioles to enter the Fall Classic—where the Mets' magic faded.

1974

Oakland (AL) 4, Los Angeles (NL) 1. In the LCS, Oakland polished off the Orioles in four games, while the Dodgers also took four games to defeat the Pirates. Then Oakland won its third straight World Series, four games to one, in this first Fall Classic played entirely on the West Coast. Also, for the third straight year, no pitcher was able to turn in a complete game.

1975

Cincinnati (NL) 4, Boston (AL) 3. In the LCS, the Red Sox eliminated the A's in a three-game sweep, as the Reds also swept the

Pirates. The hitting stars of the Series were Cincinnati third baseman Pete Rose (.370) and Boston left fielder/first baseman Carl Yastrzemski (.310).

1976

Cincinnati (NL) 4, New York (AL) 0. Cincinnati swept its LCS with Philadelphia, while the Yankees took five games to beat the Royals. This World Series was the first in which designated hitters were used. The Reds outhit the Yanks (.313 to .222) as well as outpitching them (2.00 ERA to 5.45). The Reds' Johnny Bench hit .533, while the Yankees' Thurman Munson hit .529.

1977

New York (AL) 4, Los Angeles (NL) 2. New York took Kansas City in the AL LCS, but had to wait until the last inning of the fifth game to do it. Meanwhile, the Dodgers topped the Phillies in four games. New York then captured its 21st World Series, as right fielder Reggie Jackson batted .450 with five home runs—three in succession in the last game.

1978

New York (AL) 4, Los Angeles (NL) 2. After ending in a tie with the Red Sox, the Yankees took the Eastern Division in a single-game playoff, then went on to beat the Royals, three games to one, in the LCS. In the NL LCS, the Dodgers beat the Phillies in four games. In the Series, the Yanks lost the first two games, but they fought back and won the next four games and the Series, becoming the first team to win the Fall Classic in six games after losing the first two.

1979

Pittsburgh (NL) 4, Baltimore (AL) 3. The Pirates beat the Reds in the NL LCS in a three-game sweep, while the Orioles beat the Angels in the AL, three games to one. In the Series, the Orioles were ahead, three games to one. But the Pirates roared back to take the next three games and the championship.

1980

Philadelphia (NL) 4, Kansas City (AL) 2. Kansas City beat the Yankees in a sweep in the AL LCS, and Philadelphia took its LCS from Houston in five games. When Philadelphia triumphed over the Royals, it was the first Phillies' win in the Fall Classic.

1981

Los Angeles (NL) 4, New York (AL) 2. This was the year of a strike that caused the cancellation of 712 games. It was decided that the four teams leading their divisions when the strike was called would face the four teams leading their divisions in the part of the season played after the strike. In the West in the National League, the Dodgers beat the Astros in the playoffs, three games to two, while in the East the Expos beat the Phillies, also three games to two. In the East in the American League, the Yankees beat the Brewers, three games to two, while in the West the A's swept the Royals. Then came the LCS games, with Los Angeles beating Montreal, three games to two, and New York taking Oakland in a sweep. The Dodgers then won the World Series after New York had won the first two games. For the first time the Series MVP was split three ways, going to Dodgers third

baseman Ron Cey, center fielder Pedro Guerrero, and catcher Steve Yeager.

1982

St. Louis (NL) 4, Milwaukee (AL) 3. In the AL LCS, the Brewers beat the Angels, three games to two, while in the NL the Cardinals swept the Braves. Although St. Louis won the Series, the Brewers' Paul Molitor hit .355, with the first five-hit game in Series history, and his teammate Robin Yount, who hit .414, became the first player to record two four-hit games.

1983

Baltimore (AL) 4, Philadelphia (NL) 1. In the LCS, the Phillies beat the Dodgers, three games to one, while the Orioles also topped the White Sox in four. In the "railroad" World Series, Philadelphia took the first game, then Baltimore went on to win the next four.

1984

Detroit (AL) 4, San Diego (NL) l. The Tigers swept the Royals in the AL LCS, while the Padres beat the Cubs, three games to two, for the NL crown. In the World Series the star was Detroit shortstop Alan Trammell, who collected an astonishing nine hits in five games, including two home runs, to bat .450.

1985

Kansas City (AL) 4, St. Louis (NL) 3. The League Championship Series became a best-of-seven contest. The Cardinals topped the Dodgers in the NL LCS in six games, while in the AL the Royals beat the Blue Jays in seven. In the Series, after six tight games, the Royals rolled to their first world championship in a laugher—winning the final, 11–0. Royals pitcher Bret Saberhagen won two games and posted an ERA of 0.50.

1986

New York (NL) 4, Boston (AL) 3. The Mets won their LCS over the Astros, four games to two, while the Red Sox won their pennant over the Angels, four games to three. The star of this tight Series was Mets third baseman Ray Knight, who hit .391 with nine hits in 23 at bats.

1987

Minnesota (AL) 4, St. Louis (NL) 3. The Cardinals beat the Giants in the NL LCS, four games to three, while the Twins triumphed over the Tigers, four games to one. The World Series opened in the noisy Metrodome in Minneapolis, the first time a Series game was played indoors. It turned out that the noise of the fans may have made the difference. Measured decibel levels indicated it was so noisy that many people could have suffered temporary hearing impairment. The Twins won all four games there to take their first championship, while the Cardinals won the three that were played in St. Louis.

1988

Los Angeles (NL) 4, Oakland (AL) 1. Los Angeles won the NL LCS over New York in seven tough games. Meanwhile, Oakland swept Boston. The Dodgers outhit the A's in the Series with a batting average of .246 to .177. And their pitchers' team ERA was 2.05 against Oakland's 3.89.

1989

Oakland (AL) 4, San Francisco (NL) 0. In the LCS, San Francisco beat the Cubs, four games to one, and Oakland took Toronto, also four games to one. Although the Series went only four games, it took the longest time of any Series to complete. After the first two games in Oakland, both won by the A's, the Series moved to San Francisco on October 17. But just before the game was to start, the Bay Area was hit by a massive earthquake. Play was not resumed for ten days, and then the A's went on to take the next two games and the Series.

1990

Cincinnati (NL) 4, Oakland (AL) 0. In a dazzling upset, the Reds swept the A's. The A's had dominated the AL Western Division, finishing in first place by nine games, and then won the LCS by shutting out the Red Sox, four games to none. In contrast, the Reds had had trouble with the Pirates in their LCS, eventually winning, four games to two. But in the World Series, Cincinnati batted .317 against Oakland's .207. The Reds also outhit the A's, 45 to 28, and outscored them, 22 to 8. And in the entire Series, the Reds pitchers allowed zero runs after the third inning.

1991

Minnesota (AL) 4, Atlanta (NL) 3. The Braves won the NL LCS from the Pirates, four games to three, and four of the seven games were shutouts. In the American League, the Twins took the Blue Jays, four games to one. For the first time in history, the World Series was played between two teams that had finished in last place in their divisions the year before. In 1990 the Braves had finished 26 games out of first place, while the Twins had trailed by 29 games. The Series was close. The Twins won all four games in Minneapolis, and the Braves won all three played in Atlanta. It was the first Series to have four games decided as a result of the last pitch, the first to have five games decided in a team's last at bat, the first to have three extra-inning games, and the first to have a seventh and last game go scoreless through nine innings. In addition to all this, the Series had five one-run games, including a 1–0 seventh game.

1992

Toronto (AL) 4, Atlanta (NL) 2. Atlanta was the National League champion, beating Pittsburgh, four games to three, in the LCS, while Toronto won in the American League over Oakland, four games to two. For the first time in history a foreign team (from Canada) played in the World Series. Not only that, but the Canadians went on to win the Fall Classic. It was a close Series, with four of the six games decided by one run. Along the way, the Blue Jays' bullpen went 15½ straight innings without allowing a run.

1993

Toronto (AL) 4, Philadelphia (NL) 2. The Phillies beat the Braves in the NL LCS, four games to two. Meanwhile, in the AL the Blue Jays took the White Sox, also four games to two. The Blue Jays then won their second consecutive World Series—the first time in 15 years that a team had won back-to-back championships. The fourth game, won by the Blue Jays, 15–14, was the highest scoring game in Series history and the longest in terms of time—four hours and 14 minutes. The hero of the World Series was the Blue Jays' designated hitter, Paul Molitor, who hit .500 with 12 hits in 24 at bats, including two doubles, two triples, two home runs, and eight RBIs.

1994

No Series. In 1994, baseball adopted a new format of three divisions in each league—East, Central, and West—which would have required a complicated postseason system. But the strike eliminated the last third of the season, the playoffs, and the World Series.

1995

Atlanta (NL) 4, Cleveland (AL) 2. For the first time, as a result of the new three-division format, baseball's postseason involved three stages—the best-of-five Division Series (involving wild card teams), best-of-seven LCS, and best-of-seven World Series. In the NL Division Series, Cincinnati beat Los Angeles in a three-game sweep, while Atlanta defeated Colorado (the wild card), three games to two. Atlanta then bested Cincinnati in a four-game sweep in the NL LCS. In the AL Division Series, Cleveland defeated Boston in a three-game sweep, while Seattle topped New York (the wild card) in five games. Cleveland then topped Seattle, four games to two, in the AL LCS. The Braves triumphed over the Indians, who hadn't made it to the Fall Classic since 1954. Five of the six games were decided by one run. The pitching star was Atlanta's Tom Glavine, who went 2–0 with a 1.29 ERA. Although Cleveland led the majors in batting average, home runs, and runs scored, the team hit only .179 in the Series.

The All-Star Game

The All-Star Game was first played between the greats of the American and National leagues in 1933 in Chicago. It was a promotional idea of Arch Ward, the sports editor of the Chicago *Tribune,* to hype the Chicago World's Fair of that year. It has been played every year but one (1945) since then, in a different major league ballpark each year. Since 1970, the All-Star starting players are selected by fans (rather than by a committee or the managers of the two teams). The pitchers and non-starters are selected by the two managers (the same managers who faced each other in the previous World Series). For four years (1959–1962) two games were held each year, but that proved disruptive to the schedule.

1933—American, 4–2
1934—American, 9–7
1935—American, 4–1
1936—National, 4–3
1937—American, 8–3
1938—National, 4–1
1939—American, 3–1
1940—National, 4–0
1941—American, 7–5
1942—American, 3–1
1943—American, 5–3
1944—National, 7–1
1945—No Game
1946—American, 12–0
1947—American, 2–1
1948—American, 5–2
1949—American, 11–7
1950—National, 4–3
(14 innings)
1951—National, 8–3
1952—National, 3–2
(five innings, rain)
1953—National, 5–1
1954—American, 11–9
1955—National, 6–5
(12 innings)
1956—National, 7–3
1957—American, 6–5
1958—American, 4–3
1959—National, 5–4
American, 5–3
1960—National, 6–0
National, 5–3
1961—National, 5–4
(ten innings)
Tie, 1-1 (nine innings, rain)
1962—National, 3–1
American, 9–4
1963—National, 5–3
1964—National, 7–4
1965—National, 6–5
1966—National, 2–1
(ten innings)
1967—National, 2–1
(15 innings)
1968—National, 1–0
1969—National, 9–3
1970—National, 5–4
(12 innings)
1971—American, 6–4
1972—National, 4–3
(ten innings)
1973—National, 7–1
1974—National, 7–2
1975—National, 6–3
1976—National, 7–1
1977—National, 7–5
1978—National, 7–3
1979—National, 7–6
1980—National, 4–2
1981—National, 5–4
1982—National, 4–1
1983—American, 13–3
1984—National, 3–1
1985—National, 6–1
1986—American, 3–2
1987—National, 2–0
(13 innings)
1988—American, 2–1
1989—American, 5–3
1990—American, 2–0
1991—American, 4–2
1992—American, 13–6
1993—American, 9-3
1994—National, 8-7
(ten innings)
1995—National, 3-2

Firsts and Lasts

Everything has a beginning and an end. Here are some of the major appearances and disappearances in the world of baseball.

Firsts

1834—The first instructional book to include baseball, *The Book of Sports,* was published.

September 23, 1845—The first baseball club, the amateur Knickerbocker Base Ball Club, was founded in New York.

April 22, 1876—The first National League game was played in Philadelphia at a diamond at 25th and Jefferson streets. The Boston Red Stockings beat the Philadelphia Athletics, 6–5, in front of 3,000 fans. Because it was the premier major league game, there were many major league firsts:

- Philadelphia shortstop Davy Force had the first assist.
- A Philadelphia first baseman made the first putout.
- Boston center fielder Jim O'Rourke had the first hit, a single.

⚾ Boston's Tim McGinley scored the first run on a long fly ball by Jack Manning in the second inning.

⚾ Philadelphia third baseman Levi Meyerle hit the first double, in the first inning.

April 24, 1876—Levi Meyerle hit the first major league triple.

May 2, 1876—Second baseman Ross Barnes of the Chicago White Stockings (later the Cubs) hit the first major league home run, an inside-the-parker against Cincinnati.

July 15, 1876—Cardinals pitcher George Washington "Grin" Bradley pitched the first major league no-hitter against the Hartford Dark Blues, winning by a 2–0 score.

1876—The first major league batting champion was crowned. It was second baseman Ross Barnes of the Chicago White Stockings (later the Cubs), with a .429 average.

June 2, 1883—The first night game was played in sandlot baseball in Fort Wayne, Indiana, between the Fort Wayne club and a team from Quincy, Illinois. League Park in Fort Wayne was floodlit by 17 lights of 4,000 candlepower each.

1884—The first ladies' day game was held by the New York Giants.

May 1, 1884—The first black players in major league baseball, brothers Moses Fleetwood Walker and Welday Wilberforce Walker, took the field for Toledo of the American Association, which was then considered a major league.

1885—The Chicago White Stockings (later the Cubs) were the first major league team to go south for spring training—to Hot Springs, Arkansas.

April 17, 1892—The first Sunday game in major league history was played. Cincinnati beat St. Louis, 5–1.

June 6, 1892—Benjamin Harrison was the first president of the United States to see a professional baseball game. He watched Cincinnati beat Washington, 7–4, in 11 innings.

April 24, 1901—The first American League game in history was played. The Chicago White Sox beat the Cleveland Broncos (later the Indians), 8–2, in front of 14,000 fans at the Chicago Cricket Club. Three other games were scheduled that day, but all of them were rained out.

July 19, 1909—Cleveland shortstop Neal Ball pulled off the first unassisted triple play in major league history.

April 14, 1910—William Howard Taft became the first president of the United States to throw out the first ball of the season. The game was in Washington, and there were 12,226 fans in the ballpark.

June 9, 1914—Shortstop Honus Wagner of the Pirates became the first major league player to get 3,000 base hits.

September 24, 1916—Marty Kavanagh of the Indians hit the first major league pinch-hit grand slam homer in a 5–3 triumph over the Red Sox. The ball rolled through a hole in the fence and could not be recovered in time.

June 1917—Catcher Hank Gowdy of the Boston Braves became the first major leaguer to volunteer for the armed forces in World War I.

August 5, 1921—Pittsburgh radio station KDKA provided its listeners with the first broadcast of a major league game. The Pirates beat the Phillies, 8–5, in Philadelphia, and the announcer was Harold Arlen.

June 1, 1925—Yankee first baseman Lou Gehrig appeared in the first of 2,130 straight games—a consecutive game record that stood until Cal Ripken, Jr., bettered it in 1995.

1927—The Yankees became the first club to spend the entire season in first place.

April 28, 1930—The first minor league night game in history was played at Independence, Missouri. Muskogee, Oklahoma, beat Independence, Missouri, 13–3, in this Western Association game.

July 6, 1933—The first major league All-Star Game was played at Comiskey Park in Chicago. The American League, managed by Connie Mack of the Athletics, beat the National League, managed by John McGraw of the Giants, 4–2, on Babe Ruth's two-run homer.

May 23, 1935—The first scheduled major league night game, which was to be played in Cincinnati, was postponed because of rain.

May 24, 1935—The first major league night game was played at Crosley Field in Cincinnati. The Reds beat the Phillies, 2–1, before a crowd of 25,000.

1936—Construction of the Hall of Fame in Cooperstown, New York, began, and the first group of major league players were elected. The first roster consisted of shortstop Honus Wagner of the Pirates, rightfielder Babe Ruth of the Yankees, center fielder Ty Cobb of the Tigers, pitcher Walter Johnson of the Senators, and pitcher Christy Mathewson of the Giants.

June 15, 1938—At Brooklyn's Ebbets Field, Johnny Vander Meer of the Reds pitched his second consecutive no-hitter—the only time this has been done—as Cincinnati won, 6–0.

May 16, 1939—The first American League night game was played in Philadelphia at Shibe Park.

June 12, 1939—The Hall of Fame officially opened in Cooperstown and the first inductions took place.

July 20, 1939—First baseman Johnny Mize of the Cardinals hit three home runs. It was the first time a major league player had two three-homer games in a single season.

August 26, 1939—The first televised baseball game was carried on NBC's experimental station, W2XBS. It was the first game of a doubleheader between the Reds and the Dodgers at Ebbets Field in Brooklyn, and the Reds won. The telecast had commercials for three different products—Ivory Soap, Mobil Oil, and Wheaties.

September 6, 1940—Second baseman Johnny Lucadello of the Browns became the first player to homer both right-handed and left-handed in a single game. These two homers were his only round-trippers of the season.

May 7, 1941—Left fielder Hank Greenberg of the Tigers became the first major league player to enter the armed forces as World War II came closer to the United States.

June 9, 1946—Mel Ott of the Giants became the first manager in major league baseball to be thrown out in both games of a doubleheader for arguing with the umpire. The Pirates won both games, 2–1 and 5–1.

April 15, 1947—On opening day, first baseman Jackie Robinson of the Brooklyn Dodgers became the first black player in modern major league history.

July 3, 1947—The Indians bought left fielder Larry Doby from the Newark Eagles of the Negro National League, making him the first black player in the American League.

July 8, 1947—In the 14th All-Star Game at Wrigley Field in Chicago, the Yankees' Spec Shea became the first rookie pitcher to win the classic.

August 26, 1947—The Dodgers' Dan Bankhead became the first black pitcher in the major leagues. Sent in as a relief pitcher, he gave up ten hits and six earned runs in 3$^{1}/_{3}$ innings but did not figure in the decision as the Pirates won the game, 16–3. Bankhead also hit a homer in his first appearance at the plate.

October 2, 1947—Yankees catcher Yogi Berra clouted the first World Series pinch homer.

June 30, 1948—Bob Lemon of the Indians pitched the first night-game no-hitter in the American League and beat the Tigers, 2–0.

July 11, 1950—For the first time, the All-Star Game was broadcast on network television. The game was returned to Comiskey Park in Chicago, where it had begun, and the National League won, 4–3, in 14 innings.

June 13, 1957—Left fielder Ted Williams of the Red Sox hit three home runs and drove in five runs as Boston beat the Indians, 9–3. It was the first time an American League player had two three-homer games in a single season.

May 15, 1960—Chicago Cubs pitcher Don Cardwell became the first hurler to throw a no-hitter in his first start after being traded. He had just come from the Phillies. The final score of the game was 4–0 in favor of the Cubs over the Cardinals.

May 27, 1960—The first "big mitt" used to catch knuckleball pitches was used by Baltimore's Clint Courtney, who caught for Hoyt Wilhelm. The mitt, designed by baseball executive and former catcher Paul Richards, was 50 percent larger than the standard mitt. The Orioles beat the Yankees, 3–2.

June 22, 1962—Left fielder Boog Powell of the Orioles became the first batter to hit a home run over the center field hedge at Baltimore's Memorial Stadium. It was a 469-foot shot off pitcher Don Schwall of the Red Sox.

1962—The first Sunday night game in baseball history was played in Houston, and the Colt .45s (later the Astros) beat the Giants, 3–0. Permission to play this game was granted because of the excessive heat in Houston during the day.

1966—Emmett Littleton Ashford became the first black umpire in modern major league baseball. He was hired by the American League.

July 9, 1968—The first indoor All-Star Game was played in the Houston Astrodome. It was also the first such contest to be decided by a 1–0 score, as the National League beat the American League.

October 13, 1971—The first World Series night game was played in Pittsburgh, and the Pirates beat the Orioles, 4–3.

1975—Frank Robinson became the first black manager in the major leagues as he took over the Indians.

1978—The Dodgers became the first team to draw more than 3 million fans, setting an attendance record of 3,347,845.

1981—Frank Robinson became the first black manager in the National League, taking over the Giants.

1981—Fernando Valenzuela of the Dodgers became the first player to win the Cy Young Award and become Rookie of the Year in the same season.

May 30, 1982—Baltimore's Cal Ripken, Jr., replaced Floyd Rayford at third base in the second game of a doubleheader to begin a consecutive game playing streak that had reached a record 2,153 by the end of the 1995 season.

August 20, 1985—Pitcher Dwight Gooden of the Mets struck out 16 batters in a 3–0 victory over San Francisco, becoming the first National League pitcher to strike out 200 or more batters in each of his first two years. He made it a major league record of three years in 1986.

1987—Orioles manager Cal Ripken, Sr., became the first father ever to manage two sons (Cal, Jr., and Billy) simultaneously in the major leagues.

August 8, 1988—The first scheduled night game at Wrigley Field in Chicago was rained out in the bottom of the fourth inning with the Cubs ahead of the Phillies, 3–1. Wrigley Field was the last ballpark to install lights.

August 9, 1988—The first complete night game at Wrigley Field in Chicago ended with the Cubs beating the Mets, 6–4.

1988—José Canseco became the first major leaguer to steal 40 bases and hit 40 home runs (he hit 42) in the same season.

1989—Mark McGwire of the A's became the first player to hit 30 or more home runs in each of his first four years in the major leagues.

August 31, 1990—Ken Griffey, Sr., and Ken Griffey, Jr., of the Seattle Mariners became the first father and son to play together for the same major league team.

September 14, 1990—Ken Griffey, Sr., and Ken Griffey, Jr., became the first father and son to hit back-to-back home runs.

1990—George Brett of the Royals became the first man in major league history to win a batting title in three separate decades (1976: .333, 1980: .390, 1990: .329).

1990—Willie McGee became the first man to win a batting title in one league while playing in another. By August, while he was with the Cardinals, his batting average was .335, and that held up for the National League title, even though he had been traded to the A's.

1990—Barry Bonds of the Pirates became the first man to drive in 100 runs, score 100 runs, hit 30 home runs, and steal 50 bases while batting .300.

August 19, 1992—When second baseman Bret Boone played his first major league game for the Seattle Mariners, he went one for three. But more than that, he was the first third-generation major leaguer. His grandfather, Ray Boone, was an infielder for 13 years for the Indians, Tigers, White Sox, Kansas City Athletics, Milwaukee Braves, and Red Sox. His father, Bob Boone, was a catcher for 18 years, working successively for the Phillies, Angels, and Royals.

October 14, 1992—Cito Gaston of the Toronto Blue Jays became the first black manager to win a league pennant.

October 24, 1992—Cito Gaston became the first black manager to win the World Series.

April 3, 1994—The first nighttime season opener in baseball history was played in Cincinnati, and the St. Louis Cardinals beat the Reds, 6–4.

September 6, 1995—Baltimore shortstop Cal Ripken, Jr., became the first player to appear in 2,131 consecutive games, breaking Lou Gehrig's record of 2,130 games that had stood for 56 years. Ripken's record-breaking game—in which he homered—took place at Oriole Park at Camden Yards, in a 4–2 Baltimore victory over the Angels.

October 6, 1995—Mark Lewis of Cincinnati hit the first pinch grand slam in playoff history as the Reds beat the Dodgers, 10–1, to capture the Division Series in a three-game sweep.

1995—The Colorado Rockies became the first expansion team to make it to postseason play in only three years. As the NL wild card team, they lost the Division Series to the Atlanta Braves, three games to one.

1995—Greg Maddux of the Atlanta Braves became the first pitcher to win four consecutive Cy Young Awards.

Lasts

And now for some real nostalgia:

October 15, 1892—Charles Leander "Bumpus" Jones of Cincinnati beat Pittsburgh, 7–1, in the last no-hitter pitched from a distance of 50 feet.

September 22, 1911—Cy Young, at age 44, beat the Pirates, 1–0, for his 511th and last victory, setting a record for total wins that still stands.

September 4, 1916—Pitching legends Christy Mathewson, playing with Cincinnati after a long career with the Giants, and Mordecai "Three-Finger" Brown of the Cubs, both to become Hall of Famers, faced each other in what was to be the last major league game for them both. Mathewson and the Reds won, 10–8.

October 2, 1920—The Reds and Pirates played the last major league tripleheader.

1933—On the last day of the season, Babe Ruth pitched his last game—for the Yankees. He went the distance to win, 6–5.

1934—This was the last year in which all the major league baseball games were played in the daytime.

May 25, 1935—Babe Ruth, now playing for the Boston Braves, hit the last three home runs of his career, bringing his total to 714, at Forbes Field in Pittsburgh.

May 30, 1935—Babe Ruth played his last baseball game.

April 30, 1939—Lou Gehrig played his last baseball game.

July 25, 1941—Pitcher Lefty Grove, now with the Red Sox, won his 300th and last game by beating the Indians, 10–6.

1948—Indians shortshop Lou Boudreau became the last player/manager to win a pennant.

October 1, 1950—After 50 years managing the Philadelphia Athletics, Connie Mack piloted his last game.

September 21, 1952—Only 8,822 fans saw the last game played at Braves Field in Boston before the Braves moved to Milwaukee.

September 24, 1957—Dodgers pitcher Danny McDevitt shut out the Pirates, 3–0, in the Dodgers' last game in Brooklyn's Ebbets Field before they moved to Los Angeles.

September 29, 1957—The Giants lost to the Pirates, 9–1, in their last game in New York's Polo Grounds before they moved to San Francisco.

1959—The Boston Red Sox became the last major league team to sign a black player, second baseman Pumpsie Green.

September 18, 1963—The Mets lost their last game in the Polo Grounds to the Phillies, 5–1. Only 1,752 fans showed up for the final major league game to be played at that stadium. In 1964 the Mets moved to the brand-new Shea Stadium.

September 29, 1963—Left fielder Stan Musial of the Cardinals got the last hit of his career, number 3,630.

May 8, 1966—The Cardinals played their last game in the old Busch Stadium, losing 10–5 to the Giants.

May 11, 1971—Steve Dunning of the Indians hit the last grand slam home run by an American League pitcher (before the designated hitter rule) off Diego Segui of the A's.

September 30, 1972—Right fielder Roberto Clemente of the Pirates doubled off Mets pitcher Jon Matlack for his 3,000th and last hit. He died in a plane crash in December 1972.

November 2, 1972—Shortstop Freddy Parent of the old Boston Pilgrims (later the Red Sox), the last survivor of the first World Series in 1903, died at the age of 96.

July 20, 1976—Designated hitter Hank Aaron of the Brewers hit his last home run—number 755—off Dick Drago of the Angels.

The Teams

Major league baseball today consists of 28 teams—14 in the National League and 14 in the American League. But it was not always so. For example, in its first year in 1876, the National League consisted of eight teams—Chicago, St. Louis, Hartford (Connecticut), Boston, Louisville (Kentucky), New York, Philadelphia, and Cincinnati. Over the years, teams came and teams went.

At one time or another, there were National League clubs in such cities as Providence, Indianapolis, Milwaukee, Buffalo, Cleveland, Syracuse, Detroit, Kansas City (Missouri), Washington, D.C., and Baltimore. But who remembers the Louisville Grays, the Hartford Dark Blues, the Cleveland Spiders, the Troy Haymakers, the Buffalo Bisons, the Providence Grays, or the Detroit Wolverines? When the American League was formed in 1901, Baltimore, Washington, and Cleveland left the National League to join it.

In 1998, two new teams are scheduled to join the majors, the Arizona Diamondbacks, who will play in Phoenix, and the Tampa Bay Devil Rays, who will play in St. Petersburg, Florida.

Information on the present 28 major league teams follows.

National League

The address of the National League Office is 350 Park Avenue, New York, NY 10022.

EAST DIVISION

ATLANTA BRAVES, PO Box 4064, Atlanta, GA 30302. The Braves play their home games in Atlanta–Fulton County Stadium, built in 1965, which seats 52,710. The home run distances in left, center, and right fields are 330, 402, and 330 feet, respectively, and the stadium has natural grass.

The team made its debut in the National League in 1876 as the Boston Red Stockings. The team's name changed several times from 1883 to 1952. They were the Boston Beaneaters (1883–1906), Boston Doves (1907–1908), Boston Pilgrims (1909–1911), Boston Braves (1912–1935), Boston Bees (1936–1940), and Boston Braves again (1941–1952).

In 1953 the Braves moved to Milwaukee, where they played in Milwaukee County Stadium, which today is the home of the Brewers. That year, in the first 13 games of the new season, they surpassed their total 1952 attendance in Boston of 281,278. In 1966 the Braves' owners stunned the baseball world by selling the team to broadcasting magnate Ted Turner, who moved them to Atlanta, where they have been ever since.

FLORIDA MARLINS, 2267 NW 199th Street, Miami, FL 33056. The Marlins play their games in Joe Robbie Stadium, built in 1987, which seats 47,226. The home run distances in left, center, and right fields are 335, 410, and 345, and the park has natural grass.

In 1991, Miami was granted an expansion franchise in the National League. The Marlins began their first season in 1993.

MONTREAL EXPOS, PO Box 500, Station M, Montreal, Quebec H1V 3P2, Canada. The Expos play their home games in Olympic Stadium, built in 1976, with its capacity of 46,500. Its home run distances in left, center, and right fields are 325, 404, and 325 feet. The stadium has artificial turf.

The Expos were an expansion team in 1969, when they joined the National League. For their first years they played in Jarry Park.

NEW YORK METS, Shea Stadium, Flushing, NY 11368. The Mets play their home games in Shea Stadium, which seats 55,601. It has natural grass, and the home run distances in left, center, and right fields are 338, 410, and 338 feet.

The team was one of the two expansion teams admitted to the National League in 1962. At first they played in the old Polo Grounds in New York—the ballpark that had been empty since the Giants left town. When Shea Stadium was opened in 1964, the Mets began playing their games there.

PHILADELPHIA PHILLIES, PO Box 7575, Philadelphia, PA 19101. The Phillies play their home games in Veterans Stadium, built in 1971, which has a capacity of 62,136. The turf is artificial, and the home run distances in left, center, and right fields are 330, 408, and 330 feet.

The team was one of the charter members of the National League when it was formed in 1876. Known then as the Philadelphia Athletics, they changed their name to the Phillies in 1883. In 1943 and

1944, they called themselves the Blue Jays. In 1938 they moved to Shibe Park after playing for many years in Baker Bowl, which was a tiny bandbox of a stadium. In 1971 they moved to Veterans Stadium.

CENTRAL DIVISION

CHICAGO CUBS, Wrigley Field, Chicago, IL 60613. The Cubs play their home games in Wrigley Field, which seats 38,765. In 1988 it became the last ballpark to install lights for night games. The stadium's home run distances in left, center, and right fields are 355, 400, and 353 feet, and it has natural grass.

The Chicago team, first known as the White Stockings, won the first National League pennant in 1876. The name was changed to the Cubs in 1901.

In 1914, Weeghman Park, then seating only 14,000, was built at a cost of $250,000 for the Chicago Whales of the Federal League—a league that lasted only two years. The Cubs took over Weeghman Park in 1916. The stadium was soon renamed Cubs Park. In 1926 it became Wrigley Field in honor of William Wrigley, Jr., the club's owner.

CINCINNATI REDS, 100 Riverfront Stadium, Cincinnati, OH 45202. The Reds play their home games in Riverfront Stadium, built in 1970, with its seating capacity of 52,952. The home run distances in left, center, and right fields are 330, 404, and 330 feet, and there is artificial turf.

One of the original members of the National League in 1876, the Cincinnati Redlegs were expelled from the league after the 1880 season for allowing liquor on the grounds and playing on Sunday. They then joined the new American Association before returning to the NL in 1890. They were rechristened the Reds, but from 1944 to 1945 and 1954 to 1960, they called themselves the Red Legs, probably because they feared that people might think of them as being Communists. For many years, the club played in the old Crosley Field, which held only 29,000 fans.

HOUSTON ASTROS, PO Box 288, Houston, TX 77001. The Astros play their home games in the Astrodome, the country's first indoor ballpark, which seats 54,350. The home run distances in left, center, and right fields are 325, 400, and 325, and there is artificial turf, called Astroturf.

In 1962, Houston was granted an expansion franchise in the National League and fielded a club called the Houston Colt .45s. The .45s played their games in Colt Stadium. When the Astrodome was opened in 1965, the team took on a new name—the Houston Astros.

PITTSBURGH PIRATES, Three Rivers Stadium, Pittsburgh, PA 15212. The Pirates play their home games in Three Rivers Stadium, which holds 47,972 fans. Equipped with artificial turf, its home run distances in left, center, and right fields are 335, 400, and 335 feet.

Pittsburgh joined the American Association in 1882 and moved to the National League in 1887. They were the losing team in the first World Series in 1903—losing to Boston, five games to three. For years they played in the old Forbes Field, which seated 35,000, before moving to the Three Rivers Stadium, which opened in 1970.

ST. LOUIS CARDINALS, Busch Stadium, St. Louis, MO 63102. The Cardinals play their home games in Busch Stadium, which seats 57,078 fans. The home run distances in left, center, and right fields are 330, 402, and 330 feet, and the stadium has artificial turf.

The club started play in the National League in 1882, when they were known as the Brown Stockings or Browns. The name was changed to the Cardinals in 1889. For years they shared old Sportsman's Park with the St. Louis Browns of the American League. After the Cards were bought by August Busch, the beer baron, that park's name was changed to Busch Stadium in the 1950s. The new Busch Stadium opened in 1966.

WEST DIVISION

COLORADO ROCKIES, Coors Field, 2001 Blake Street, Denver, CO 80205. The Rockies play their home games in Coors Field, which seats 50,200. The home run distances in left, center, and right fields are 347, 415, and 350, and the park has natural grass.

In 1991, Denver was granted an expansion franchise in the National League, and the Rockies began their first season in 1993. They played their home games in Mile High Stadium until Coors Field opened in 1995.

LOS ANGELES DODGERS, Dodger Stadium, Los Angeles, CA 90012. The Dodgers play their home games in Dodger Stadium, built in 1962, which seats 56,000. Its home run distances in left, center, and right fields are 330, 395, and 330, and it has natural grass.

The team that was to become the Los Angeles Dodgers entered the American Association in 1884, under the name Brooklyn Bridegrooms. They joined the National League in 1890. The team had various names, including the Superbas and Robins. Because people in Brooklyn at that time often called themselves "trolley dodgers," the club finally became the Dodgers. For years they played ball in cozy Ebbets Field.

In 1958 the team left Brooklyn and settled in Los Angeles. Their first ballpark there was the Los Angeles Memorial Coliseum; they moved to Dodger Stadium in 1962.

SAN DIEGO PADRES, PO Box 2000, San Diego, CA 92112. The Padres play their home games in San Diego Jack Murphy Stadium, built in 1967, which seats 46,510. Its home run distances in left, center, and right fields are 327, 405, and 327, and it has natural grass. The team joined the National League in 1969 as an expansion team.

SAN FRANCISCO GIANTS, Candlestick (3Com) Park, San Francisco, CA 94124. Candlestick (or 3Com) Park, where the Giants play their home games, can accommodate 63,000 people. Its home run distances in left, center, and right fields are 335, 400, and 330 feet, and it has natural grass.

The franchise entered the National League in 1876 as the New York Giants. For years they played in the Polo Grounds in New York. But in 1957 it was announced that they were moving to San Francisco, and they began play there in 1958. The Giants took over a former minor league park, the old Seals Stadium, and in 1960 moved to the new Candlestick Park, which was given the name 3Com Park in 1995.

American League

The address of the American League Office is 350 Park Avenue, New York, NY 10022.

EAST DIVISION

BALTIMORE ORIOLES, Oriole Park at Camden Yards, 333 West Camden Street, Baltimore, MD 21201. The Orioles play their home games in Oriole Park at Camden Yards, which has a capacity of 48,262. The home run distances in left, center, and right fields are 333, 400, and 318, and it has natural grass.

The Orioles began play in 1901 as the Milwaukee Brewers. In 1902 they moved to St. Louis and became the Browns. For years they shared the old Sportsman's Park in St. Louis with the Cardinals of the National League. But the Browns were never a success, and in 1954 they moved to Baltimore and changed their name to the Orioles. They played in Memorial Stadium until 1992, when they moved to their new ballpark.

BOSTON RED SOX, 4 Yawkey Way, Boston, MA 02215. The Red Sox play their home games in the fine old stadium known as Fenway Park, opened in 1912. The park seats 33,871, its surface is natural grass, and its home run distances in left, center, and right fields are 315, 390, and 302 feet.

The team was a charter member of the American League when it was formed in 1901. The Red Sox played their early games at the Huntington Avenue Grounds. They were also known in their early years as the Pilgrims, Puritans, Plymouth Rocks, and Somersets.

DETROIT TIGERS, Tiger Stadium, Detroit, MI 48216. The Tigers play their home games in Tiger Stadium, which has a seating capacity of 52,416. It has natural grass, and its home run distances in left, center, and right fields are 340, 440, and 325 feet.

The team was in at the formation of the American League in 1901. For years the Tigers played in the old Bennett Park before Tiger Stadium (known for some years as Navin Field and Briggs Stadium) was built in 1912.

NEW YORK YANKEES, Yankee Stadium, The Bronx, NY 10451. The Yankees play their home games in Yankee Stadium, with its seating capacity of 57,545. The stadium has natural grass, and its home run distances in left, center, and right fields are 318, 408, and 314 feet.

In 1892 a team called the Baltimore Orioles joined the National League from the American Association, where it

remained until the organization of the American League in 1901, when it skipped to the junior circuit. The team stayed in Baltimore until moving to New York to open the 1903 season. The team called itself the Highlanders until 1912, when the name was changed to the Yankees. The team played in various parks, for some years sharing the Polo Grounds with the Giants, until Yankee Stadium was opened in 1923.

TORONTO BLUE JAYS, 1 Blue Jays Way, Toronto, Ontario M5V 1J1, Canada. The Blue Jays play their home games in the SkyDome, opened in 1989, which has a seating capacity of 50,516. It has artificial turf, and its home run distances in left, center, and right fields are 328, 400, and 328 feet. Toronto first took the field in 1977 after the city had received an expansion team franchise from the American League, playing during the early years in Exhibition Stadium.

CENTRAL DIVISION

CHICAGO WHITE SOX, 333 West 35th Street, Chicago, IL 60616. The Sox play their home games in Comiskey Park, which seats 44,321. Its home run distances in left, center, and right fields are 347, 400, and 347, and it has natural grass.

Formerly, the club played in Southside Park and then in the old Comiskey Park, which opened in 1910 as White Sox Park. The team, which moved into its new stadium in 1991, was a charter member of the American League in 1901, and it won the first American League pennant.

CLEVELAND INDIANS, 2401 Ontario Street, Cleveland, OH 44115. The Indians play their home games in Jacobs Field, which opened in 1994. The park has a seating capacity of 42,865. Its home run distances in left, center, and right fields are 325, 405, and 325 feet, and it has natural grass.

The team began as the Cleveland Spiders in the National League but switched to the American League when that circuit was formed in 1901. The team had a little trouble with names for a while—they were called the Broncos, Blues, Naps, and Molly McGuires before becoming the Indians in 1915. They originally played in League Park and from 1932 until 1993 in Cleveland Stadium.

KANSAS CITY ROYALS, PO Box 419969, Kansas City, MO 64141. The Royals play their home games in Ewing Kauffman Stadium, built in 1973, which holds 40,625 fans. It has artificial turf, and the home run distances in left, center, and right fields are 330, 410, and 330 feet. The team came into being as an expansion club in the American League in 1969 and played its first years in Municipal Stadium.

MILWAUKEE BREWERS, Milwaukee County Stadium, Milwaukee, WI 53214. The Brewers play their home games in Milwaukee County Stadium, built in 1953, which has a seating capacity of 53,192. The home run distances in left, center, and right fields are 315, 402, and 315 feet, and the park has natural grass.

In 1969, Seattle fielded an expansion club in the American League—the Seattle Pilots. The team lasted there but one year, playing in Sick's Stadium, before it moved to Milwaukee, taking the field as the Brewers in 1970.

MINNESOTA TWINS, 501 Chicago Avenue South, Minneapolis, MN 55415. The Twins play their home games in the Hubert H. Humphrey Metrodome, built in 1982, which holds 56,783 people. Its home run distances in left, center, and right fields are 343, 408, and 327 feet, and it has artificial turf.

The Twins' ancestors, the Washington Senators, were charter members of the American League when the league was founded in 1901. But in 1961, after years of falling attendance, the team moved to Minnesota and changed its name to the Twins. From 1961 to 1981 they played in Metropolitan Stadium in Bloomington, Minnesota.

WEST DIVISION

CALIFORNIA ANGELS, Anaheim Stadium, Anaheim, CA 92803. The Angels play their home games in Anaheim Stadium, built in 1966, with its seating capacity of 64,593. Its home run distances in left, center, and right fields are 333, 404, and 333 feet, and it has natural grass.

The team made its debut in 1961 as an expansion team called the Los Angeles Angels. They played in what had been Los Angeles's small minor league park, Wrigley Field. The club in 1962 moved to Chavez Ravine Stadium in Los Angeles (later called Dodger Stadium). The team moved south to Anaheim in 1966 and became the California Angels.

OAKLAND ATHLETICS, Oakland Coliseum, Oakland, CA 94621. The Athletics, commonly called the A's, play their home games in Oakland–Alameda County Coliseum, built in 1968, which can seat 47,313. The stadium has natural grass, and its home run distances in left, center, and right fields are 330, 400, and 330 feet.

The team began in Philadelphia as the Philadelphia Athletics—one of the charter members of the American League in 1901. The Athletics first occupied Columbia Park and from 1909 to 1954 played in Shibe Park, later renamed Connie Mack Stadium. But the fans didn't show up because of the team's poor record, and it was moved to Kansas City in 1955. While there, the Athletics played in Municipal Stadium. In 1968 the team moved yet again and opened the season in Oakland, California.

SEATTLE MARINERS, PO Box 4100, Seattle, WA 98104. The Mariners play at the Kingdome, built in 1976, which holds 59,166 fans. It has artificial turf, and its home run distances in left, center, and right fields are 331, 405, and 312 feet. The team was formed as an expansion club in the American League to open the 1977 season.

TEXAS RANGERS, PO Box 90111, Arlington, TX 76004. The Rangers play their home games in The Ballpark in Arlington, opened in 1994. It holds 49,292, has natural grass, and has home run distances in left, center, and right fields of 332, 400, and 325 feet.

When the Washington Senators left the District of Columbia for Minnesota after the 1960 season, a new Washington Senators team was immediately granted an American League expansion franchise for the 1961 season. The team played in Washington's Griffith Stadium and then RFK Stadium. But after some unsuccessful seasons, the team left for Texas, where it opened the 1972 season as the Texas Rangers. Until the new park was opened, the Rangers played in Arlington Stadium.

Spring Training

All major league ball clubs have spring training either in Florida or Arizona. Here are the locations.

NATIONAL LEAGUE

Atlanta Braves—Municipal Stadium, West Palm Beach, FL

Chicago Cubs—Ho Ho Kam Park, Mesa, AZ

Cincinnati Reds—Plant City Stadium, Plant City, FL

Colorado Rockies—Hi Corbett Field, Tucson, AZ

Florida Marlins—Space Coast Stadium, Melbourne, FL

Houston Astros—Osceola County Stadium, Kissimmee, FL

Los Angeles Dodgers—Holman Stadium, Vero Beach, FL

Montreal Expos—Municipal Stadium, West Palm Beach, FL

New York Mets—St. Lucie County Sports Complex, Port St. Lucie, FL

Philadelphia Phillies—Jack Russell Memorial Stadium, Clearwater, FL

Pittsburgh Pirates—McKechnie Field, Bradenton, FL

St. Louis Cardinals—Al Lang Stadium, St. Petersburg, FL

San Diego Padres—Peoria Stadium, Peoria, AZ

San Francisco Giants—Scottsdale Stadium, Scottsdale, AZ

AMERICAN LEAGUE

Baltimore Orioles—Huggins-Stengel Complex, St. Petersburg, FL

Boston Red Sox—Red Sox Stadium, Fort Myers, FL

California Angels—Tempe-Diabolo Stadium, Tempe, AZ

Chicago White Sox—Ed Smith Stadium, Sarasota, FL

Cleveland Indians—Chain O' Lakes Park, Winter Haven, FL

Detroit Tigers—Joker Marchant Stadium, Lakeland, FL

Kansas City Royals—Baseball City Stadium, Baseball City, FL

Milwaukee Brewers—Compadre Stadium, Chandler, AZ

Minnesota Twins—Lee County Sports Complex, Fort Myers, FL

New York Yankees—Fort Lauderdale Stadium, Fort Lauderdale, FL

Oakland Athletics—Municipal Stadium, Phoenix, AZ

Seattle Mariners—Peoria Sports Complex, Peoria, AZ

Texas Rangers—Charlotte County Stadium, Port Charlotte, FL

Toronto Blue Jays—Dunedin Stadium, Dunedin, FL

What Did He Say?

Baseball people throughout history have always had something to say. More than in any other sport, baseball players, managers, umpires, writers, and executives have felt called upon to offer their reading or listening public some pithy comments, flaky observations, and probing musings. Here are a few gems.

Managers

SPARKY ANDERSON

Manager of the Reds and Tigers

"My biggest job as manager is that I don't trip the players going down the runway."

ALVIN DARK

Manager of the Giants, Kansas City Athletics, Indians, Oakland A's, and Padres

"The Lord taught me to love everybody, but the last ones I learned to love were the sportswriters."

LEO DUROCHER

Manager of the Dodgers, Giants, Cubs, and Astros

"You don't save a pitcher for tomorrow. Tomorrow it may rain."

"Nice guys finish last."

"Baseball is like church. Many attend. Few understand."

TOMMY LASORDA

Manager of the Dodgers

Describing his 43-year-old pitcher: "We've timed Don Sutton's fastball at 92 miles an hour—46 going in to [catcher] Rick Dempsey, 46 coming back."

"Managing a baseball team is like holding a dove in your hand. Squeeze too hard and you kill it, not hard enough and it flies away."

CONNIE MACK

Manager of the Pirates and Athletics

On his retirement after 50 years as Philadelphia manager: "I am not quitting because I am too old. I am quitting because I think the people want me to quit."

MARTY MARION

Manager of the Cardinals, Browns, and White Sox

"I'd say that [Mickey] Mantle today is the greatest player in either league. No weaknesses? Let's see—uh, yes. There's one thing he can't do very well. He can't throw left-handed." (Mantle was right-handed.)

DANNY OZARK

Manager of the Phillies and Giants

About an inferior ballplayer: "His limitations are limitless."

After a losing streak: "Even Napoleon had his Watergate."

WILBERT ROBINSON

Manager of the Orioles and Dodgers

After three Dodgers ended up on third base at the same time: "Leave them alone. That's the first time those guys got together on anything all season."

CASEY STENGEL

Manager of the Dodgers, Braves, Yankees, and Mets

"I was not so successful as a ball player, as it was a game of skill."

"Pitchers are selfish men."

"The secret of managing is to keep the guys who hate you away from the guys who are undecided."

On the Mets' 40–120 season in 1961, their first year in the National League: "I won with this club what I used to lose."

During his first year managing the Mets: "Can't anybody here play this game?"

DON ZIMMER

Manager of the Padres, Red Sox, Rangers, and Cubs

After a road trip in which the Cubs finished with four wins and four losses: "It just as easily could have gone the other way."

Hitters

ERNIE BANKS

Hall of Fame Cubs infielder

"It's a beautiful day—let's play two."

YOGI BERRA

Hall of Fame catcher for the Yankees and manager of the Yankees and Mets

Upon striking out looking, after being told to think when he was at bat: "I can't think and hit at the same time."

After facing Dodgers pitcher Sandy Koufax in the 1963 World Series: "I can see how he won 25 games. What I don't understand is how he lost five."

"You've got to be very careful if you don't know where you're going, because you might not get there."

About the shortening of the days in the autumn: "It gets late early out there."

On the game of baseball: "It ain't over till it's over."

After the Yankees lost the 1960 World Series to the Pirates: "We made too many wrong mistakes."

On playing the game: "You observe a lot by watching."

When taking on the job of managing the Yankees for the first time: "My big problem as manager will be to see if I can manage."

After a state dinner: "How could you get a conversation started in there? Everybody was talking too much."

After an elderly woman told him after a game that he looked "mighty cool today": "Thank you, ma'am. You don't look so hot yourself."

When asked, "What time is it?": "You mean now?"

"If the people don't want to come to the park, nobody's going to stop them."

TERRY FRANCONA

First baseman for the Expos and other teams

At the Hall of Fame Game in Cooperstown in 1988: "I wonder how many more ten RBI seasons I need to get back here."

WILLIE KEELER

Hall of Fame right fielder, primarily for the Dodgers and Yankees

On his batting technique: "Hit 'em where they ain't."

RALPH KINER

Slugging Hall of Fame left fielder, primarily for the Pirates

"Home run hitters drive Cadillacs, singles hitters drive Fords."

STAN MUSIAL

Hall of Fame outfielder/first baseman for the Cardinals

On his position as senior vice president of the Cardinals: "I have a darn good job, but please don't ask me what I do."

GRAIG NETTLES

Third baseman for the Yankees and other teams

"When I was a little boy, I wanted to be a baseball player and join a circus. With the Yankees, I've accomplished both."

GERALD PERRY

First baseman for the Braves and other teams

After being told that the Braves drew only 848,089 fans in 1988: "This would have been a good year to paint the seats."

PETE ROSE

All-around player for the Reds, Phillies, and Expos, and manager of the Reds

"There is one more important reason that I slide [into base] head first. It gets my picture in the newspaper."

On one of his few regrets: "I wish there was some way I could have gotten a college education. I'm thinking about buying a college, though."

On the appointment of Bart Giamatti, the president of Yale University, as president of the National League: "He's an intellectual from Yale, but he's very intelligent."

BABE RUTH

Hall of Fame Yankees slugger

After it was pointed out that he earned more than President Herbert Hoover in 1931: "Well, I had a better year."

On his system for hitting home runs: "All I can tell 'em is I pick a good one and sock it. I get back to the dugout and they ask me what it was I hit and I tell 'em I don't know except it looked good."

Pitchers

JIM BOUTON

Pitcher for the Yankees and other teams and author of Ball Four

On why baseball is better than football: "Baseball is played by normal human beings. You don't have to weigh 270 pounds or bench press the team bus."

"Baseball players are smarter than football players. How often do you see a baseball team penalized for having too many players on the field?"

"Baseball sets a better example for kids. When the announcers say that a player 'likes to hit,' they're not talking about assault and battery."

DIZZY DEAN

Hall of Fame pitcher for the Cardinals and Cubs

"It's only bragging when you say you're going to do something and then can't do it."

After he won a three-hit game in a doubleheader and his brother, Paul (known as Daffy), pitched a no-hitter in the second game: "If I'd known Paul was going to do that, I'd have pitched a no-hitter, too."

As a baseball broadcaster, when he was told that his syntax greatly distressed educators: "Sin tax? Are them jokers down in Washington puttin' a tax on that, too?"

When broadcasting a steal: "They woulda had him at second, but he slud."

DOCK ELLIS

Pitcher for the Pirates and other teams

"Good pitching beats good hitting—and vice versa."

NED GARVER

Pitcher for the fanless Browns and other teams

"The crowd didn't boo us because we had them outnumbered."

LEFTY GOMEZ

Hall of Fame pitcher for the Yankees

When asked by his catcher what he wanted to throw slugger Jimmie Foxx: "To tell you the truth, Bill [Dickey], I don't want to throw him anything at all."

"I'd rather be lucky than good."

OREL HERSHISER

Pitcher for the Dodgers and Indians

After winning the Cy Young Award in 1988: "I worked hard with the talent I was given and everything just worked out perfect. My career will go downhill from here."

TUG McGRAW

Relief pitcher for the Mets and Phillies

When the Mets were in last place on August 30, 1973: "Ya gotta believe!" (The Mets won 20 of their last 28 games and took the National League pennant.)

SATCHEL PAIGE

Hall of Fame pitcher who was legendary in the Negro Leagues

"You win a few, you lose a few. Some are rained out. But you got to dress for all of them."

On the six steps to eternal youth (Paige was noted for his longevity):

"1. Avoid fried meats which angry up the blood.
2. If your stomach disputes you, lie down and pacify it with cool thoughts.
3. Keep the juices flowing by jangling around gently as you move.
4. Go very light on the vices, such as carrying on in society. The social rumble ain't restful.
5. Avoid running at all times.
6. Don't look back. Something might be gaining on you."

ROBIN ROBERTS

Hall of Fame pitcher, primarily for the Phillies

"I had a high fastball, and I either overpowered them or they overpowered me."

CURT SIMMONS

Pitcher for the Phillies, Cardinals, Cubs, and Angels

On throwing a fastball past Henry Aaron: "It's like trying to sneak the sunrise past a rooster."

DON SUTTON

Pitcher primarily for the Dodgers

After being sent to the minors for conditioning and then pitching into the seventh inning for the first time in months: "I finally got to hear 'Take Me Out to the Ball Game.'"

Executives

HARRY FRAZEE

Owner of the Red Sox

After selling Babe Ruth to the Yankees in 1920: "Ruth had become simply impossible, and the Boston club could no longer put up with his eccentricities. I think the Yankees are taking a gamble."

JIM FREY

General manager of the Cubs

On installing lights at Wrigley Field in 1988: "Would someone tell me when tradition starts? What do they want us to do, play without gloves because they didn't use them in the 19th century?"

CLARK GRIFFITH

Owner of the Washington Senators

On the installation of lights at Cincinnati's Crosley Field in 1935: "There is no chance of night baseball ever becoming popular in the bigger cities because high-class baseball cannot be played under artificial lights."

KENESAW MOUNTAIN LANDIS

First commissioner of baseball

To Yankee owner Colonel Jacob Ruppert after Ruppert complained that Giants outfielder Casey Stengel had thumbed his nose at him after he had hit a home run to beat the Yankees in the 1923 World Series: "When a man hits a home run to win a World Series game, he is entitled to a certain amount of exuberance. Especially if he's Casey Stengel."

BRANCH RICKEY

General manager of the Cardinals and Dodgers

"It's better to get rid of a player too soon than too late."

KEN SHEPARD

General manager of the minor league Geneva, New York, Cubs

After promising to sleep in the stadium press box until his club won (they went on to lose 18 straight games): "Every day I get crankier and crankier. There's no air conditioning up there. The mosquitoes are terrible. I want to go home."

HARVEY WALKEN

Part owner of the Pittsburgh Pirates

On the Cubs' failure to win a World Series since 1908: "Any team can have a bad century."

Writers

WARREN BROWN

Sportswriter for the Chicago Tribune

On which team, the Cubs or the Tigers, would win the 1945 World Series, when most of baseball's stars were in the armed forces: "I don't think either of them can."

HENRY CHADWICK

Baseball editor of the New York Clipper *in 1876*

"Say what you will, gentlemen of the league, you must come down in your price; you must come down to the 25¢ admission fee; and you must proportionately lower your salaries. One thousand dollars for seven months of such services as the professional ballplayer is called upon to perform, even when he is not indisposed, is amply sufficient."

JAMES MICHENER

Author of such novels as Hawaii *and* Centennial

"Young man, when you root for the Phillies, you acquire a sense of tragedy."

DAN SHAUGHNESSY

Sportswriter for the Boston Globe

"Defensively the Red Sox are a lot like Stonehenge. They are old, they don't move, and no one is certain why they are positioned the way they are."

MARK TWAIN

Nineteenth-century author of such novels as The Adventures of Tom Sawyer *and* The Adventures of Huckleberry Finn

"[Baseball is] the very symbol, the outward and visible expression of the drive and push and rush and struggle of the raging, tearing, booming 19th century."

Miscellaneous

ANONYMOUS ADVERTISEMENT

For the Cal Ripken Baseball School

As the Orioles were going through 21 straight losses at the beginning of the 1988 season: "Learn to play baseball the Oriole way."

DAVE CAMPBELL

ESPN sportscaster

On the quickness of Blue Jays second baseman Roberto Alomar: "He gets to the ball quicker than Cinderella's sisters."

RON LUCIANO

American League umpire

On the spitball: "One of the few things about baseball that hasn't changed since the turn of the century is the fact that pitchers cheat. They break the rules. They flaunt authority. And worse, they are unsanitary about it."

MARTIN MULL

Comedian

On why baseball is better than football: "There are fewer people named Bubba."

"The players needn't pose as college graduates."

"There is plenty of time to absorb the thought-provoking spectacle of a man in a chicken suit."

"You can wear the hat backwards."

"On a rainy day, there's a darn good chance that you might get to see an acre of land covered by rubber sheeting—if you're into that sort of thing."

RICHARD NIXON

President of the United States

Recalling his days as a Washington baseball fan: "The Senators were never very good, but not much has changed in Washington. The senators they have there still aren't very good."

FRANKLIN D. ROOSEVELT

President of the United States

Answering suggestions in 1942 that baseball should be canceled for the duration of World War II: "I honestly feel that it would be best for the country to keep baseball going."

PAUL TSONGAS

Senator from Massachusetts and presidential candidate

When on the campaign trail: "I hold no public office. I can't even get you Red Sox tickets. Of course, you wouldn't want them."

Just Plain Trivia

In the more than 100 years since the beginning of professional major league baseball, there have been a number of unusual events. Here's a lineup of little known facts, along with some hardball nostalgia.

Oldest and Youngest

- On October 3, 1897, **Cap Anson** closed out a career, begun in 1871, by hitting two home runs for the Cubs against St. Louis. He was 46, the oldest player to homer in a major league game.
- On August 31, 1906, the Tigers, crippled by injuries, called 46-year-old **Sam Thompson** out of retirement for help in the outfield. He batted in two runs in a 5–1 victory over the Browns.
- In 1985, **Dwight Gooden** of the Mets became the youngest pitcher, at age 21, to win 20 games. He was also the youngest to win the Cy Young Award.

Noteworthy Achievements

- **Ernie Banks** of the Chicago Cubs, although elected to the Hall of Fame and a player in 2,528 games in his 19-year career, never played in a World Series.
- **Philadelphia** is the home of the cellar dwellers. In the American League, the Athletics finished last 17 times before moving to Kansas City in 1955, and the Phillies have finished last 27 times in the National League.
- Outfielder **Minnie Minoso**, primarily a White Sox player, is the only man to play in the majors in five different decades—beginning in 1949 and ending in 1980.
- **Connie Mack** managed the Philadelphia Athletics for 50 years.
- In 1946 the **St. Louis Browns** drew only 93,000 fans, and at one game only 34 people showed up.
- **Bill Sharman,** who played basketball for the Boston Celtics and made Pro Basketball Hall of Fame, also played baseball, batting .286 for Fort Worth in the Texas League. He was called up to the Brooklyn Dodgers in 1951 and was sitting on their bench when

he was ejected by the umpire, who had cleared the bench. Sharman never got into a game in the major leagues.

⚾ **Joe Sewell,** the Cleveland Indians shortstop, was struck out twice in the same game on May 26, 1930. He finished the season with only one more strikeout, for a total of three.

⚾ **Fred Tenney,** who played for the Boston Braves and New York Giants, in a 1908 game stole second and then turned around and stole first in an attempt to confuse the pitcher and allow a teammate to score from third. Five weeks later, **Germany Schaefer,** who played for various teams from 1901 to 1918, also reached second base (on a double) and then, a few moments later, stole first. The play was soon declared illegal.

⚾ On June 23, 1963, when he was playing for the New York Mets, outfielder **Jimmy Piersall** celebrated his 100th career homer by running the bases backward.

⚾ In 1953, the **St. Louis Browns'** last season before moving to Baltimore, the team had lost 14 games in a row. And they were to face the Yankees, who had won 18 in a row. Manager Marty Marion of the Browns ran into sportswriter Milt Richman in the clubhouse. Marion was so discouraged he handed his empty lineup card to Richman and said, "Here, you make it out." Richman declined, but Marion was insistent. "Pick out any nine you like." Richman did, and the Browns won the game.

- On July 30, 1937, Phillies first baseman **Dolf Camilli** played the entire game without a putout as Philadelphia beat the Reds, 1–0.
- Sixteen-time Gold Glove winner **Brooks Robinson,** third baseman for the Orioles, made three errors in the sixth inning of a game against the A's on July 28, 1971.
- In 1968, **Tom Tresh,** the Yankees' shortstop, played three straight games without having a fielding chance.
- On August 23, 1952, during a game against the Cardinals, the Giants' **Bob Elliott** complained about a called strike two and kicked dirt on umpire Augie Donatelli. He was ejected, and **Bobby Hoffman** finished the at bat by being called out on strikes. Hoffman was then also ejected for arguing the call.
- In his only major league appearance on September 29, 1963, **John Paciorek** of the Colt .45s went three for three with three runs batted in and four runs scored against the Mets. A back injury ended his career.
- In 1950 utility infielder **Pete Castiglione** of the Pirates made ten errors—one at first base, two at second base, three at third base, and four at shortstop.

⚾ Every major league franchise except the Angels, Astros, Expos, Mariners, Marlins, Rangers, and Rockies has won at least one **league pennant**. Here are the pennant winners, in order of number of flags won, as of the 1995 season:

Yankees	33
Dodgers *(Brooklyn 9, Los Angeles 9)*	18
Giants *(New York 14, San Francisco 2)*	16
Cardinals	15
A's *(Philadelphia 8, Oakland 6)*	14
Cubs	10
Pirates	9
Reds	9
Red Sox	9
Tigers	9
Braves *(Boston 2, Milwaukee 2, Atlanta 3)*	7
Orioles *(Saint Louis Browns 1, Baltimore 6)*	7
Twins *(Washington Senators 3, Minnesota 3)*	6
Phillies	5
Indians	4
White Sox	4
Mets	3
Blue Jays	2
Royals	2
Brewers	1
Padres	1

⚾ Every major league franchise except the Angels, Astros, Brewers, Expos, Mariners, Marlins, Padres, Rangers, and Rockies has won at least one **World Series**. Here are the Series winners, in order of number of Series won, as of the 1995 season:

Yankees	22
A's *(Philadelphia 5, Oakland 4)*	9
Cardinals	9
Dodgers *(Brooklyn 1, Los Angeles 5)*	6
Giants *(New York 5)*	5
Pirates	5
Reds	5
Red Sox	5
Tigers	4
Braves *(Boston 1, Milwaukee 1, Atlanta 1)*	3
Orioles	3
Twins *(Washington Senators 1, Minnesota 2)*	3
Blue Jays	2
Cubs	2
Indians	2
Mets	2
White Sox	2
Phillies	1
Royals	1

More Baseball Bits

The record for number of **World Series games umpired** belongs to Hall of Famer Bill Klem of the National League—104.

On July 4, 1912, **Ty Cobb** of the Tigers stole second, third, and home in the first inning against the St. Louis Browns.

Cal Hubbard, the American League umpire who was elected to the Hall of Fame in 1976, was also elected to the Pro Football Hall of Fame (1963) and the College Football Hall of Fame (1963).

Bill McKechnie was the only manager to win the World Series with two different National League clubs—the 1925 Pirates and the 1940 Reds.

Bucky Harris was the only manager to win the World Series with two different American League clubs—the 1924 Senators and the 1947 Yankees.

Sparky Anderson was the only manager to win the World Series in both leagues—with the Reds in the National (1975–1976) and the Tigers in the American (1984).

In circling the bases running out his record 755 home runs, **Hank Aaron** trotted a total of 51.5 miles.

In running to first base for his record 3,215 singles, **Pete Rose** covered 54.8 miles.

Ty Cobb of the Tigers set a record by getting five or more hits in 14 different games.

On July 13, 1896, **Ed Delahanty,** the Phillies left fielder, hit four home runs—one to left, one to right, one to center, and one inside the park.

Catcher **Luke Sewell** of the Senators tagged out two runners at home plate on the same play on April 29, 1933. Lou Gehrig of the Yankees had held up, thinking a fly ball would be caught. But the ball fell in for a hit, and both Gehrig and Dixie Walker right behind him were tagged out trying to score.

Pete Rose of the Reds was named to the All-Star Game at five different positions—first base, second base, third base, left field, and right field.

The **Chicago Cubs** have won more regular-season games than any other professional team in any sport—9,058 as of the end of the 1995 season.

Center fielder **Bob Johnson** drove in all of Philadelphia's runs as the Athletics beat the Browns, 8–3, on June 12, 1938.

First baseman **Bob Watson** was the first to hit for the cycle (getting a single, double, triple, and homer in one game) in both leagues—with the Astros in 1977 and the Red Sox in 1979.

A total of **17 runs** were scored in the ninth inning—seven by the Giants and ten by the Braves—on June 20, 1912, as the Giants won the game, 21–12.

On April 20, 1988, center fielder **Claudell Washington** hit the 10,000th homer in Yankee history, off the Twins' Jeff Reardon.

On June 24, 1962, **Jack Reed,** a utility outfielder for the Yankees, hit a home run in the 22nd inning for a 9–7 victory over the Tigers. It was the only homer he hit in his three-year career.

On June 29, 1986, the Tigers beat the Brewers to give manager **Sparky Anderson** his 600th American League win. He became the first manager to win 600 games in each league, since he had won 863 with the Reds in the National League.

The **Cubs** and the **Reds** played a nine-inning game with just one baseball on June 29, 1916.

On July 11, 1954, third baseman **Jim Command** of the Phillies hit a grand slam home run against the Dodgers for his first major league hit. In the rest of his two-year career, he got only three more hits.

Pitcher **Doc Medich** of the Rangers, a medical student in the off-season, saved the life of a 61-year-old fan who suffered a heart attack just before a game in Baltimore on July 17, 1978. Medich administered heart massage until emergency help arrived.

The National League home run crown of 1902 was won by Pirates third baseman **Tommy Leach.** He hit a grand total of six four-baggers, and all six of them were inside-the-park jobs.

Hank Aaron might have had 756 career home runs instead of his record 755. On August 18, 1965, he hit a pitch on top of the pavilion roof in St. Louis, but umpire Chris Pelakoudas called him out for being out of the batter's box when he hit the ball.

Early in the 20th century, manager Connie Mack of the Philadelphia Athletics awarded star pitcher **Rube Waddell** a contract that stated that Waddell's battery mate, Ossee Schreckengost, could not eat crackers in bed when the pair shared a room on the road. In those days, players had to share not only a hotel room when traveling but the same bed as well.

Two Hall of Famers each had their numbers retired by two teams in the same city in different leagues. **Hank Aaron's** number 44 was retired by his first and last teams, the Atlanta/Milwaukee Braves and the Milwaukee Brewers, and **Casey Stengel's** 37 was retired by the New York Yankees and the New York Mets.

Frank Baker, the slugger for the Athletics and the Yankees whose nickname was "Home Run" Baker, hit only 96 homers in his 13-year career (1908–1914, 1916–1922). That wasn't a bad record because in those days homers were rare.

Rusty Staub and **Ty Cobb** were the only two players to hit their first home runs as teenagers and their last after they were 40 years old.

Whitey Lockman was the only player to hit a home run in his first (1945) and last (1960) major league at bats.

The player who holds the record for most home runs in the world is **Sadaharu Oh,** of the Tokyo Giants in Japan, who hit 868 round-trippers in his 22-year career.

Hall of Fame hitter **Rogers Hornsby** (who played 1915–1937) guarded his eyesight by not going to the movies. He thought the flickering movement on the screen would hurt his eyes.

Frank Robinson and **Rusty Staub** share the record for most stadiums in which they hit home runs in regular-season games—32.

On August 4, 1982, **Joel Youngblood** got hits for two teams on the same day. He singled and knocked in two runs for the Mets in Chicago in an afternoon game. He was then told that he had been traded to the Expos. He flew to Philadelphia, where Montreal was playing a night game, and got a single for his new team.

In 1957 first baseman **Julio Becquer** of the Senators led the team in stolen bases with three. The club had a total of only 13.

Not only was **Frank Robinson** the first black man to manage in both the National and the American leagues, he was the first man to be named Most Valuable Player in both leagues, the first to hit 200 or more home runs in both leagues, and the first to hit homers for both leagues in the All-Star Game.

On April 22, 1959, the **White Sox** scored 11 runs in one inning while getting only one hit. In the seventh inning they drew ten walks off the A's, and eight of them came with the bases loaded. There were also three errors and a hit batsman, and the Sox still left three men on base in the inning.

The one-millionth major league run was scored by first baseman **Bob Watson** of the Astros on May 4, 1975.

On August 4, 1919, the **Indians,** with one out to go, scored nine runs in the ninth inning, thus beating the Yankees, 14–6.

In one of the wildest games ever played, the **Cubs** beat the Phillies, 26–23, on August 25, 1922. Chicago had led, 25–6, in the fourth inning and were able to hold on as the game ended with the Phillies leaving the bases loaded.

In 1986, for the first time ever, every major league team drew over **1 million fans.**

On July 17, 1990, the **Minnesota Twins** set a record by pulling off two triple plays in one game against the Boston Red Sox, but they still lost the game, 1–0.

Andre Dawson was given a record five intentional walks by opposing pitchers as the Chicago Cubs beat the Cincinnati Reds, 2–1, on May 22, 1990.

Billy Hatcher, the Reds' outfielder, set the record for most consecutive World Series hits—seven—in 1990.

Billy Hatcher also tied a record of five consecutive extra-base hits in two games of a World Series in 1990. Lou Brock had accomplished this in 1968.

Don Baylor, who played for 19 years in the American League, set the record for most times being hit by a pitch—267.

When **Ken Griffey, Jr.**, won the MVP Award in the 1992 All-Star Game, he and his father became the first father-son winners of the award. Ken Griffey, Sr., won it in 1980.

The 1993 **Toronto Blue Jays** became the first team since Philadelphia in 1893 to have the league's top three hitters: John Olerud (.363), Paul Molitor (.332), and Roberto Alomar (.326).

Pitchers

On June 7, 1938, Indians pitcher **Johnny Allen** walked off the mound in the second inning after umpire Bill McGowan asked that his dangling sweatshirt sleeve be cut off because it was distracting to Red Sox hitters. Allen was fined $250 by manager Ossie Vitt, and the shirt ended up in the Hall of Fame.

The three pitchers with the **worst career batting averages** were Ron Herbel (Giants, Padres, Mets, and Braves, 1963–1971)—.029 (six for

206); Andy McGaffigan (Yankees, Giants, Expos, Reds, and Royals, 1981–1988)—.048 (six for 126); and Ed Klepfer (Yankees, White Sox, and Indians, 1911, 1913, 1915–1917, 1919)—.048 (six for 125).

The single-season record of hitless at bats in a row is 70 straight, set by pitcher **Bob Buhl** of the Braves and Cubs in 1962.

In 1923, **Lefty O'Doul** of the Red Sox allowed 13 runs in the first six innings of a game as the Indians won, 27–3. This effectively ended his four-year major league pitching career. But in 1928, he came back as a great hitting outfielder and played seven more years for the Giants, Phillies, Dodgers, and Giants again.

On July 22, 1906, **Bob Ewing** of the Reds beat the Phillies, 10–3, without a single assist being registered by his teammates on the ball club.

Joe "Iron Man" McGinnity of the Giants won both ends of a doubleheader twice in one week in 1903.

Warren Spahn of the Braves struck out 18 Cubs in a 15-inning game on June 14, 1952, but lost the game, 3–1.

The **St. Louis Browns** used nine pitchers in nine innings against the White Sox on October 2, 1949, as the Sox beat them, 4–3.

On April 16, 1940, **Bob Feller** of the Indians beat the White Sox, 1–0, as he pitched a no-hitter—the only opening day no-hitter in major league history.

On September 26, 1908, **Ed Reulbach** of the Cubs became the only pitcher to throw two shutouts in a doubleheader. He beat Brooklyn, 5–0 and 3–0, in two nine-inning games.

Dizzy Dean of the Cardinals was the last National League pitcher to win at least 30 games in one season in 1934 (30–7). In the American League, the feat was last accomplished by **Denny McLain** of the Tigers in 1968 (31–6).

The highest composite win totals of two pitchers who faced each other were featured on June 9, 1986, when **Tom Seaver** of the White Sox (306 wins) opposed **Don Sutton** of the Angels (298 wins). Sutton won, 3–0.

In 1945, **Dick Fowler** of the Athletics threw a no-hitter at the Browns on September 9, winning 1–0. It was the only game he won all year.

On May 1, 1991, **Nolan Ryan** of the Rangers became the first pitcher ever to throw seven no-hit, no-run games, with a 3–0 victory over the Blue Jays. He was 44 years old.

Walter Johnson of the Senators pitched his third consecutive shutout in four days on September 7, 1908, with a two-hit victory over the New York Highlanders. He might have done it in three days, but Washington had had a day off on September 6.

On May 26, 1959, **Harvey Haddix** of the Pirates pitched 12 hitless innings before losing to the Braves, 1–0, in the 13th inning on an error, a sacrifice hit, and Joe Adcock's double.

Cincinnati pitchers **Johnny Klippstein, Hersh Freeman,** and **Joe Black** combined for 9⅓ hitless innings on May 26, 1956, but the Reds still lost an 11-inning decision to the Phillies, 2–1.

On May 13, 1942, Braves pitcher **Jim Tobin** hit three straight home runs as Boston beat the Cubs, 6–5.

When **Bob Feller,** the Indians' future Hall of Fame pitcher, was only 17 years old in 1936, he struck out 15 batters in his first appearance in the major leagues. Soon after, he set an American League record at that time by striking out 17. Then he returned home to Van Meter, Iowa, to finish high school. He had signed with the Indians for a bonus of a $1 bill and an autographed baseball.

Before the 1963 season, future Hall of Fame pitcher **Early Wynn** had won 299 games in his career and wanted to get his 300th. He went to spring training with the White Sox in 1963, but he could not make the team. One of his old teams, the Indians, took him on, and in his fifth start, he won number 300.

In 1995, **Hideo Nomo** of the Dodgers became the first Japanese native to play major league baseball in North America after playing professional ball in Japan. In 1990 he was Rookie of the Year of Japan's Pacific League for the Kintetsu Buffaloes, and he led the league in wins and strikeouts four times (1990–1993). In his first year with the Dodgers, Nomo started in the All-Star Game, led the NL in strikeouts (236) and shutouts (3), was second in ERA (2.54), and was NL Rookie of the Year. "Nomomania" struck Japan hard; Dodger games were even televised on giant public TV screens in Tokyo and other cities whenever Nomo pitched.

Browns pitcher **Harry Kimberlin** won his first game in 1939—but it was during his fourth year with the club. It was his only win.

Perhaps the toughest no-hit, no-run game ever pitched was thrown by **Sam Jones** of the Cubs on May 12, 1955. In the ninth inning, he walked the bases full and then struck out the next three Pirates batters to win, 4–0.

Money Matters

Hall of Famer **Ralph Kiner** led the National League in home runs in 1952 with 37, but Pirates general manager Branch Rickey pointed out that the team had finished in last place, which they could have done without Kiner. So the left fielder took a pay cut.

First baseman **Jimmie Foxx** of the Philadelphia Athletics hit 48 home runs, scored 125 runs, and batted in 163 runs with a batting average of .356 in 1933. He was also voted Most Valuable Player in the American League. But Athletics manager and owner Connie Mack, who was notoriously tight with a dollar, cut his salary from $16,333 to $16,000.

The **first umpires** in the National League were paid $5 a day.

In 1900 the National League established a **player salary** limitation of $2,400 per year.

In 1933 the **Boston Braves** earned a modest $5,000 from the radio broadcasts of their games. In 1936 the Giants sold their radio broadcasting rights for $100,000.

The **1947 World Series** was the first to be televised, and the rights were sold for $65,000.

In 1988 major league teams **bought baseballs** that cost about $38 a dozen.

The **Cubs,** who installed lights in Wrigley Field in 1988, paid less than $600 per night game to illuminate the field.

In a 1992 survey, it was calculated that the **average family of four** spent $85.85 to go to a baseball game. The cheapest costs were at Riverfront Stadium in Cincinnati ($72.28), and the most expensive were at the SkyDome in Toronto (US $112.83). These figures included the prices of four seats, two beers, four hot dogs, four soft drinks, two caps, two programs, and parking.

The **average pay** to major league baseball players in 1993 was $1.5 million.

Miscellaneous

All-Star pitcher **Sandy Koufax** had a clause in his contract that he would not pitch on the Jewish High Holy Days. So in the first game of the 1965 World Series, on October 6, the Dodgers star, who had gone 26–8, did not throw against the Twins because it was Yom Kippur.

Hall of Fame executive **Branch Rickey,** a devout Christian, did not play on Sundays when he was a major league catcher (1905–1907, 1914).

The **National League** goes through about 4,000 dozen baseballs per year.

Wilbert "Uncle Robbie" Robinson, while the manager of the Dodgers in the 1920s, tried to keep his players on their toes by forming a "Bonehead Club." A Dodger who pulled a "bonehead" play was obliged to pay a fine to the club. The first member was Robinson himself, who walked up to home plate prior to a game and handed the umpire the wrong lineup card.

On September 15, 1946, the Dodgers beat the Cubs, 2–0, in five innings. The game was called because of **gnats**, which had become a problem for the players, umpires, and fans.

Probably the most even game ever played was between the **Brooklyn Superbas** and the **Pirates** on August 13, 1910. They played to an 8–8 tie, with each team getting 38 at bats, 13 hits, 12 assists, two errors, five strikeouts, three walks, one hit batsman, and one passed ball.

Hall of Fame outfielder **Edd Roush,** who played for various teams, including the Reds and Giants, during his 18-year career, used a 48-ounce bat—the heaviest ever in the major leagues.

First baseman **Ted Kluszewski** of the Reds had such muscular arms that he had to cut the sleeves of his uniform to get into it.

Bert Campaneris of the Kansas City Athletics played all nine positions in a single game on September 8, 1965.

Babe Ruth named his bat "Black Beauty."

"Wee Willie" Keeler, at 5'4½" tall and 140 pounds, is the smallest player in the Hall of Fame.

In 1934 the confident Giants manager **Bill Terry,** when asked about the Dodgers, said, "Brooklyn? Is Brooklyn still in the league?" Then, with two games to go in the season, the Giants were tied with the Cardinals for first place. But the Dodgers beat them in both games, and the Giants lost the pennant. This caused sportswriter John Kieran of the New York *Times* to write a poem:

> Why Mister Terry, oh!, why did you ever
> Chortle the query that made Brooklyn hot?
> Just for the crack that you thought was so clever,
> Now you stand teetering right on the spot!
> Vain was your hope they forgave or forgot;
> Now that you're weary and bowed with fatigue.
> Here is the drama and this is the plot:
> Brooklyn, dear fellow, is still in the league.

On August 2, 1938, the **Dodgers** and the **Cardinals** used a yellow baseball as an experiment in the first game of a doubleheader at Brooklyn's Ebbets Field. The Dodgers won the game, 6–2. The yellow ball was used in three more Dodgers games in 1939, but it was never used again after that.

When old **Comiskey Park** was built in Chicago in 1910, the owner of the White Sox modestly called it "Charles A. Comiskey's Baseball Palace."

On June 26, 1944, in an effort to raise funds for war bonds, the **Giants, Dodgers,** and **Yankees** played against each other in a six-inning game at the Polo Grounds in New York. More than 50,000 fans turned out as each team played successive innings against the other two teams, then sat out an inning. The final score was Dodgers 5, Yankees 1, Giants 0.

During **World War II,** American soldiers in their foxholes taunted their Japanese adversaries with nasty references to Emperor Hirohito. The Japanese frequently replied with what they considered the only fitting retort: "To hell with Babe Ruth."

The Hall of Fame received a letter from *The Sporting News* in 1985 addressed to **Abner Doubleday,** the alleged originator of baseball. The letter informed Doubleday that his subscription had been canceled.

When the seventh edition of *The Baseball Encyclopedia* was published in 1988, **Lou Proctor**, listed in previous editions as a member of the 1912 Browns, was missing. It had been discovered that Proctor was actually a press box telephone operator who decided to enter his name in the box score. He remained a "Player" with a one-game career until researchers weeded him out. All those years he was listed as having no hits, no at bats, and one walk.

Marge Schott, the owner of the Reds, required her scouts to make calls from pay phones rather than from their rooms to avoid hotel surcharges.

In 1988, **Marge Schott** went to Rome and took a gift for the Pope—a Reds warm-up jacket with "John Paul II" on the back.

In an exhibition game in Raleigh, North Carolina, Wake Forest and North Carolina State played a nine-inning game with a **mechanical pitcher**. Each team stationed a man near the machine to do the fielding. Wake Forest won, 8–0, getting 11 hits to North Carolina's three. The robot was also charged with seven walks and one wild pitch.

When he owned the Oakland A's, **Charles O. Finley** bought a mascot—a mule named Charlie O.

In 1985, **Art Ditmar,** the former Yankees pitcher, sued a beer company and an advertising agency that had mistakenly identified him in a TV commercial as the pitcher who had given up Pirate Bill Mazeroski's home run that won the 1960 World Series. Actually, it was Ralph Terry, but the judge ruled that Ditmar failed to provide more than speculation that the commercial had caused him any financial harm, such as reduced opportunities for playing in old-timers' games and golf tournaments.

In 1987 the Cardinals, the National League pennant winners, had so many injuries that they voted **Dr. Stan London,** their team doctor, a half-share in their World Series winnings. It amounted to $28,026.26.

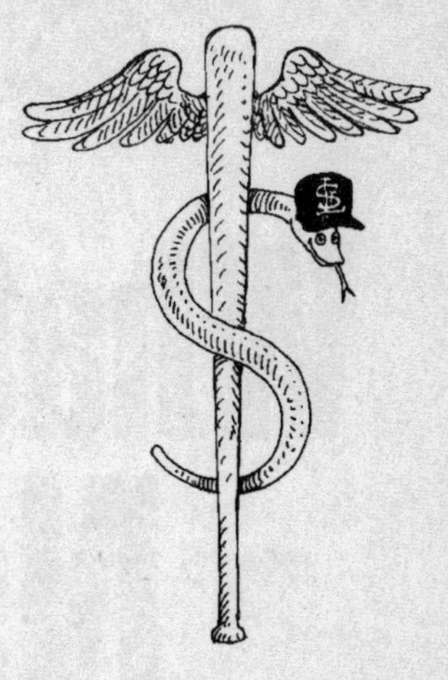

On July 11, 1990, during the last year of their old Comiskey Park, the **Chicago White Sox** played a baseball nostalgia game. They wore uniforms like their 1917 world champion forerunners and used a hand-operated scoreboard. Popcorn cost 5¢, and general admission tickets went for 50¢. The Milwaukee Brewers won the game, 12–9, in 13 innings.

On September 23, 1990, American League umpire **Ken Kaiser**'s luggage was lost by an airline on its way to Kansas City. Kaiser umpired at second base dressed in a sweatsuit with "Royals" on the shirt and pant legs. Kansas City beat Oakland, 10–3.

When the Republican National Convention was held in the Houston Astrodome in August 1992, the **Astros** had no place to play their home games. They were forced to go on a 28-game road trip that lasted from July 27 to August 23.

When the pitcher, catcher, and umpire get into an argument, baseball announcers call it a "**rhubarb**." The word comes from a sound effects technique used in early radio dramas. Whenever a director wanted the sound of an angry, menacing crowd, he would have five or six actors mutter "rhubarb-rhubarb-rhubarb" over and over, which created the sound of a large and belligerent mob. Ever since, the word "rhubarb" has meant a loud and heated dispute.

The score of a **forfeited ball game** is 9–0.

What's in a Name?

One of the best things about baseball has been—and always will be—the players' names and nicknames. Only in baseball will you find a pitcher named Rollie Fingers, a shortstop called "Scooter" (Phil Rizzuto), or a slugger called the "Sultan of Swat" (Babe Ruth). Below are some of the best names in baseball.

He's Not Who You Think He Is

Because of the sheer number of players in major league baseball, it's no surprise that some of them would have the same names as famous personalities. Here are some of the better ones and the teams and positions they are most closely associated with.

HE'S NOT THE PRESIDENT

James Buchanan, Browns pitcher
John Kennedy, Red Sox third baseman
John Tyler, Braves outfielder
George Washington, White Sox outfielder

HE'S NOT THE SENATOR, CONGRESSMAN, OR GOVERNOR

Howard Baker, Cleveland Molly McGuires third baseman
Bill Bradley, Cleveland Broncos third baseman
John Calhoun, Cardinals third baseman
John Glenn, Cardinals outfielder
Robert Kennedy, White Sox/Indians outfielder
Ted Kennedy, Cubs pitcher
Tip O'Neill, Reds outfielder
Al Smith, Indians/White Sox outfielder

HE'S NOT THE TRAILBLAZER OR SCOUT FROM U.S. HISTORY

Daniel Boone, Padres pitcher
Kit Carson, Indians outfielder
Davey Crockett, Tigers first baseman

HE'S NOT THE GENERAL

Ethan Allen, Reds outfielder
Mark Clark, Cardinals pitcher

HE'S NOT THE WRITER

Ben Johnson, Cubs pitcher
Earl Wilson, Red Sox pitcher

HE'S NOT THE SINGER

James Brown, Cardinals infielder
Dave Clark, Indians pitcher
Phil Collins, Phillies pitcher
Eddie Fisher, White Sox pitcher
Tom Jones, Browns first baseman
Ricky Nelson, Mariners outfielder
Johnny Ray, Pirates second baseman
Kenny Rogers, Rangers pitcher

HE'S NOT THE PERFORMER

Jack Barry, Athletics shortstop
Ed Begley, Giants pitcher

Ken Berry, White Sox outfielder
Brett Butler, Indians/Dodgers outfielder
Robert Reed, Tigers pitcher

HE'S NOT THE MOVIE STAR

Matthew Broderick, Brooklyn Superbas second baseman
Gary Cooper, Braves outfielder
John Houseman, Cardinals infielder
William Powell, Pirates pitcher
George C. Scott, Red Sox first baseman
Robert Shaw, White Sox/Giants pitcher
Jimmy Stewart, Cubs outfielder
Robert Taylor, Giants outfielder

HE'S NOT THE COMEDIAN

George Burns, Indians first baseman
George Burns, Giants outfielder
Eddie Murphy, White Sox outfielder
Bill Murray, Senators second baseman
Danny Thomas, Brewers outfielder

HE'S NOT THE AUTO RACING CHAMPION

Johnny Rutherford, Dodgers pitcher
Al Unser, Tigers catcher

HE'S NOT THE BASKETBALL STAR

Michael Jordan, Pirates outfielder
Bill Russell, Dodgers shortstop

HE'S NOT THE BOXER

Joe Frazier, Cardinals outfielder
Archie Moore, Yankees outfielder
John L. Sullivan, Braves outfielder
Mike Tyson, Cardinals second baseman

HE'S NOT THE NEWSMAN

Mike Wallace, Cardinals pitcher

HE'S NOT THE MOTEL FOUNDER

Howard Johnson, Mets third baseman

HE'S NOT THE TEAM OWNER

Charles Finley, Angels pitcher
Ted Turner, Cubs pitcher

HE'S NOT THE BOY IN THE SHOE

Buster Brown, Braves pitcher

Neat Nicknames

Baseball players have always had interesting nicknames. There have been clever ones, such as the nickname given to Doug Gwosdz, the Padres catcher, who was called "Eyechart," and disgusting ones, such as the nickname given to Nick Cullop, the Reds outfielder—"Tomato Face." Even those players who seemed to have enough names to begin with were often given an extra one or two. Take Christian Frederick Albert John Henry David Betzel, the Cardinals second baseman, who was called "Bruno"; Indians pitcher Calvin Coolidge Julius Caesar Tuskahoma McLish, called "Cal" and "Buster"; and Alan Mitchell

Edward George Patrick Henry Gallagher, the Giants third baseman, who was called "Dirty Al." Below are some of the more amusing nicknames in baseball. The teams and positions are the ones the players are most commonly associated with.

WOMEN'S NAMES

"Beverly" Bayne, Browns pitcher
"Tilly" Bishop, Athletics second baseman
"Lu" Blue, Tigers first baseman
"Kitty" Bransfield, Phillies first baseman
"Mary" Calhoun, Braves first baseman
"Rosy" Carlisle, Red Sox outfielder
"Molly" Craft, Senators pitcher
"Dolly" Gray, Pirates first baseman
"Bubbles" Hargrave, Reds catcher
"Zaza" Harvey, Indians outfielder
"Bonnie" Hollingsworth, Senators pitcher
"Sadie" Houck, Braves outfielder
"Little Eva" Lange, Cubs outfielder
"Polly" McLarry, Cubs first baseman
"Molly" Meloan, White Sox outfielder
"Minny" Mendoza, Twins third baseman
"Mollie" Milosevich, Yankees shortstop
"Molly" Molinaro, Tigers outfielder
"Ivy" Olson, Dodgers shortstop
"Rosy" Ryan, Giants pitcher
"Tillie" Shafer, Giants third baseman
"Dolly" Stark, Dodgers shortstop
"Lil" Stoner, Tigers pitcher
"Tilly" Walker, Phillies outfielder

FOOD NAMES

"Liver" Ancker, Athletics pitcher
"Sweetbreads" Bailey, Cubs pitcher
"Chops" Broskie, Braves catcher
"Soup" Campbell, Indians outfielder
"Cookie" Cuccurullo, Pirates pitcher
"Chili" Davis, Giants outfielder

"Pickles" Dillhoefer, Cardinals catcher
"Pea Soup" Dumont, Senators pitcher
"Pickles" Gerken, Indians outfielder
"T-Bone" Giordano, Athletics second baseman
"Noodles" Hahn, Reds pitcher
"Cracker" Hamby, Giants catcher
"Hot Potato" Hamlin, Dodgers pitcher
"Pork Chop" Hoffman, Astros catcher
"Tomatoes" Kafora, Pirates catcher
"Beans" Keener, Phillies pitcher
"T-Bone" Koski, Pirates pitcher
"Cookie" Lavagetto, Dodgers third baseman
"Peanuts" Lowrey, Cubs outfielder
"Spinach" Melillo, Browns second baseman
"Peach Pie" O'Connor, Browns catcher
"Little Potato" Pascual, Twins pitcher
"Ham" Patterson, Browns first baseman
"Pretzels" Pezzullo, Phillies pitcher
"Soup" Polivka, Reds pitcher
"Cookie" Rojas, Athletics second baseman
"Ham" Schulte, Phillies second baseman
"Cheese" Schweitzer, Browns outfielder
"Pie" Traynor, Pirates third baseman
"Goober" Zuber, Yankees pitcher
"Noodles" Zupo, Orioles catcher

Baseball in the Media

Baseball has never been the hottest subject in films or on TV. In the movies, it has always taken a backseat to boxing and thoroughbred racing, and it's never been a very popular subject for TV series. But there are many enjoyable movies, as well as books, songs, and a few poems, on the subject of baseball. Here are some of them.

At the Movies

EARLY FILMS

Casey at the Bat, a short based on the classic poem about the star of the Mudville Nine, was probably the first baseball movie ever made. And, believe it or not, it was made by the great inventor Thomas Edison.

Somewhere in Georgia (1916) starred the great Tigers outfielder Ty Cobb and is said to be the worst baseball film ever made. In it, Cobb is attacked by bad guys and tied up. He makes his escape just in time to race to the ballpark on a mule and save the old ball game for the home team. This is one of the few baseball movies from the silent film era worth mentioning (and not necessarily because it was good).

Babe Ruth had a modest movie career, too. First came ***Headin' Home*** (1920), followed by ***The Babe Comes Home*** (1922). For the latter picture he was paid an astronomical (especially in those days) $25,000 for a mere 17 days of shooting. He also had cameo roles in Harold Lloyd's ***Speedy***, a 1928 comedy, and as himself in ***The Pride of the Yankees*** (1942), the biographical picture about his old Yankees teammate Lou Gehrig.

BIOPICS

The Babe (1992). John Goodman, Kelly McGillis, Bruce Boxleitner. Goodman plays Babe Ruth in this picture about the man whose appetites were as gigantic as his talent. But the critics, although admitting it was better than ***The Babe Ruth Story,*** scored it as a double rather than a home run.

The Babe Ruth Story (1948). William Bendix, Claire Trevor, Charles Bickford. Bendix stars as the Bambino in this sentimental, inaccurate biography.

Cobb (1994). Tommy Lee Jones, Robert Wuhl. Jones plays the legendary mean-spirited Hall of Famer in this film about the last years of the old man's life.

Don't Look Back: The Story of Leroy "Satchel" Paige (TV movie, 1981). Louis Gossett, Jr., Cleavon Little, Ossie Davis. This is the biography of the legendary pitcher, based on his own book, *Maybe I'll Pitch Forever.*

Fear Strikes Out (1957). Anthony Perkins, Karl Malden, Norma Moore. Perkins brilliantly plays the fine Red Sox outfielder Jimmy Piersall, whose career was affected by a mental breakdown. Malden plays his ambitious father.

It's Good to Be Alive (TV movie, 1974). Paul Winfield, Louis Gossett, Jr., Ruby Dee. This is the story of Roy Campanella, the Hall of Fame Dodgers catcher, who was crippled in an automobile accident.

The Jackie Robinson Story (1950). Jackie Robinson, Ruby Dee. Robinson plays himself in this biopic that tells of the early years of the first black man in modern major league baseball.

One in a Million: The Ron LeFlore Story (TV movie, 1978). LeVar Burton, Madge Sinclair, Paul Benjamin, Billy Martin. Burton plays Tigers outfielder LeFlore, who rose from the Detroit ghetto and a prison term to play in the major leagues.

The Pride of St. Louis (1952). Dan Dailey, Joanne Dru, Richard Crenna. This is the biography of Dizzy Dean, the famed Cardinals pitcher. Dailey does a fine job as Dean.

The Pride of the Yankees (1942). Gary Cooper, Teresa Wright, Walter Brennan, Dan Duryea, Babe Ruth. Cooper plays the legendary Lou Gehrig, the Yankees' first baseman. Although Cooper was a natural right-hander, he wore a mirror-image uniform and seemed to be left-handed when the film was reversed, and his acting was first-rate.

The Stratton Story (1949). James Stewart, June Allyson, Frank Morgan, Bill Williams. This is the biopic of the outstanding White Sox pitcher Monty Stratton, who made a successful minor league comeback after losing his leg in a hunting accident.

The Winning Team (1952). Ronald Reagan, Doris Day, Frank Lovejoy. Reagan plays Grover Cleveland Alexander, the Hall of Fame pitcher for the Phillies and Cubs.

MOVIE MUSICALS

Damn Yankees (1958). Gwen Verdon, Tab Hunter, Ray Walston. This musical features a die-hard, middle-aged Washington Senators fan who sells his soul to the Devil. The Devil transforms him into a youthful superstar who leads the Senators to the pennant over the hated Yankees.

Take Me Out to the Ball Game (1949). Frank Sinatra, Esther Williams, Gene Kelly, Betty Garrett, Jules Munshin. This is a fun musical about the early days of baseball in which Williams owns a ball club with a versatile double play combination ("O'Brien to Ryan to Goldberg").

COMEDIES, DRAMAS, AND FANTASIES

Angels in the Outfield (1951). Paul Douglas, Janet Leigh, Keenan Wynn. This fantasy about the Pittsburgh Pirates features an orphan who sees angels who give advice about how to win baseball games.

Angels in the Outfield (1994). Danny Glover, Brenda Fricker, Tony Danza. In a movie loosely based on the 1951 film, this time the inept team is the California Angels. Two small boys pray for heavenly help, and suddenly the team begins to play like a group of All-Stars.

The Bad News Bears (1976). Walter Matthau, Tatum O'Neal, Vic Morrow, Joyce Van Patten, Brandon Cruz, Jackie Earle Haley. Matthau plays Morris Buttermaker, a former minor league player who cleans swimming pools and signs on to coach a losing Little League team. He recruits the best pitcher he can, an 11-year-old girl (O'Neal). There were two sequels—both of them pretty bad.

Bang the Drum Slowly (1973). Robert De Niro, Michael Moriarty. This is the story of a simpleton catcher (De Niro) dying of Hodgkin's disease and his protector, a hustling star pitcher (Moriarty). One of the best sports pictures of all time.

The Bingo Long Traveling All-Stars and Motor Kings (1976). Billy Dee Williams, James Earl Jones, Richard Pryor. This is a comedy about a barnstorming black baseball team of the 1930s that tries to outdo local white teams.

Blue Skies Again (1983). Mimi Rogers, Harry Hamlin, Robyn Barto, Kenneth McMillan. A young woman (Rogers) wants to play professional baseball and is given a trial.

Bull Durham (1988). Kevin Costner, Susan Sarandon, Tim Robbins. Life in the minors is accurately depicted in this film about a love triangle among the three main characters.

The Comrades of Summer (TV movie, 1992). Joe Mantegna. Mantegna is Sparky Smith, an arrogant player/manager who is tossed out of the major leagues. He then takes a job as the manager of the Russian national baseball team.

Cooperstown (TV movie, 1993). Alan Arkin, Hope Lange, Ed Begley, Jr. Arkin is a baseball scout and former major league pitcher. An embittered man, he tries to learn why he has never been elected to the Hall of Fame.

Eight Men Out (1988). John Cusack, Clifton James, Christopher Lloyd, David Strathairn, D. B. Sweeney, Charlie Sheen. This film explores the motivations of the eight men involved in the infamous 1919 Black Sox Scandal.

Field of Dreams (1989). Kevin Costner, Amy Madigan, James Earl Jones, Burt Lancaster. Costner is believable as an Iowa farmer who has a vision that if he builds a baseball diamond, Shoeless Joe Jackson and other deceased great players will come to play there.

It Happens Every Spring (1949). Ray Milland, Jean Peters, Paul Douglas. Milland is a chemistry professor who discovers a compound that makes baseballs repel wood, and he becomes a star pitcher who can strike out any batter holding a wooden bat.

The Kid From Left Field (1953). Dan Dailey, Anne Bancroft, Lloyd Bridges. Dailey plays a baseball park vendor who uses his son, a bat boy, to break the St. Louis Cardinals' slump.

The Kid From Left Field (TV movie, 1979). Gary Coleman, Robert Guillaume, Tab Hunter. This appealing remake of the 1953 film switches to the San Diego Padres.

A League of Their Own (1992). Geena Davis, Tom Hanks, Madonna. This warm, funny, and sentimental film tells the story of the rocky first season of the Rockford Peaches in the All-American Girls Professional Baseball League in the 1940s. It is the fictional account of a real team in a real league.

Little Big League (1994). Jason Robards, Timothy Busfield. A fatherless 12-year-old inherits the Minnesota Twins from his grandfather (Robards) and appoints himself manager.

Major League (1989). Tom Berenger, Charlie Sheen, Corbin Bernsen, Bob Uecker. A lovable band of misfits and loonies turn around the fate of the hapless Cleveland Indians.

Major League II (1994). Charlie Sheen, Bob Uecker, Tom Berenger. In this sequel to the 1989 film, the boys are back, just as crazy as ever.

Mr. Baseball (1992). Tom Selleck, Ken Takakura. This is a comedy about an American baseball player who learns about playing in Japan.

Moochie of the Little League (1959). Kevin Corcoran, Frances Rafferty, James Brown, Reginald Owen, Stuart Erwin. In this Disney comedy, Moochie (Corcoran) organizes a baseball team with the help of a British gentleman (Owen).

The Natural (1984). Robert Redford, Robert Duvall, Glenn Close, Richard Farnsworth, Kim Basinger, Wilford Brimley, Barbara Hershey. Roy Hobbs (Redford), an all-American hero, strives for perfection as a baseball player, but he is shot with a silver bullet by a young woman. He makes a comeback 15 years later. Based on a novel by Bernard Malamud.

Pastime (1991). William Russ. Russ is Roy Dean Bream, a 41-year-old pitcher on a losing minor league team in the 1950s. He is generous in helping the younger players, but the film ends on a sad note.

Rhubarb (1951). Ray Milland, Jan Sterling, Gene Lockhart. A millionaire who owns a baseball team dies and wills the team to his cat, Rhubarb, who becomes the mascot and inspires the team to a pennant.

Rookie of the Year (1993). Thomas Ian Nicholas, Gary Busey. Nicholas, a 12-year-old boy, breaks his arm. And when it heals, he is able to throw a baseball 100 miles per hour. He soon becomes the star of the Chicago Cubs.

Safe at Home! (1962). Mickey Mantle, Roger Maris, Don Collier, Bryan Russell, William Frawley. This is a story about a kid who runs away from home to the Yankees' training camp to try to get Mantle and Maris to come to his Little League team's banquet.

The Sandlot (1993). James Earl Jones, Tom Guiry. This is a nostalgic movie about young boys who play baseball and are helped by Jones.

The Scout (1994). Albert Brooks, Dianne Wiest, Brendan Fraser. This comedy features Brooks as a New York Yankees scout who signs a young pitcher who is something of a kook.

The Slugger's Wife (1985). Michael O'Keefe, Rebecca DeMornay, Martin Ritt, Randy Quaid. This is the story of a rude, boorish baseball player who falls in love with a singer.

Stealing Home (1988). Jodie Foster, Mark Harmon, Blair Brown. This movie tells of the longtime romance between a girl and a baseball player, and her eventual suicide.

Baseball on TV

For some reason, there have been very few television series featuring baseball. ***Cheers,*** in which Ted Danson plays a former Red Sox pitcher, and ***Who's the Boss?,*** in which Tony Danza plays a former Cardinal, don't really count since those shows are not about baseball.

Baseball series have never lasted long. The sitcom ***The Bad News Bears*** appeared from 1979 to 1980, and ***Ball Four*** (1976) collapsed after running for less than a full season, as did the drama ***The Bay City Blues*** (1983). There was also a short-lived series called ***Hardball*** (1994), in which Rose Marie played a sort of Marge Schott–type baseball owner.

The exception to all this mediocrity was Ken Burns's 1994 PBS series ***Baseball***. Divided into nine episodes—one for each inning— it faithfully traced the history of the national pastime.

Baseball Books

Baseball has been appearing in books for much longer than most people imagine. In the 18th century, a 1744 alphabetical book of sports for English children, the kind that starts "A is for Archery," chose to represent the letter B with "Baseball." A Lady Hervey in England described what the family of Frederick, the Prince of Wales, were doing: "They were diverting themselves with baseball, a play all who are or have been schoolboys are well acquainted with." Even the great English novelist Jane Austen referred to the game in 1798 in her book *Northanger Abbey.*

BOOKS FOR KIDS

Last Sunday, by Robert Newton Peck, is about sandlot baseball in the 1930s. It tells of a girl and her dreams of baseball.

Noonan, by Leonard Everett Fisher, is a wonderful science fiction novel about baseball in the future. It tells the story of a young man who plays for the Chicago Cubs in the 21st century, when people watch the games on three-dimensional television instead of at the ballpark.

OTHER BASEBALL STORIES

Bang the Drum Slowly, by Mark Harris, is one of the most moving of all baseball stories. It is about the friendship between an intelligent star baseball pitcher and a dull-witted, second-rate catcher who is suffering from a fatal disease. It was made into a wonderful movie.

The Curious Case of Sidd Finch, by George Plimpton, began as an article in *Sports Illustrated* intended to be an April Fool's joke on the American public. It tells the story of Finch, an English orphan trained in the Himalayas in the ways of Zen, who shocks the major leagues with his ability to throw a baseball 168 miles per hour.

The Natural, by Bernard Malamud, tells of the rise and fall of a talented baseball player. It was later made into a movie starring Robert Redford.

Shoeless Joe, by W. P. Kinsella, tells what happens when an Iowa farmer hears a voice that says, "If you build it, he will come." "It" turns out to be a stadium, and "he" turns out to be Shoeless Joe Jackson. This novel is the basis for the film *Field of Dreams*.

The Year the Yankees Lost the Pennant, by Douglas Wallop, is a funny book about a middle-aged Washington Senators fan who sells his soul to the Devil to become a young Senators superstar who finally leads his team to the pennant—breaking the Yankees' dynasty. The musical comedy *Damn Yankees* was based on this book.

You Know Me, Al, by Ring Lardner, is about an illiterate and selfish but extremely talented baseball player. This book was the first success for Lardner, one of the greatest of American humorists.

NONFICTION

Ball Four, by Jim Bouton, is the first and still the best of the baseball exposé autobiographies. Pitcher Bouton provides new insights into baseball life off the field and is very funny at the same time.

Baseball: An Illustrated History, by Geoffrey C. Ward and Ken Burns, is the lavishly illustrated companion volume to Burns's 1994 TV documentary on the game.

The Boys of Summer, by Roger Kahn, is part remembrance of the Brooklyn Dodgers during the 1940s and 1950s, part a bittersweet look at where some of the Dodgers stars were years later.

The Summer Game, by Roger Angell, is the first of Angell's wonderful books on baseball. The *New Yorker* writer is arguably the best sports interviewer in the baseball business, with an ability to talk to the players and get them to give him their innermost thoughts, poignant memories, fears, and humorous stories. Some of Angell's other books are ***Five Seasons***, ***Season Ticket***, and ***Late Innings***.

Poetic Musings

"PRAY FOR RAIN"

One of the worst pieces of doggerel was the poem created about the 1948 Boston Braves. They had a pretty mediocre pitching staff, with the exception of Warren Spahn and Johnny Sain, and the poem was "Spahn and Sain and pray for rain." The Braves managed to win the National League pennant that year.

POETRY IN SONG

Songs can qualify as poetry too, and the most famous of all is "Take Me Out to the Ball Game." It was first heard in 1908 and had words by Jack Norworth and music by Albert Von Tilzer. At the time they wrote it, neither one had ever seen a baseball game.

TINKER TO EVERS TO CHANCE

Franklin Pierce Adams, a transplanted Chicagoan, was a columnist for the New York *Daily Mail.* On a July day in 1910, because he needed eight lines to fill out his column, he wrote a poem called "Baseball's Sad Lexicon," which turned a no better than capable Cubs double-play combination of Joe Tinker, Johnny Evers, and Frank Chance into a legend:

These are the saddest of possible words
  Tinker to Evers to Chance.
Trio of Bear Cubs and fleeter than birds
  Tinker to Evers to Chance.
Thoughtlessly pricking our gonfalon bubble,
  Making a Giant hit into a double,
Words that are weighty with nothing but trouble
  Tinkers to Evers to Chance.

This bit of doggerel may have made the reputations of all three players and helped get them into the Hall of Fame.

CASEY AT THE BAT

The most famous poem of all—a poem that has been beloved for more than 100 years—is "Casey at the Bat." It was written by Ernest Lawrence Thayer, a Harvard graduate and a close friend of William Randolph Hearst, editor of the San Francisco *Examiner,* who hired Thayer to write a humor column for the paper. His final piece was written in May 1888, and Thayer said it took only two hours to write. It appeared on Sunday, June 3, under a pseudonym, and Thayer was paid $5.

The piece made little stir at first. But that summer in New York, a tall, handsome, 30-year-old singer and comedian named William DeWolf Hopper was appearing at Wallach's Theater. He was a fan of the New York Giants and decided to stage a "Baseball Night" at the theater. Two days before the scheduled night, a friend shared the poem with him. Hopper presented the poem at the festivities, and the New York *Times* reported that "a thrilling ode entitled 'Casey's at the Bat' was most uproariously received." The poem became Hopper's trademark.

In 1895, Thayer sheepishly admitted that he was the author and later said, "For this, perhaps my greatest of sins, I am exclusively to blame." Mudville, it was said, was really Boston.

The outlook wasn't brilliant for the Mudville nine that day;
The score stood four to two, with but one inning more to play.
And then when Cooney died at first, and Barrows did the same,
A sickly silence fell upon the patrons of the game.

A straggling few got up to go in deep despair. The rest
Clung to that hope which springs eternal in the human breast;
They thought, if only Casey could but get a whack at that—
We'd put up even money, now, with Casey at the bat.

But Flynn preceded Casey, as did also Jimmy Blake,
And the former was a lulu and the latter was a cake;
So upon that stricken multitude grim melancholy sat,
For there seemed but little chance of Casey's getting to the bat.

But Flynn let drive a single, to the wonderment of all,
And Blake, the much despis-ed, tore the cover off the ball;
And when the dust had lifted, and the men saw what had occurred,
There was Jimmy safe at second and Flynn a-hugging third.

Then from 5,000 throats and more there rose a lusty yell;
It rumbled through the valley, it rattled in the dell;
It knocked upon the mountain and recoiled upon the flat,
For Casey, mighty Casey, was advancing to the bat.

There was ease in Casey's manner as he stepped into his place;
There was pride in Casey's bearing and a smile on Casey's face.
And when, responding to the cheers, he lightly doffed his hat,
No stranger in the crowd could doubt 'twas Casey at the bat.

Ten thousand eyes were on him as he rubbed his hands with dirt;
Five thousand tongues applauded when he wiped them on his shirt.
Then while the writhing pitcher ground the ball into his hip,
Defiance gleamed in Casey's eye, a sneer curled Casey's lip.

And now the leather-covered sphere came hurtling through the air,
And Casey stood a-watching it in haughty grandeur there.
Close by the sturdy batsman the ball unheeded sped—
"That ain't my style," said Casey. "Strike one," the umpire said.

From the benches, black with people, there went up a muffled roar,
Like the beating of the storm-waves on a stern and distant shore.
"Kill him! Kill the umpire!" shouted someone on the stand;
And it's likely they'd a-killed him had not Casey raised his hand.

With a smile of Christian charity great Casey's visage shone;
He stilled the rising tumult; he bade the game go on;
He signaled to the pitcher, and once more the spheroid flew;
But Casey still ignored it, and the umpire said, "Strike two."

"Fraud!" cried the maddened thousands, and the echo answered fraud;
But one scornful look from Casey and the audience was awed.
They saw his face grow stern and cold, they saw his muscles strain,
And they knew that Casey wouldn't let that ball go by again.

The sneer is gone from Casey's lip, his teeth are clenched in hate;
He pounds with cruel violence his bat upon the plate.
And now the pitcher holds the ball, and now he lets it go,
And now the air is shattered by the force of Casey's blow.

Oh, somewhere in this favored land the sun is shining bright;
The band is playing somewhere, and somewhere hearts are light,
And somewhere men are laughing, and somewhere children shout,
But there is no joy in Mudville—mighty Casey has struck out.

Arts and Letters

That same poem, "Casey at the Bat," keeps popping up, even on the higher artistic level of opera and dance.

In 1953 the American composer William Schuman premiered his one-act opera *The Mighty Casey,* which contained as the libretto the Thayer poem. It is still performed occasionally, usually by college music schools.

The world premiere of a ballet also called *The Mighty Casey* was presented in Pittsburgh on October 6, 1990. Danced by the Pittsburgh Ballet Theatre, the choreographer was Lisa de Ribère. It was good enough to cause one critic to rave that it was "the first choreographic attempt to combine the moves of the game with the steps of the art for an entire ballet, and it does so with enough style, wit, and accuracy to satisfy fans of both ballpark and theater."

Colleges have even got into the act of making baseball intellectually acceptable. For example, in 1990 the New School for Social Research in New York offered two new courses. "The History of Baseball in America" reviewed the sport from 1839 to the present, using a timeline of American history as a scorecard, and "The Mystique of Baseball" examined the karma and mythology of the game.

Odds and Ends

Five Strikes and They're Not Out

Strikes in baseball don't go back a long way—just to 1972. That year, players in both leagues went on strike during spring training to demand that the owners contribute more to the medical and pension funds. The strike ended after only 13 days, but not before 86 regular-season games had been missed. Rather than try to make them up, different teams ended up playing different numbers of games that year.

In 1973 the owners locked out the players for 17 days during spring training—an action that ceased after labor arbitration. No games were lost that year.

The "reserve clause" was a major issue in baseball in the early 1970s. In June 1972, the U.S. Supreme Court ruled that the reserve clause was binding on all players, thus guaranteeing each club a player's services for as long as it wishes. But by 1975 the reserve clause had been struck down, which meant that all players sooner or later were free to negotiate as free agents. In 1976 the owners staged another lockout during the spring over free agency. This lasted for 17 days, but again no games were missed.

In 1979 the owners laid down a new condition: A club that lost a free agent had to be compensated by being allowed to choose a player from the club that signed the free agent. The players rejected this, claiming that it would put a brake on the bidding for free agents. During the final week of spring training in 1980, the players staged an eight-day walkout and threatened to go on strike during the season, in May, if there was no agreement. Just before the deadline a committee studied the situation and set a new deadline for 1981. Once again, no games were lost.

Because the players and owners still had not resolved their differences by the beginning of the 1981 season, the players set a deadline for a strike at June 12, 1981—a promise they kept. This strike lasted 50 days, finally ending on July 31. The free agent compensation ruling was relaxed by the owners, but 712 games had been missed. The playoff solution was that the teams leading their respective divisions when the strike began were to play the respective division leaders from the second half of the season, thus producing a division champion. But in the National League West, the Cincinnati Reds finished second in both halves and still won more games than either first place club, yet the Reds failed to make the playoffs despite having the best overall record.

In 1985 there was a two-day strike in August over salary arbitration. But not much harm was done, since most of the missed games were made up during the season. The ones of no importance to the pennant races were simply not played.

During spring training in 1990 the owners staged another lockout. This time it was over their desire to install a salary cap on each team, meaning that no team could pay more than a total given amount for all salaries, thus cutting down on the astronomical salaries paid to some players. The lockout lasted 32 days, but no games were lost.

Then came the big one—the disastrous strike of 1994. The problem again was that the owners demanded a salary cap in order to adopt a revenue-sharing plan to distribute $58 million to low-revenue teams. The players rejected this plan on July 18. The owners refused to budge, and the last games that season were played on August 11, with the players going out on strike immediately after the conclusion of those games. Both sides remained adamant, and on September 14 it was announced that the rest of the season had been canceled, with a loss of 669 games. And it meant that, for the first time since 1904, there would be no World Series.

Progress in the negotiations was so slow that a member of Congress from Ohio, James Traficant, made a suggestion. "Negotiators should be locked in a room with no windows and air conditioning, and should be fed baked beans, fried cheese, hard-boiled eggs, and chocolate Kisses. In eight hours they'll be pleading 'Play Ball!'"

Needless to say, his suggestions were not taken, and talks still went on at a snail's pace. In 1995 the owners (except for those of the Baltimore Orioles) began fielding teams of replacement players in spring training. Finally, on March 31, 1995, a U.S. District Court judge ruled in favor of the players, and the players offered to return to work. The owners agreed, and baseball was ready to begin on April 25.

But great damage had been done. Spring training with the regular players had to begin again, and the season had to be reduced to 144 games. And no one will ever know how many records might have been broken if there had been a complete 1994 season. Would Tony Gwynn of the Padres have hit .400? (He was batting .394.) Would anyone have broken Roger Maris's season record of 61 home runs? (In the running were Matt Williams of the Giants with 43; Ken Griffey, Jr., of the Mariners with 40; Jeff Bagwell of the Astros with 39; Frank Thomas of the White Sox with 38; Barry Bonds of the Giants with 37; and Albert Belle of the Indians with 36.)

The Last Legal Spitball

The last legal spitball was thrown by Hall of Fame member Burleigh "Ol' Stubblebeard" Grimes, a right-handed pitcher for the Yankees, in 1934. That might not seem too important, but the spitball had been declared illegal in 1920.

Grimes began his career with the Pirates in 1916 and moved to the Brooklyn Dodgers in 1918. He continued to play for the Dodgers until

1926. He then pitched for the New York Giants (1927), Pirates again (1928–1929), Boston Braves (1930), Cardinals (1930–1931), Cubs (1932–1933), Cardinals again (1933–1934), Pirates again (1934), and Yankees (1934). For 15 years he used what was technically an illegal pitch.

The catch was that when the anti-spitball rule was passed, there were several pitchers who relied on it, and each of the major league teams was permitted to name up to two members of its pitching staff as exemptions for the 1920 season. In the 1921 season, 17 pitchers were granted the right to use the spitball for the rest of their careers.

The nine exempted in the American League, with their 1920 won-lost records, were: Stan Coveleski (24–14) and Ray Caldwell (20–10) of the Indians, Red Faber (23–13) of the White Sox, Jack Quinn (18–10) of the Yankees, Urban Shocker (20–10) and Allen Sothoron (8–15) of the Browns, Allan Russell (5–6) of the Red Sox, and Doc Ayers (7–14) and Dutch Leonard (10–17) of the Tigers. In the National League, the eight exempted were: Burleigh Grimes (23–11) and Clarence Mitchell (5–2) of the Dodgers, Phil Douglas (14–10) of the Giants, Ray Fisher (10–11) of the Reds, Bill Doak (20–12) and Marv Goodwin (3–8) of the Cardinals, and Dana Fillingim (12–21) and Dick Rudolph (4–8) of the Braves.

Grimes outlasted them all, pitching through 1934, and ended his career with 270 wins. He also made it to the Hall of Fame.

The Chicago Black Sox

In 1919 the Chicago White Sox, who had won the American League pennant in 1917, won it again under manager Kid Gleason. In the National League, the Reds won the pennant for the first time, and this created a great deal of Midwest interest in the World Series. Who knew that some of the Sox had made a deal with big-time gamblers to fix the Series in exchange for a large sum of money? They became known as the Black Sox.

The White Sox—an unhappy and underpaid team—were favored, but they lost the Series, five games to three. Many people apparently knew the fix was in, since the odds went from 3–1 White Sox to 8–5 Reds. Supposedly the signal to the gamblers telling them the Series was to be thrown was to have the Sox pitcher hit the first batter in game number one. This was done by Sox starter Eddie Cicotte, and the Reds won the game, 9–1.

Many people think that after the first game, the Series was played more or less honestly, even though Claude "Lefty" Williams did walk three men in one inning in the second game, which was very unusual for him. The Reds also won that game, 4–2. The Sox did win the third game, 3–0, but cynics say it was because the gamblers were not paying the players what had been agreed on—$10,000 of the $100,000 total after each game.

Cicotte was on the mound again in the fourth game and lost, 2–0, making two errors himself. The fifth game was won by the Reds, 5–0, and the sixth was won by the Sox, 5–4. In the seventh game, Cicotte—who had begged to start—actually beat the Reds, 4–1. But the final game was all Reds as they won the game, 10–5, and the Series.

The fixing of the Series took almost a year to surface. In September 1920, a Chicago grand jury began investigating gambling and corruption in baseball. At the same time, rumors were circulating that eight Sox players had been involved in fixing the 1919 Series: left fielder "Shoeless Joe" Jackson, third baseman George "Buck" Weaver, first baseman Chick Gandil (the apparent organizer of the fix), shortstop Charles "Swede" Risberg, Cicotte, Williams, center fielder Oscar "Happy" Felsch, and utility infielder Fred McMullin.

Cicotte broke down when he was confronted by manager Gleason and Sox owner Charles Comiskey. He, Jackson, and Williams then confessed to the grand jury, and Comiskey suspended all eight players, although it was argued that Weaver was guilty only by association, since he had sat in on the negotiations and then decided not to participate in the fix. As Jackson was leaving the courthouse, a small boy supposedly came up to him and said, with tears in his eyes, "Say it ain't so, Joe."

Criminal indictments followed, but the players' written confessions somehow disappeared, and the eight were all acquitted in 1921. According to the letter of the law, they all could have been reinstated. But there was a new man in baseball—its first commissioner, Kenesaw Mountain Landis. He took quick and decisive action: "Regardless of the verdict of juries, no player who throws a ball game, no player that undertakes or promises to throw a ball game, no player that sits in conference with a bunch of crooked players and gamblers where the ways and means of throwing a game are discussed and does not promptly tell his club about it, will ever play professional baseball!"

Some people felt that some of the players deserved a pardon. Weaver never shared in the bribe money and hit .324 in the Series. Ten thousand fans signed a petition calling for his reinstatement, but Landis turned a cold shoulder. Jackson had tried to give back the money he got and batted .375 in the Series, the highest average of a regular on either team. But when word got to Landis that Jackson had been hired to coach a Class D minor league team, he ordered him fired.

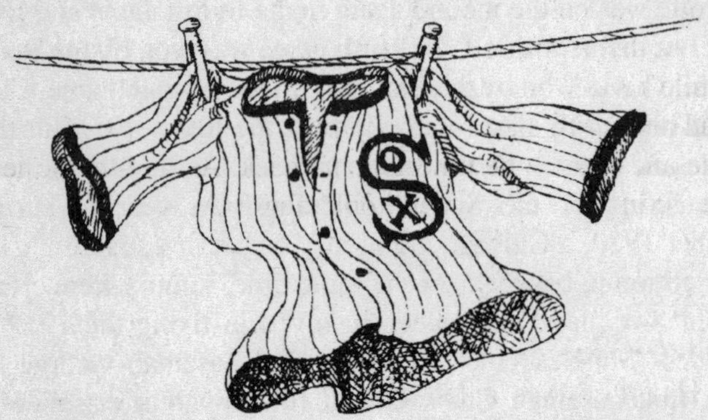

Double-Barreled Stars

Here are a few fine baseball players who were also stars in other sports.

DANNY AINGE: FROM BATS TO HOOPS

Danny Ainge was an outstanding player in several sports for Brigham Young University. At 6'4" and 175 pounds, he seemed an ideal player for either baseball or basketball. Ainge tried baseball first as a utility player at second base, third base, shortstop, the outfield, and even as a designated hitter for the Toronto Blue Jays (1979–1981). But because he was only a .220 hitter and appeared in a mere 211 games in those three years, he decided that basketball was his sport. He went on to become a fast, hustling guard for the Boston Celtics, Sacramento Kings, Portland Trail Blazers, and Phoenix Suns and a deadly free-throw and three-point shooter.

GENE CONLEY: SPLIT PERSONALITY

Gene Conley, a 6'8" right-handed pitcher, threw for the Braves in Boston and Milwaukee (1952, 1954–1958), Phillies (1959–1960), and Red Sox (1961–1963). Conley won 91 while losing 96 and carried an earned run average of 3.82. Amazingly, during most of that time he was also a standout professional basketball player, appearing as the center for the Boston Celtics (1952–1953, 1958–1961) and New York Knicks (1962–1964).

LOU GEHRIG: ALL-AROUND ATHLETE

Lou Gehrig, the Hall of Fame Yankees first baseman, was an amazing athlete. At the age of 11 he was able to swim across the Hudson River, and while he was a student at Columbia University, he was a baseball star and an outstanding football player. He played part of the time as a tackle and part of the time as a halfback. As a lineman, he hit hard on offense and was resourceful on defense. As a triple-threat man, he was a fine blocker but an even better punter.

STEVE HAMILTON: FROM HURLING TO HOOKSHOTS

Steve Hamilton was a left-handed pitcher for the Indians (1961), Senators (1962–1963), Yankees (1963–1970), White Sox (1970), Giants (1971), and Cubs (1972). In his 12 years as a pitcher, he won 40 games while losing 31, and also saved 42. He also played professional basketball with the Minneapolis Lakers (1958–1960). He went on to become the baseball coach and later the athletic director at Morehead State University in Kentucky.

BO JACKSON: DOUBLE DRAFT PICK

Bo Jackson was an outstanding running back for Auburn University, winning the Heisman Trophy in 1985. Drafted by the Royals in baseball as well as number one in football, he astonished the sports world by choosing to play baseball. In 1986 this 6'1", 222-pound athlete joined the Kansas City Royals and became their regular left fielder in 1987. In 1988 he astonished the sports world again by declaring he would also play for the Los Angeles Raiders. He said that professional football was like a hobby to him, and so he reported late to the National Football League. (His contract with the Raiders provided for a ten-day break after the conclusion of the Royals' baseball season.)

Jackson was the first athlete to be named to both baseball's All-Star squad and football's Pro Bowl game. But on January 13, 1991, during a playoff game with the Cincinnati Bengals, he sustained what may have been a career-ending injury to his left hip. Dropped by the Royals, he was picked up as a DH by the White Sox in 1991. Things still did not go right, and in March 1992 the Sox put him on waivers, not so much to get rid of him but rather to resign him to a new contract without exercising his $910,000 option. That same month, the superstar decided to have a hip replacement, and on April 4, 1992, surgeons gave him a new artificial hip. He played for the Sox in 1993 and the California Angels in 1994, retiring after the season.

VIC JANOWICZ: FINALLY A FOOTBALLER

Vic Janowicz, 5'9" halfback for Ohio State and 1950 Heisman Trophy winner, at first chose to play professional baseball. Primarily a catcher, he played for the Pirates (1953–1954) but batted only .214 in 83 games. He decided to switch to professional football. In 1954 and 1955, he played for the Washington Redskins and in the latter year led the team in rushing and scoring. He retired after a serious auto accident in 1956.

DEION SANDERS: THE NEON MAN

A baseball/football star who has caught the attention of all sports fans today is "Prime Time" "Neon" Deion Sanders—the first athlete to play in both the World Series and the Super Bowl. Sanders has played baseball for the Yankees (1989–1990), Braves (1991–1994), Reds (1994–1995), and Giants (1995–). He has also played pro football for the Atlanta Falcons (1989–1993), San Francisco 49ers (1994–1995), and Dallas Cowboys (1995–). He would generally play baseball until the football season began, and then he would join his gridiron team—unless his baseball team was engaged in postseason play.

To illustrate his importance to both teams, here is an example of a unique day in his life. Sanders had left the Braves in late summer 1991, when the Falcons started training camp. After the fourth game of the NFL season, he was named defensive player of the week for his part in his team's 21–17 defeat of the Los Angeles Raiders. Then came an urgent request from the Braves, who were in the thick of the National League West pennant race. The Braves had just lost their leadoff man, Otis Nixon, who was leading the major leagues in base stealing with 60, and they needed some help from the fleet-footed Sanders. He spent the morning of September 25 at football practice, going through calisthenics, catching drills, and pass coverage drills. Then he showered and went to a Falcons team meeting. Usually he would go home after all this and take a nap. But not this time. After the meeting broke up, Sanders boarded a news helicopter from an Atlanta television station and flew southward to downtown Atlanta, where he landed in a parking lot near the state capitol. A television station car then took him to the ballpark, where he arrived wearing a sweatsuit and carrying a football. There he was, ready for a baseball game on the same day he had practiced with his football team. In the first game of a doubleheader with the Cincinnati Reds, Sanders was inserted at first base as a pinch runner and promptly stole second base.

In 1992, the Braves were involved in a pennant race so Sanders decided to remain with them until the end of the season. The Braves made it to the World Series, where Sanders batted .533 with eight hits and four runs scored. In 1994–1995, Sanders shone as a defensive back for the San Francisco 49ers. In January 1995, the 49ers won the Super Bowl; "Neon" Deion had an interception and became the first and only man to play in both a World Series and a Super Bowl!

JIM THORPE: OLYMPIC STAR

Jim Thorpe, whose Indian name was Bright Path, attended the Carlisle Indian School in Pennsylvania, where he was an all-around athlete. This 6', 200-pound star played minor league baseball for Rocky Mount and Fayetteville, North Carolina, in the Eastern Carolina League in 1909 and 1910. In 1912 he went to the Olympic Games in Stockholm, Sweden, where he was the first person to win both the decathlon and the pentathlon. Later, officials took back his Olympic medals after discovering that he had been a professional baseball player. (He was finally reinstated as champion and his medals returned to his family in the early 1980s, years after his death.) Thorpe then played the outfield for the New York Giants (1913–1915), Reds (1917), Giants again (1917–1919), and Boston Braves (1919), batting .252.

In 1919, Thorpe left baseball to play professional football, which had just begun. He played in the backfield for the Canton Bulldogs (1915–1920), Cleveland Indians (1921), Oorang Indians of Marion, Ohio (1922–1923), Toledo Maroons (1923), Rock Island (Illinois) Independents (1924), New York Giants (1925), and Bulldogs again (1926). In many of those years he was player/coach. Thorpe was elected to the Pro Football Hall of Fame in 1963.

A Dream Field

Field of Dreams, a 1989 film, was so good it was nominated for the Academy Award for best picture. It was a warm, nostalgic baseball movie that became everybody's favorite father-son reconciliation saga. Ray Kinsella (Kevin Costner), a down-to-earth, likable Iowa farmer, feels that he might be becoming stodgy. He hears a mysterious voice telling him, "If you build it, he will come." Then a vision shows him a baseball diamond in the middle of his cornfield.

The baseball field built by Universal Studios for the picture, at a cost of about $5 million, was created outside Dyersville, Iowa, a small town northeast of Iowa City, and it straddled a property line between two farms. After the film was shot, Don Lansing, the farmer who owned right field and most of the infield, proved to be rather sentimental. He kept the grass trimmed and his part of the field in repair. Al Ameskamp, who owned left and center field, tore out the sod and planted corn again. But true to the voice's prediction, people began to come, and Ameskamp relented. Today, visitors can see a white farmhouse with a picket fence in front on a hillock above the baseball field. Little wooden bleachers sit behind the first baseline, and in the summer the outfield fence is a two-acre field of corn.

There is no admission charge or tour guide, and the field is free to anyone who wants to use it for a game. There is a small souvenir stand on the third base side of the field, and a stand behind home plate, plus an unmanned donation box. Visitors can even take an ear of corn from the farms at no charge. It has been estimated that some 65,000 people come to see the field each year.

Stand for Your Team

Even people who have never been to a baseball game may have seen Harry Caray, the broadcaster of the Chicago Cubs games on television, stand up in the seventh inning to sing "Take Me Out to the Ball Game" to cheer his Cubbies on. The seventh-inning stretch has become a part of the game wherever it is played. But where and when did the practice start?

For years it was thought that President William Howard Taft, whose tenure ran from 1909 to 1913, was the cause of the ceremony. (See the section on "Baseball and U.S. Presidents" on page 207 for the traditional explanation.) But that may not be true.

In June 1869 the New York *Herald* reported on a game between the Cincinnati Red Stockings and the Brooklyn Eagles: "At the close of the long second inning, the laughable stand up and stretch was indulged in all round the field." And later that year, the Cincinnati *Commercial* told of a break in a game between the Red Stockings and the Eagle Club of San Francisco: "One thing noticeable in this game was a ten minutes' intermission at the end of the sixth inning—a dodge to advertise and have the crowd patronize the bar."

In June 1882, during a game between Manhattan College and the New York Metropolitans, a Christian Brother named Jasper Brennan, who was Manhattan's coach, noticed that his team was becoming restless on the bench. When it was their turn to bat in the seventh inning, he encouraged the students to stand up and stretch.

Then came the first game of the 1889 championship series between the New York Giants of the National League and the Brooklyn Bridegrooms of the American Association. *The Sporting News* reported: "As the seventh opened, somebody cried, 'Stretch for luck!' And instantly the vast throng on the grand stand rose gradually and then settled down, just as long grass bends to the breath of the zephyr." That was 20 years before Taft took office.

Doctoring the Ball—Legally

As far as baseball pitchers have been concerned, brand-new baseballs direct from the factory have always been too slick to be gripped properly. The remedy in the good old days was to rub them down with a combination of home plate dirt and tobacco juice. But the problem with this method was that the dirt produced scratches in the horsehide, causing some pretty wobbly pitches. And the tobacco juice made irregular stains that made it more difficult for the batter to follow the path of the ball.

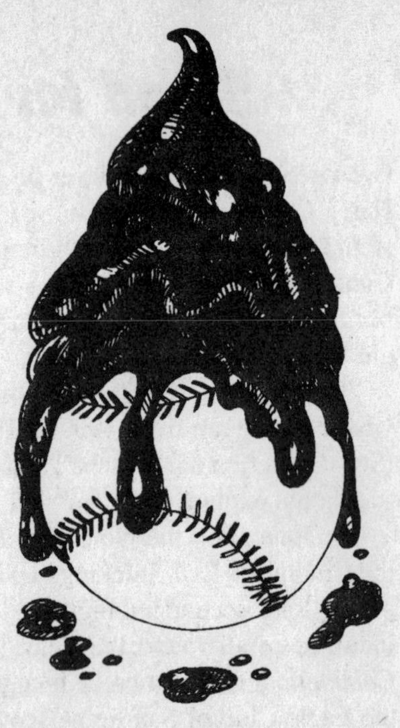

For the last 50 years or so, the answer to the problem has been a kind of gunk called Lena Blackburne Baseball Rubbing Mud. All major league teams, plus some minor league teams, use the stuff to make the ball more grippable.

Lena Blackburne was not a woman. He was a man who had been a White Sox shortstop and later a Sox manager. He developed a "secret formula" to remove the slipperiness from new baseballs. According to Burns Bintliff, the man who inherited the formula after Blackburne died, "You just dab some mud on and rub it all over the ball. It takes the gloss off without scoring the surface."

This gooey, blackish-brown stuff is as thick as cold cream and is collected in southern New Jersey every autumn. Bintliff won't tell exactly where his mud mine is, and he certainly won't tell what he does with the mud to make it more smooth so that it doesn't scratch the ball. He won't even tell the price he charges. But he does admit that he stores it over the winter in plastic garbage cans. All winter long his neighbors deliver empty coffee cans to his door, and in the spring,

Bintliff packs the mud into the coffee cans and seals them with duct tape. Then he sends them off to every major league club. The standard order is 15 pounds per team, although some of them need a bit more.

"I'm not getting rich," Bintliff says. "In fact, I'm probably losing money on it. But I'm not doing it for the money. I'm doing it for the love of baseball." His efforts will be remembered. There is a can of Lena Blackburne Rubbing Mud in the Baseball Hall of Fame in Cooperstown, New York.

The Cartwright Rules

Alexander Joy Cartwright, Jr., was a young man who, early in the 19th century, played the English game of rounders and other contests involving a ball and bases. By 1842, when he was 22, he was one of a group of young New York men who played a new game called "base ball." By 1846, Cartwright had set up a new set of rules for the game, dropping the rounders regulations that provided for a runner to be retired by being hit with a thrown ball. The new rules provided for foul lines, nine players to a team, and nine innings to a game. Here are the regulations that the "Father of Baseball" laid down.

1. Members must strictly observe the time agreed upon for exercise, and be punctual in their attendance.
2. When assembled for practice, the President, or in his absence, the Vice President, shall appoint an Umpire, who shall keep the game in a book provided for that purpose, and note all violations of the By-Laws and Rules during the time of exercise.
3. The presiding officer shall designate two members as Captains, who shall retire and make the match to be played, observing at the same time that the players put opposite each other should be as nearly equal as possible; the choice of side to be tossed for, and the first in hand to be decided in a like manner.
4. The bases shall be from "home" to second base, forty-two paces; from first to third base, forty-two paces, equidistant. [Forty-two paces equals 90 feet.]
5. No stump match shall be played on a regular day of exercise.
6. If there should not be a sufficient number of members of the Club present at the time agreed upon to commence exercise, gentlemen

not members may be chosen in to make up the match, which shall not be broken up to take in members who may afterwards appear; but in all cases, members shall have the preference, when present, at the making of a match.

7. If members appear after the game is commenced they may be chosen in if mutually agreed upon.
8. The game is to consist of twenty-one counts, or aces, but at the conclusion an equal number of hands must be played.
9. The ball must be pitched, and not thrown, for the bat.
10. A ball knocked out of the field, or outside the range of the first or third base, is foul.
11. Three balls being struck out and missed and the last one caught is a hand out; if not caught is considered fair, and the striker is bound to run.
12. A ball being struck or tipped and caught either flying or on the first bound is a hand out.
13. A player running the bases shall be out, if the ball is in the hands of an adversary on the base, or the runner is touched with it before he makes his base; it being understood, however, that in no instance is a ball to be thrown at him.
14. A player running who shall prevent an adversary from catching or getting the ball before making his base, is a hand out.
15. Three hands out, all out.
16. Players must take their strike in regular turn.
17. All disputes and differences relative to the game, to be determined by the Umpire, from which there is no appeal.
18. No ace or base can be made on a foul strike.
19. A runner cannot be put out in making one base, when a balk is made by the pitcher.
20. But one base allowed when a ball bounds out of the field when struck.

Baseball and U.S. Presidents

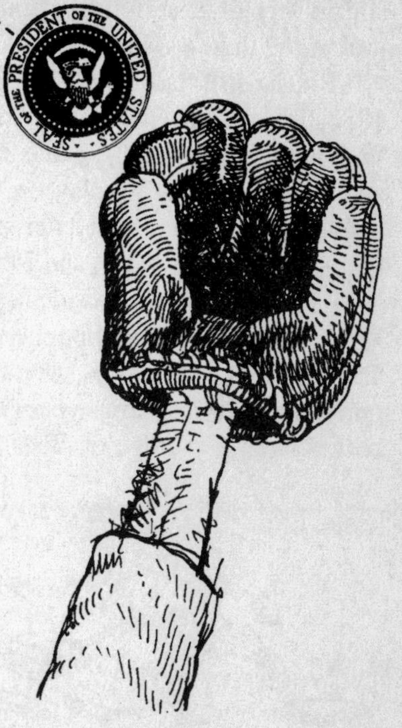

There have been ten presidents who played baseball in their youth—Ulysses S. Grant, Benjamin Harrison, William Howard Taft, Woodrow Wilson (who also briefly coached the football team at Wesleyan University), Herbert Hoover (who also managed the football team at Stanford University), Dwight D. Eisenhower, John F. Kennedy, Jimmy Carter (who preferred softball), Ronald Reagan, and George Bush.

Taft was the first presidential baseball fan. He was the first chief executive to throw out the first ball to open the baseball season. (Carter was the first president to break that tradition.) In 1910, Taft arrived at the ballpark to see the Washington Senators' home opener against the Philadelphia Athletics and was asked by umpire Billy Evans to do the honors.

Taft may have been responsible for beginning another baseball tradition. The story says he was attending a game in Pittsburgh and rose to stretch in the middle of the seventh inning. The crowd, thinking he was leaving, got up to honor him. Taft sat down, the crowd sat down, and the seventh-inning stretch was born.

Ronald Reagan was deeply involved in baseball. His first professional job was as an announcer on radio station WOC (the letters stood for World of Chiropractic) in Davenport, Iowa. The job paid $5 a week plus bus fare. He went on to become a sportscaster for WHO in Des Moines, Iowa, where he was paid $75 a week. The job involved recreating Cubs games as they came in over the ticker tape.

When Reagan got to Hollywood, he played baseball with the Leading Men, a team made up of actors. In a 1949 charity game against the Comedians, he hit a grounder toward the shortstop, comedian Donald O'Connor. Seeing that the play would be close, Reagan slid in feet first, suffering a multiple fracture of the right thigh that took more than a year to heal.

But he still had a soft spot in his heart for the Cubs. In October 1988, he was in Chicago to make a speech and decided to go to Wrigley Field to watch a game. He ended up throwing out the first ball and doing the play-by-play on television for part of the first inning and all of the second. He later said, "You know, in a few months I'm going to be out of work, and I thought I might as well audition."

The most skillful presidential ball player of all was George Bush. When he was in prep school he was named Best Athlete at the school. Then he went on to Yale, where he became the regular first baseman on the team in his junior year (1947), batting right and throwing left, with a batting average of .264. The team went on to the finals of the

NCAA tournament, losing the national championship to the University of California. The next year he was captain of the Yale team that again went to the finals of the NCAA tournament, this time losing to Southern California.

His coach, Ethan Allen, said of him, "If you told him to bunt, he bunted." And Dodgers scout Whitey Piurek said of his play in the NCAA, "By professional standards, he wasn't a prospect. He could run, but he lacked real power."

Gehrig's Famous Farewell

On June 1, 1925, Yankees first baseman Lou Gehrig appeared in the first of 2,130 consecutive games, an amazing record that was not broken until 1995. During his career, Gehrig hit a record 23 grand slam home runs, and he had a career batting average of .340.

In 1938 his batting average dropped to .295, and it was obvious that he was sick. He had lost weight and seemed to be losing his muscle tone. In 1939 he opened as usual at first base, but after collecting only four hits in his first eight games, Gehrig, as team captain, asked to speak to manager Joe McCarthy. "I think I'm hurting the team," he said. "Maybe it would be better if I took a rest for a while." So he benched himself on May 2, 1939. Babe Dahlgren took over first, and Gehrig never took the field for a major league game again.

Gehrig entered the Mayo Clinic in Rochester, Minnesota, in June, and tests showed that he was suffering from an incurable disease, amyotrophic lateral sclerosis—now often referred to as Lou Gehrig's disease. He was given two years to live. On July 4, 1939, the Yankees held Lou Gehrig Appreciation Day in Yankee Stadium before 61,808 fans.

Gehrig gave a memorable speech: "Fans, for the past two weeks you have been reading about a bad break I got. Yet today I consider myself the luckiest man on the face of the earth. I have been in ballparks for 17 years, and I have never received anything but kindness and encouragement from you fans. Look at these grand men [his teammates and former teammates, including Babe Ruth]. Which of you wouldn't consider it the highlight of his career just to associate with them for even one day? Sure I'm lucky. Who wouldn't have considered it an honor to have known Jacob Ruppert? Also, the builder of baseball's greatest empire, Ed Barrow? To have spent six years with that wonderful little fellow, Miller Huggins? Then to have spent the next nine years with that outstanding leader, that smart student of psychology, the best manager in baseball today, Joe McCarthy? Sure, I'm lucky. When the New York Giants, a team you would give your right arm to beat and vice versa, sends you a gift, that's something. When everybody down to the groundskeepers and those boys in white coats remember you with trophies, that's something. When you have a father and mother who work all their lives so that you can have an education and build your body, it's a blessing. When you have a wife who has been a tower of strength and shown more courage than you dreamed existed, that's the finest I know. So I close in saying that I might have had a bad break, but I have an awful lot to live for."

The Yankees retired Gehrig's uniform number 4 that year—the

first Yankee ever to be so honored. Lou Gehrig died June 2, 1941, in Riverdale, New York. In 1989 the U.S. Postal Service issued a Lou Gehrig commemorative stamp.

Equipment and Rule Changes

Over the years, there have been many changes in the rules and the equipment for the game of baseball, but few of them have violated the original intent of the Cartwright rules. Here are a few of the more important ones.

1845—The ball is required to weigh 3 ounces. The pitching distance is to be 45 feet.

1854—The weight of the ball is increased to between 5½ to 6½ ounces and it must be 2¾ to 3½ inches in diameter.

1859—Bats are to be no more than 2½ inches in diameter.

1860—Whitewash is to be used to mark the foul lines.

1863—Bats must be round and made of wood.

1868—The bat is to be no more than 42 inches long.

1869—The pitcher's box is to be a 6-foot square.

1872—The ball is to weigh not less than 5 or more than 5½ ounces. The ball's circumference is to be not less than 9 or more than 9¼ inches.

1875—The unpadded glove may be used.

1877—The bases are to be canvas covered and 15 inches square. Home plate is to be located just within the diamond at the intersection of the first and third baselines.

1881—The pitcher's box is to be 50 feet from the plate.

1882—The 3-foot baseline is to be used.

1884—The pitcher is allowed to pitch overhand.

1885—Home plate may be made of marble or whitened rubber. The bat may have one flattened side.

1886—The pitcher's box is to be 4 feet by 7 feet. First and third bases are to be within the foul lines. Stolen base statistics are introduced, and a runner is credited with a stolen base for each base advanced on another player's hit.

1887—A batter can no longer call for a high or low pitch. Home plate must be made of rubber and must be 12-inches square. The pitcher's box must be 4 feet by 5½ feet. A walk will count as a hit and a time at bat.

1888—The number of strikes for a strikeout will be three, rather than five.

1889—The number of balls for a walk will be four. (It ranged from five to nine during the 1880s.)

1891—Substitutions other than for injury or with the permission of the other team are allowed.

1893—The pitcher's plate is to be made of rubber, and the box is eliminated. The rubber is to be 12 inches by 4 inches, located 60 feet and 6 inches from home plate. The bat must be round.

1895—Foul tips are to be counted as strikes. The pitcher's rubber is to be 24 inches by 6 inches. The bat diameter is to be 2¾ inches.

1898—Stolen bases are not to be given for advancing on a teammate's hit.

1900—The plate is to be five-sided and 17 inches wide.

1901—Foul balls will be counted as strikes.

1910—The ball will be cork-centered.

1920—The spitball is abolished. The lively ball will be used, with its Australian yarn and tighter winding.

1926—The cushioned cork-center ball will be used.

1934—Both major leagues will use the same brand of baseball.

1950—The pitcher's mound will be a standard 15 inches higher than the baselines.

1954—The bat may be made of laminated wood.

1959—New ballparks must be built with fences at least 325 feet down the lines and 400 feet in center field.

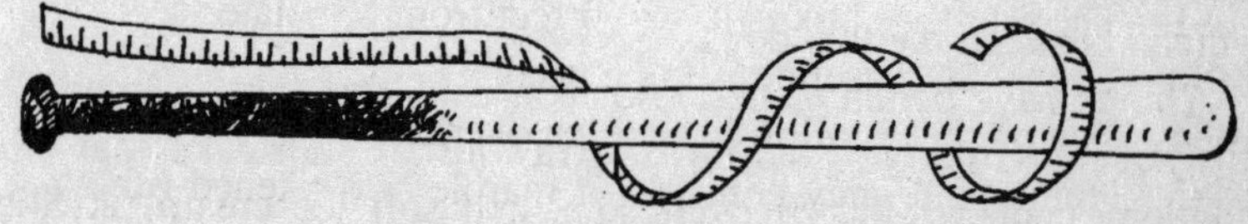

1962—Oversized gloves may not be used by pitchers, infielders, and outfielders. Players may use a grip-improving substance on their bats, but not for more than the first 18 inches beginning at the handle.

1968—The pitcher's mound will be 10 inches higher than the baselines.

1973—The American League may use designated hitters.

1975—The ball may be made of cowhide or horsehide. Cupped bats may be used.

Food at the Ballpark

Americans have always had definite traditions when it comes to eating at the ballpark. Take the hot dog, or frank, or red hot, depending on where you live.

There is a question as to when hot dogs were introduced to ballparks. There are those who claim that the owner of the St. Louis Browns, Chris Von der Ahe, started selling them at Sportsman's Park 100 years ago. Others think that Harry M. Stevens started selling them at the Polo Grounds in New York in 1900. He called them dachshunds and sold them by yelling, "Get 'em while they're hot." It is said that Tad Dorgan, a cartoonist for the New York *Evening Journal*, was at the game, and he drew cartoon characters of the sausages, giving them tails and feet and the label "hot dogs."

There are variations on the plain old hot dog. Several ballparks in the Midwest offer bratwurst sandwiches. And there is the double dog sandwich found in Baltimore's Oriole Park at Camden Yards, which is a sandwich with two franks in a bun that is cut twice, leaving a wall of bread between the two dogs.

Things have begun to get wild. You could buy chef's salads (at Milwaukee County Stadium); strawberry shortcake (at the Kingdome); pizzarolls, fried chicken, and soft ice cream (at Shea

Stadium); Buffalo chicken wings and 14 kinds of imported beer (at Yankee Stadium); sushi (at Anaheim Stadium); vegetarian burgers with blue cheese dressing (at the Oakland Coliseum); Rib-B-Que, yogurt, and tofu hot dogs (at Candlestick Park); and Evian Water and yogurt (at Dodger Stadium). Some outstanding culinary failures have been noted, of course. These include salads (in several ballparks) and a raw seafood bar (at Yankee Stadium).

Candy has baseball connections, too. But the chances are that the Baby Ruth candy bar was not named after the baseball player. However, the similarity of the names certainly didn't hurt sales. The commonly accepted story is that it was named in honor of a daughter of President Grover Cleveland. Then there was the Reggie! candy bar. When Reggie Jackson was with the Orioles, he said, "If I ever played in New York, they'd name a candy bar after me." Sure enough, he went to the Yankees and the candy bar appeared.

Some Crazies and Con Men

VOODOO IN SAN DIEGO

In 1988 the Astros lost 11 straight games, and the losing pitcher of the 11th game, Jim Deshaies, decided to do something about it. He bought a book on witchcraft and performed a curse-breaking ceremony in the visitors' clubhouse. He took twigs from four different trees, spit on them, and threw them into a fire while chanting a curse. Deshaies asked his teammates if anyone didn't believe in the curse, and only first baseman Glenn Davis said yes. The Astros beat the Padres, 4–1, that night, and Davis strained a hamstring muscle.

GLOVE BURNING

When Iona College pitcher Phil McKiverkin lost seven games in a row in 1988, he blamed his losing streak on his new glove, a Bret Saberhagen model. McKiverkin decided to perform an exorcism (a ceremony to get rid of evil spirits). He poured alcohol all over the glove and set it afire along the left field foul line. His teammates helped by uttering incantations. The next day McKiverkin went in to relieve wearing a borrowed glove and got credit for a win over Brooklyn College. He was modest about it, saying, "I'm grateful to my teammates. They could have burned my right arm instead."

BIRD STREAK BROKEN

Baltimore disc jockey Mike Filippelli was a die-hard Orioles fan. In 1988 the Birds set a record by losing the first 21 games of the season. When they were halfway through the streak, Filippelli bet Vince Edwards, his broadcast partner, that the Orioles' streak would not reach 13, and the two let the listeners decide the punishment if the team did lose its 13th. The Orioles lost, and Filippelli's punishment was to crawl and walk a 6.2-mile stretch of Maryland's Coastal Highway. It took him four hours. He also had to dress in an Orioles jersey and helmet, sit in a plastic kiddie pool, and have 30 gallons of chocolate syrup poured over him. Observers decorated him with cherries, pineapple, sprinkles, nuts, and whipped cream. Filippelli commented that it was "something not to tell my grandchildren about."

CHARLIE O

One of the strangest team owners was Charlie Finley, the owner of the Kansas City Athletics who later moved the team to Oakland. Finley was the first to fit out his team in rainbow-colored uniforms. He also elected a mule (named Charlie O) to be the team mascot and installed a mechanical rabbit (named Harvey), which popped up from the ground to deliver new baseballs to the home plate umpire. Finley also brought sheep to Kansas City's Municipal Stadium and a shepherd to tend them. The sheep were put between the right field fence and the outer wall where they helped to keep the grass short.

VEECK MADNESS

Probably the most brilliant baseball team promoter of all time was Bill Veeck. In 1948, when he was the owner of the Indians, the club received a letter from a Cleveland baseball fan named Joe Earley, who claimed that he, an average fan, deserved a night in his honor. Veeck was intrigued with the idea, and on September 28, 60,405 fans showed up for Good Old Joe Earley Night. Earley, a 24-year-old night guard at an auto plant, was presented with a new convertible, clothing, luggage, books, and appliances. Other fans received livestock, poultry, and other gifts. Veeck spent $30,000 to have orchids flown in from Hawaii and gave them to the first 20,000 women entering the stadium.

On May 31, 1949, another crazed Indians fan, Charley Lupica, climbed a flagpole, sat on a platform at the top, and promised he would not come down until Cleveland was in first place in the American League. On September 25, Veeck had the platform moved to the Indians' ballpark for a ceremony in which Lupica gave up his hopeless 117-day stunt. The team finished third that year.

Toward the end of the 1949 season, on September 23, Veeck, having realized that the Indians were out of the running after winning the World Series the year before, staged a funeral for the 1948 pennant. Wearing a top hat, he drove a horse-drawn coffin-containing hearse at the head of a funeral procession to a grave behind the center field fence. Manager Lou Boudreau and his coaches were the pallbearers, and the club's business manager read the last rites from *The Sporting News*.

On August 24, 1951, when Veeck was owner of the St. Louis Browns, he gave over 1,000 fans behind the Browns dugout YES and NO placards so they could take part in the strategy of the game. The fans flashed the cards when asked by the coaches what the Browns should do—steal, sacrifice, and so on. It worked. The Browns beat the Philadelphia Athletics, 5–3.

But perhaps Veeck's most famous stunt occurred when he was the owner of the Browns—the worst club in organized baseball. He hired a midget, Edward Carl "Eddie" Gaedel, who stood 3'7" tall and weighed 65 pounds. On August 19, 1951, Gaedel made his first and only appearance at the plate. The Browns were playing the Tigers, and Gaedel was sent in to pinch-hit for outfielder Frank Saucier. Ed Hurley, the plate umpire, permitted him to bat when Zack Taylor, the Browns' manager, showed him a contract signed by Gaedel. Naturally, because of his tiny strike zone, Gaedel—wearing number 1/8—was walked on four pitches by pitcher Bob Cain. Gaedel was then replaced by outfielder Jim Delsing, who ran for him. He never appeared again in the major leagues. Later, on opening day in 1961, Gaedel and several other midgets served as vendors in the box seat section of Comiskey Park. Veeck, who now owned the White Sox, had received letters from fans complaining that the regular vendors were blocking their view.

Baseball Cards

The baseball card, with its picture of a player along with his personal statistics, is almost as old as the professional game itself. One of the earlier distributors of baseball cards was the maker of a cigarette called Sweet Caporal. To get the card, a person had to buy a package of cigarettes, and this so enraged Honus Wagner of the Pirates, the future Hall of Fame shortstop, that he demanded in 1909 that his cards be destroyed. A nonsmoker, he realized that young people were the real baseball card collectors, and he didn't want them to be corrupted by the Sweet Caporal people. In 1992 one of those rare surviving Wagner cards sold for $451,000.

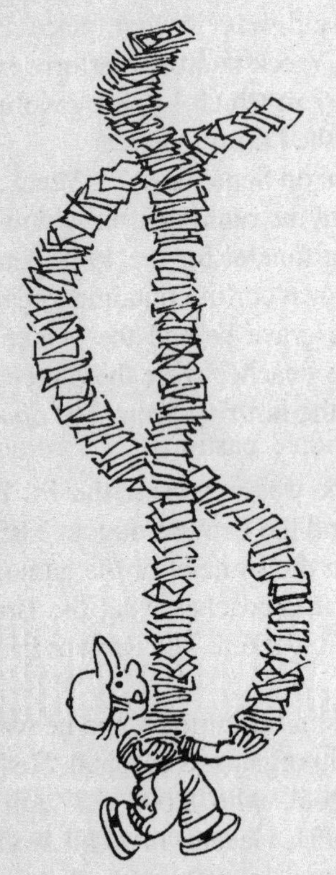

Other companies got into the baseball card business. In 1932 the U.S. Caramel Company had 32 cards printed and offered a baseball ("value $1") to anyone who had a collection of all 32. But hardly anyone could find card number 16, and for a while many thought that the company was so stingy that it purposely didn't print that card. In fact, card collectors didn't even know whose picture was on it. The mystery was solved in 1988. One number 16 card was found, and it had the picture of Hall of Fame Giants third baseman Freddie Lindstrom. Experts guess that it is worth $35,000.

The Topps Chewing Gum Company soon got into the production of cards to package with their gum, and in 1952 they bought out their chief rival, Bowman Gum. Topps pretty much had the field to itself until 1981, when Fleer Corporation and the Donruss Company began to issue their own sets of cards. Then, in 1988, Major League Marketing began to produce its own set under the name of Score.

Today, baseball cards are big business. Dealers often buy and sell at top dollar, but they demand that the card be in almost mint condition. A 1952 Topps Mickey Mantle may go for $8,500, and a 1953 Topps Mickey Mantle is worth $1,400. A 1963 Topps Pete Rose can cost $550. The problem is that the real worth of a card depends on how much someone is willing to pay for it, and it can cost $1,500 to $2,000 just to get a collection started. Gone are the days when kids just flipped the cards in competitive games and then shoved them into a dresser drawer or shoe box.

Baseball's Big Bucks

Paychecks for those who play the national pastime have ballooned since George Wright was paid $1,400 by the Cincinnati Red Stockings for the entire year of 1869. Many people were stunned when they learned that Babe Ruth was paid more than President Herbert Hoover in 1931. But baseball salaries today make all this look like small potatoes. In 1992, Ryne Sandberg, the Chicago Cubs second baseman, astonished the baseball world by signing a contract for $28.4 million over a period of four years. That came to $7.1 million a year when it took effect in 1993, and he made much more when advertising endorsement money was figured in. (Sandberg retired for 1½ seasons beginning in June 1994, and that contract was no longer in effect when he returned.) By 1992 the sky seemed to be the limit, as the New York Mets paid their players an average salary of $1,711,615 per year.

After the baseball strike of 1994, it was hard to get accurate figures on what the various baseball players were earning. So many of them were registered as free agents, and salary negotiations took a long time. Still, at the beginning of the 1995 season, although salaries had shown a 10 percent decline, these seemed to be the highest paid players and their annual salaries:

Cecil Fielder, Detroit Tigers first baseman $9,237,500
Barry Bonds, San Francisco Giants left fielder $8,000,183
David Cone, Toronto Blue Jays pitcher
(traded to the Yankees in mid-1995) $8,000,000
Joe Carter, Toronto Blue Jays left fielder $7,500,000
Ken Griffey, Jr., Seattle Mariners center fielder $7,500,000
Frank Thomas, Chicago White Sox first baseman $7,150,000
Mark McGwire, Oakland A's first baseman $6,900,000
Jeff Bagwell, Houston Astros first baseman $6,875,000
Cal Ripken, Jr., Baltimore Orioles shortstop $6,871,671
Lenny Dykstra, Philadelphia Phillies center fielder $6,200,000
Kirby Puckett, Minnesota Twins right fielder............. $6,200,000
Ruben Sierra, Oakland A's right fielder
(traded to the Yankees in mid-1995) $6,200,000

The club-by-club payroll on opening day in 1995 went like this:

Toronto Blue Jays $49,853,500
New York Yankees $46,598,516
Atlanta Braves $45,295,500
Baltimore Orioles $42,193,691
Chicago White Sox $39,495,333
Detroit Tigers $36,280,950
Oakland A's $35,917,500
Chicago Cubs $35,625,833
San Francisco Giants $35,238,350
Cincinnati Reds $35,060,667
Cleveland Indians $35,056,500
Seattle Mariners $33,039,260
Texas Rangers $32,611,726
Colorado Rockies $31,415,549
Houston Astros $31,288,000
St. Louis Cardinals $30,918,000
California Angels $30,469,167
Boston Red Sox $30,353,850
Kansas City Royals $30,261,333
Philadelphia Phillies $28,623,000

Los Angeles Dodgers	$27,504,167
San Diego Padres	$26,103,500
New York Mets	$25,943,990
Minnesota Twins	$24,850,500
Florida Marlins	$23,491,500
Pittsburgh Pirates	$17,672,000
Montreal Expos	$15,710,833
Milwaukee Brewers	$15,273,600

After the strike, the annual salaries for first-year players went up from $109,000 to $115,000. That amount is more than the salaries of the governors of 44 of the 50 states.

Even the salaries of umpires have gone up. Previously, the salary scale was $60,000 to $155,000, depending on years of service. Beginning in 1995, the scale went to $75,000 to $175,000.

The Language of Baseball

Baseball is a gold mine of colorful words and phrases. Many of them have crept into everyday English. Here are a few of them.

Ace: The best pitcher on the ball team. The Cincinnati Red Stockings, the first professional team in the game, won 56 games (with one tie) in 1869, and their only pitcher was Asa Brainard. Therefore, any pitcher who was outstanding was called an "Asa," which was soon shortened to "ace."

Around the horn: When an out is made with no one on base, the opposing infielders throw the ball around the infield from third to first. This term was taken from the route that ships had to take around Cape Horn in South America before the Panama Canal was opened.

Boot: An error made while fielding a ground ball. This sometimes includes accidentally kicking the ball.

Bull pen: The place on the field where relief pitchers warm up. This word was used partly because of the Bull Durham tobacco ads painted on the outfield walls.

Can of corn: A fly ball that is easy to catch, taken from a grocer's practice early in the century of stacking cans on high shelves, to be tipped with a long stick and caught by the grocer.

Country-fair hitter (also **pretty fair country hitter**): A good hitter, taken from the strong farmers who played ball at fairs.
Ducks on the pond: The bases are loaded.
Farm team: A minor league club owned or subsidized by a major league team. The phrase came from the small rural towns where these minor league clubs played.
Hot dog: A player who shows off.
Iron man: A durable ball player.
Major league: The top level.
Minor league: Inferior.
Muff: To misplay the ball. The word came from the early baseball slang word "muffin," meaning an inept player. 
On deck: Next to bat—ready and waiting.
Out of left field: Unexpected. This phrase came about because of the vastness of the outfield and its distance from the infield.
Pinch hitter: One who is used to take another batter's place. This is often used incorrectly in common speech to imply that the pinch hitter is not as talented, since a baseball pinch hitter is usually a better hitter than the man he hits for.
Play ball: To cooperate.
Play-by-play: A running commentary on the baseball action.
Rain check: The part of a baseball ticket to be used on another day if a game is rained out. Thus, a reinvitation to an event in the future.
Rain out: A rain that is hard enough to cause postponement of a game. Thus, any lack of success.
Relieve: To take over for another player or take over another's job.
Root: To encourage a team. The word may come from the idea that a fan is rooted to his or her team.
Southpaw: A left-hander, especially a pitcher. Whenever possible, ballparks were built so that home plate was in the west. That way, the batter didn't have to stare into the afternoon sun. So a pitcher's left arm was on the south side as he stood on the mound.

Strikeout: To be out after being charged with three strikes. Thus, any failure.

MORE BASEBALL WORDS AND PHRASES

There are also many words and terms that arose in baseball and are part of the national game. Here are some.

Alley: The section of the outfield between center and left or center and right.
Aspirin: A fastball—so called because it looks as small as an aspirin.
Bag: A base. Bases are made of canvas bags.
Baltimore chop: A topped fair ball that bounces in front of the plate and high enough in the air so that the batter can reach first. In the 1890s, Baltimore kept its infield hard and many hits like this were made.
Battery: The pairing of the pitcher and the catcher—after the military term for a group of big guns.
Bleachers: Unsheltered seats, usually beyond the outfield wall, so called because of the exposure to the sun.
Cleanup: The player fourth in the batting order who is powerful enough to drive runners home and "clean" the bases.
Collar: A batter who got no hits in a game once "wore the collar," since wagon horses' collars looked like zeroes.

Designated hitter (or **DH**): A player who bats for the pitcher (without causing the pitcher to be removed from the game) but does not play in the field.
Earned run: A run scored before the third out in an inning that is not the result of an error.
Earned run average (or **ERA**): A statistic that tells the average number of earned runs given up by a pitcher for every nine innings.

Fireman: A relief pitcher who can "put out the fire" when he enters the game with men on base.

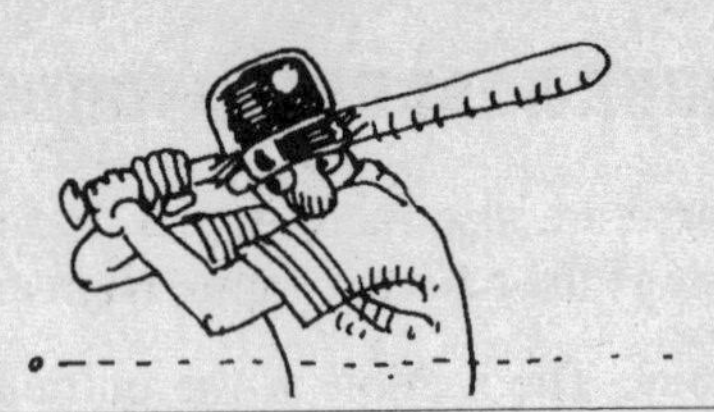

Fungo: A practice game in which a man throws a ball into the air and bats it himself to fielders. He uses what is called a fungo bat. There are three theories as to where the term came from. One says that in early versions of the game the hitter would recite the rhyme, "One go, two goes, fun goes." Or it may have come from the word "fungus," referring to the soft wood used in the fungo bat. It also might have come from the Scottish word "fung," which means "to toss."

Gopher ball: A pitched ball hit for a home run. Yankees pitcher Lefty Gomez was the first to use the term, saying that bad pitches might "go fer" a home run.

Hit for the cycle: To hit a single, double, triple, and home run in a single game.

Hot corner: Third base, since the third baseman, often playing close to the batter, has to field many hard-hit balls.

Junior Circuit: The American League, which was founded later than the National League.

Keystone sack: Second base, since it is the center of the infield.

Modern era: In baseball, it is usually dated from 1903, when the two leagues played the first World Series.

Pepper: A practice game in which a player tosses the ball to a second player who taps it to another player, who fields it and tosses it to other players.

Pull the ball: To hit the ball toward the outfield on the same side of the plate where the batter stands.
Ribby: A run batted in—pronouncing the abbreviation RBI.
Rookie: A first-year player. The word comes from the army term, which was probably a shortened form of "recruit."
Rubber: The pitcher's mound, since it is made of rubber.
Screwball: A breaking ball that curves in the opposite direction from a curveball.
Senior Circuit: The National League, which was founded before the American League.
Slugging average: A statistic measuring extra-base hitting. The total bases reached safely are divided by the total times at bat, carried to three decimal places.
Switch hitter: A player who can bat both right-handed and left-handed.
Texas leaguer: A softly hit ball that goes just over an infielder's head and falls in for a hit. In the 1890s, it was the specialty of Art Sunday of Toledo of the American Association, who had been a veteran of the Texas League.
Triple Crown: Won by a player who leads the league at the end of the season in batting average, home runs, and runs batted in.
Unearned run: A run scored after an error or interference call that should have caused the end of an inning. It is not charged against the pitcher in computing his earned run average.
Worm burner: A hit that skims along the ground.

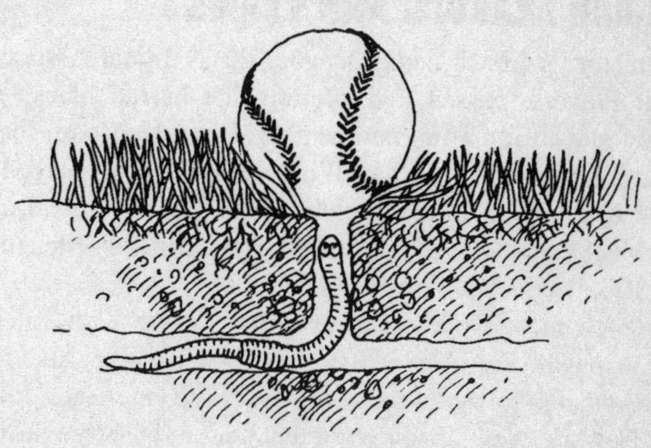

Men of COURAGE

Over the years there have been countless baseball players who demonstrated more courage than the average person can comprehend. Hundreds of players have overcome bigotry, poor health, and physical handicaps. They are inspirations to all of us.

Blacks in Baseball

ALL-BLACK LEAGUES AND TEAMS

In 1867 history's first baseball league, the National Association of Base-Ball Players, passed a resolution that barred blacks and the teams they played for from membership. Even so, Moses Fleetwood Walker and his brother, Welday Wilberforce Walker, played for the American Association's Toledo club in 1884, and there were at least 20 other blacks who played ball on mostly white major league clubs. Before 1900, over 30 had played.

In 1884, Chicago played an exhibition game with Toledo. The Chicago manager, Cap Anson, saw Fleetwood Walker take his position, and Anson bellowed a racist remark. Five years later he refused to play a Newark, New Jersey, team that featured George Stovey, perhaps the best black pitcher of all time. In 1887 the New York Giants tried to bring Stovey up to the majors, but Anson was able to prevent it.

In 1901 the Orioles tried to sneak black second baseman Charlie Grant into the lineup by passing him off as a Cherokee Indian, but White Sox owner Charlie Comiskey made sure that this didn't happen. Similar events met similar fates.

These situations set a precedent that would last for many years and was to force the creation of all-black teams and leagues. The Negro National League was formed in 1920, and it was followed by the Negro Eastern League and the Negro American League. Out of this came the Negro World Series.

PLAYERS SPEAK OUT

In addition to playing others in their own league, these black teams often played, and often beat, teams of white professionals in exhibition games. One of the early giants of black baseball, John Henry "Pop" Lloyd, was often compared to Hall of Fame shortstop Honus Wagner. Wagner himself commented, "It's a privilege to have been compared to him." Wagner also considered Andrew "Rube" Foster, who pitched for the Chicago Lelands and later founded the Negro National League, "the smartest pitcher I have ever seen in all my years in baseball."

Yankees first baseman Lou Gehrig was to say, "I've seen many Negro players who should be in the major leagues. There is no room in baseball for discrimination. It is our national pastime and a game for all." Cubs catcher and later manager Gabby Hartnett agreed: "If managers were given permission, there'd be a mad rush to sign up Negroes." And Cardinals pitcher Dizzy Dean commented, "I have played against a Negro All-Star team that was so good, we didn't think we had an even chance against them." But these remarks were made during the 1930s, and baseball had years to go before the color line was broken.

ROBINSON BREAKS THE COLOR BARRIER

The player to break the color barrier, of course, was the immortal Jackie Robinson. On August 29, 1945, he was signed by the general manager of the Brooklyn Dodgers, Branch Rickey, and sent to the Dodgers' Montreal Royals farm club in the International League. Rickey tried to prepare him for what was going to happen once Robinson was brought up to the parent team:

"I want a ball player with guts enough not to fight back . . . I want you to know, Jackie, that there is no way for us to fight our way through this situation. There is virtually no group on our side. No umpires, no club owners, maybe a few newspapermen. We will be in a very tough spot. I have a great fear that there will be some fans who will be highly hostile to what we are doing. Jackie, it will be a tough position to be in, an almost impossible position. But we can win if we can convince everyone that you are not only a great ballplayer but also a great gentleman."

Robinson pointed out that this sounded like a battle. "Yes, exactly, a battle!" Rickey replied. "But it's one we won't be able to fight our way through. We have no army, no soldiers. Our weapons will be base hits and stolen bases and swallowed pride. Those will do the job and get the victory—that's what will win . . . and, Jackie, nothing, nothing else will do it."

Robinson was called up to the Dodgers in 1947. Manager Leo Durocher was with the team at spring training in Panama, and he got wind of a planned players' strike against Robinson. Durocher got the news after he had undressed to go to bed, but he dressed and called a late team meeting. "If you do this, if you have this strike," he told the men, "you can [expletives deleted]. He's a fine ball player, and he'll put money in your pocket and in my pocket, and he's going to play. And furthermore, *he's just the first. Just the first.*" (Durocher was fired as Dodgers manager for other reasons shortly afterward.)

Robinson did suffer hatred and bigotry. The whole St. Louis Cardinals team also threatened to strike just before the Dodgers were to open a series with them. National League President Ford Frick lost no time in setting the Cardinals straight: "You will find that the friends you think you have in the press box will not support you, that you all will be outcasts. I do not care if half the league strikes. Those who do it will encounter quick retribution. They will be suspended, and I don't care if it wrecks the National League for five years. This is the United States of America and one citizen has as much right to play as another. The National League will go down the line with Robinson whatever the consequence. You will find if you go through with your intention that you have been guilty of complete madness."

Jackie Robinson went on to become one of the greatest players of all time, and blacks were no longer outcasts. But breaking the color barrier was not over. In the National League, the Phillies were the last team to sign a black—John Kennedy, in 1957—ten years after Robinson's major league debut. It was 12 years after Robinson's debut that the last American League team to hold out, the Red Sox, signed Pumpsie Green in 1959. And it was not until 1975 that Frank Robinson became the first black manager when he took over the Indians. It wasn't until 1989 that Bill White became president of the National League.

They Also Overcame

PITCHERS

JIM ABBOTT: OLYMPIAN ACHIEVER

Jim Abbott first gained the public's attention as a one-handed pitcher for the University of Michigan. He was born without a right hand, yet

he was able to become a baseball star. Abbott was the winner of the 1987 Sullivan Award as the nation's top amateur athlete and was the winning pitcher in the final baseball game of the 1988 Olympics, which gave the U.S. team the gold medal. He had said of his disability, "I don't think people should make too much of it. I was blessed with a good left arm and a not so good right one. I don't think of myself as different, I don't think of myself as courageous. I grew up learning to do things within my capabilities. I've had a good time doing what I've done." Abbott was drafted in the first round by the California Angels in 1988. Late in 1992 he joined the New York Yankees (for whom he threw a no-hitter), and then the Chicago White Sox and Angels again in 1995.

HUGH DAILY: ONE-ARMED HURLER

Hugh Daily was a pitcher who had one arm. He spent six years in the majors with several teams, from 1882 to 1887, winning 73 games while losing 89. While he was with the Cleveland Spiders, he threw a 1–0 no-hitter against Philadelphia on September 13, 1883. He also struck out 16 men in one game at a time when four strikes were needed for a strikeout.

BOB OJEDA: AMAZIN' MET

Late in the 1988 season, Bob Ojeda, then a Mets pitcher, nearly cut off part of a finger on his pitching hand in a freak accident with a power hedge trimmer in his garden. After microsurgery and a lot of physical therapy during the off-season, he came back to start for the Mets in 1989, going 13–11 with a 3.47 ERA.

TOAD RAMSEY: ACCIDENT VICTIM

Thomas "Toad" Ramsey of the Louisville Colonels and Cardinals won 114 games and lost 124 in his six years of play. His best years were 1886 (38–27) and 1887 (37–27, leading the league in strikeouts with 355). Ramsey had a disfigured pitching hand. He had been a bricklayer and cut through the tendon of his index finger with a trowel. Later, that liability became an asset because it gave him a natural knuckleball, although the pitch was unknown in his day.

HERB SCORE: COMEBACK MIRACLE

On May 7, 1957, pitcher Herb Score of the Indians was struck in the right eye by a line drive off Gil McDougald of the Yankees. He almost lost the sight in that eye but came back the next year. He won 17 games for the Indians and White Sox before he retired in 1962.

BERT SHEPARD: WAR HERO

Bert Shepard of Dana, Indiana, had been a fighter pilot in World War II whose plane was shot down. After the amputation of his right leg below the knee, he wore an artificial leg. On August 4, 1945 (in his only major league appearance), he went 5 1/3 innings for the Washington Senators against the Red Sox, giving up three hits and one run.

MONTY STRATTON: COMEBACK KID

Monty Stratton pitched for the White Sox from 1934 to 1938. He was one of the rising stars of the American League, winning 15 games in 1937 and another 15 in 1938. In November 1938, a hunting accident caused the amputation of his right leg. But wearing an artificial leg, he made a comeback in the minor leagues and won 18 games in 1946 for Sherman in the East Texas League.

OUTFIELDERS

PETE GRAY: EXPERT FIELDER

Born Peter J. Wyshner, Pete Gray played for the Browns in 1945, although he had lost his right forearm in a childhood accident, retaining only a stub above the elbow. When he caught a ball in the outfield, he would toss the ball up in the air, throw the glove off his hand, catch the ball, and throw it back into play. In his 77 games in the majors, he batted .218 before he returned to the minor leagues, retiring in 1950. When asked how good he might have been if he had had two arms, he said, "Who knows? Maybe I wouldn't have done as well. I probably wouldn't have tried as hard and practiced as much as I did. And I probably wouldn't have been as determined."

DUMMY HOY: BRILLIANT OUTFIELDER

William Ellsworth "Dummy" Hoy was a sterling outfielder for many clubs in his 14-year career (1888–1902), although he was hearing and speech impaired. Totally deaf, he had a lifetime batting average of .288 and was a brilliant fielder and base runner. This was in the days before hand signals were used by managers, coaches, and umpires.

Other Leagues

It has been said: "Toss a ball to a European, and he or she will kick it. Toss a ball to an American, and he or she will catch it and throw it." To a great degree, we owe that to baseball, since basketball and football came later. At any rate, baseball is designed to be played by people of all ages, all shapes, all sizes, and all degrees of proficiency. Here are some of the organizations that provide everyone with opportunities to play baseball.

The Minors

In the beginning, the minor league clubs were not deliberately organized. They were simply composed of teams in the smaller cities, particularly outside the northeast quarter of the United States where the two major leagues were first based. Over the decades, many minor league teams were formed. At first, they were totally independent clubs whose players were under contract to them. To obtain these players, the major league teams had to negotiate with the minor league teams.

THE "FARM CLUBS"

Gradually, more and more of the minor league teams came to be bought outright by the major league teams, or at least to have a working agreement under which the major league team would give them some financial and instructional support in return for top priority in acquiring players. And it is because of this that the minor leagues have come to be regarded as "farm clubs," nurturing the young talents for the great harvest of the major leagues.

It was Branch Rickey who was the father of the high-powered use of the minor leagues to provide men for the majors. As the general manager of the Cardinals in the 1920s and 1930s, he sought out young talent, signed the players to fairly cheap contracts, and placed them on minor league teams until they were ready to come to St. Louis or were sold to other teams. The other clubs soon followed suit.

ALPHABET DIVISION

At one time the minors were divided into seven classes, but in 1963, they were reorganized into four: AAA (or Triple A), AA (or Double A), A, and Rookie (limited to players in their first or second season of professional play). By the 1970s, the many minor league teams were organized into various leagues. Now, Class AAA has the American Association, International League, Mexican League, and Pacific Coast League. Class AA has the Eastern League, Southern League, and Texas League. Class A has the California League, Carolina League, Florida State League, Midwest League, New York-Penn League, Northwest League, and South Atlantic ("Sally") League. The Rookie leagues are the Appalachian League, Arizona League, Dominican Summer League, Gulf Coast League, and Pioneer League.

Each season, minor league teams are allowed to draft players from the class below, and the major league teams are also allowed to bring up players at set times during the year.

During the 1930s and 1940s, there were some 60 minor leagues with teams in over 400 cities in the United States, Mexico, and Cuba. But with the advent of television sports and the spreading of the major leagues from coast to coast, they went into decline. But things are looking up. According to the National Association of Professional Baseball Leagues, the governing body of minor league baseball, attendance in the minors in 1994 hit 33,892,773 (perhaps because of the devastating strike in major league ball).

Let's take a look at the minor leagues located in the United States. Here are the teams, league by league, with their locations, stadiums, stadium capacities, and major league affiliations.

AAA

AMERICAN ASSOCIATION

Buffalo (NY) Bisons, Pilot Field (21,050), Cleveland
Indianapolis (IN) Indians, Busch Stadium (12,934), Cincinnati
Iowa (Des Moines, IA) Cubs, Sec Taylor Stadium (10,500), Chicago NL
Louisville (KY) Redbirds, Cardinal Stadium (33,500), St. Louis
Nashville (TN) Sounds, Herschel Greer Stadium (17,000), Chicago AL
New Orleans (LA) Zephyrs, Privateer Park (5,116), Milwaukee
Oklahoma City (OK) 89ers, All-Sports Stadium (15,000), Texas
Omaha (NE) Royals, Rosenblatt Stadium (19,500), Kansas City

INTERNATIONAL LEAGUE

EASTERN DIVISION

Ottawa (ONT, Canada) Lynx, Rec Complex (10,000), Montreal
Pawtucket (RI) Red Sox, McCoy Stadium (6,010), Boston
Rochester (NY) Red Wings, Silver Stadium (11,000), Baltimore
Scranton/Wilkes Barre (Scranton, PA) Barons, Lackawanna County Stadium (10,800), Philadelphia
Syracuse (NY) Chiefs, MacArthur Stadium (8,316), Toronto

WESTERN DIVISION

Charlotte (Fort Mill, SC) Knights, Knights Castle (10,917), Florida
Columbus (OH) Clippers, Cooper Stadium (15,000), New York AL
Norfolk (VA) Tides, Harbor Park (12,000), New York NL
Richmond (VA) Braves, The Diamond (12,500), Atlanta
Toledo (OH) Mud Hens, Ned Skeldon Stadium (10,025), Detroit

PACIFIC COAST LEAGUE

NORTHERN DIVISION

Calgary (ALTA, Canada) Cannons, Burns Stadium (7,500), Pittsburgh
Edmonton (ALTA, Canada) Trappers, Edmonton Stadium (10,000), Oakland
Salt Lake (Salt Lake City, UT) Buzz, Franklin Quest Field (15,000), Minnesota
Tacoma (WA) Rainiers, Cheney Stadium (8,002), Seattle
Vancouver (BC, Canada) Canadians, Nat Bailey Stadium (6,500), California

SOUTHERN DIVISION

Albuquerque (NM) Dukes, Albuquerque Sports Stadium (10,510), Los Angeles
Colorado Springs (CO) Sky Sox, Sky Sox Stadium (6,130), Colorado
Las Vegas (NV) Stars, Cashman Field (9,370), San Diego
Phoenix (Scottsdale, AZ) Firebirds, Scottsdale Stadium (10,000), San Francisco
Tucson (AZ) Toros, Hi Corbett Field (9,500), Houston

AA

EASTERN LEAGUE

NORTHERN DIVISION

Binghamton (NY) Mets, Municipal Stadium (6,064), New York NL
Hardware City (New Britain, CT) Rock Cats, Beehive Field (4,700), Minnesota

New Haven (CT) Ravens, Yale Field (6,200), Colorado

Norwich (Yantic, CT) Navigators, Senator Thomas Dodd Stadium (6,000), New York AL

Portland (ME) Sea Dogs, Hadlock Field (6,000), Florida

SOUTHERN DIVISION

Bowie (MD) Baysox, Prince George's Stadium (10,000), Baltimore

Canton-Akron (Canton, OH) Indians, Thurman Munson Memorial Stadium (5,765), Cleveland

Harrisburg (PA) Senators, Riverside Stadium (5,600), Montreal

Reading (PA) Phillies, Municipal Stadium (7,500), Philadelphia

Trenton (NJ) Thunder, Waterfront Park (6,200), Boston

SOUTHERN LEAGUE

EASTERN DIVISION

Carolina (Zebulon, NC) Mudcats, Five County Stadium (6,000), Pittsburgh

Greenville (SC) Braves, Municipal Stadium (7,027), Atlanta

Jacksonville (FL) Suns, Wolfson Park (8,200), Detroit

Orlando (FL) Cubs, Tinker Field (6,000), Chicago NL

Port City (Wilmington, NC) Roosters, Brooks Field (4,000), Seattle

WESTERN DIVISION

Birmingham (AL) Barons, Hoover Metropolitan Stadium (10,000), Chicago AL

Chattanooga (TN) Lookouts, Engel Stadium (7,500), Cincinnati

Huntsville (AL) Stars, Joe W. Davis Stadium (10,200), Oakland

Knoxville (TN) Smokies, Bill Meyer Stadium (6,412), Toronto

Memphis (TN) Chicks, Tim McCarver Stadium (10,000), San Diego

TEXAS LEAGUE

EASTERN DIVISION

Arkansas (Little Rock, AR) Travelers, Ray Winder Field (6,082), St. Louis

Jackson (MS) Generals, Smith-Willis Stadium (5,200), Houston

Shreveport (LA) Captains, Fairgrounds Field (6,200), San Francisco

Tulsa (OK) Drillers, Drillers Stadium (10,500), Texas

WESTERN DIVISION

El Paso (TX) Diablos, Cohen Stadium (10,000), Milwaukee
Midland (TX) Angels, Angels Stadium (4,000), California
San Antonio (TX) Missions, Municipal Stadium (6,500), Los Angeles
Wichita (KS) Wranglers, Lawrence-Dumont Stadium (6,100), Kansas City

A

CALIFORNIA LEAGUE

NORTHERN DIVISION

Bakersfield (CA) Blaze, Sam Lynn Ballpark (3,200), Independent
Modesto (CA) A's, Thurman Field (2,500), Oakland
San Jose (CA) Giants, Municipal Stadium (4,500), San Francisco
Stockton (CA) Ports, Billy Hebert Field (3,500), Milwaukee
Visalia (CA) Oaks, Recreation Park (2,000), Independent

SOUTHERN DIVISION

High Desert (Adelanto, CA) Mavericks, Maverick Stadium (3,500), Baltimore
Lake Elsinore (CA) Storm, Lake Elsinore Diamond (6,000), California
Rancho Cucamonga (CA) Quakes, R. C. Sports Complex (4,600), San Diego
Riverside (CA) Pilots, Sports Center (3,500), Seattle
San Bernadino (CA) Spirit, Fiscalini Field (3,500), Los Angeles

CAROLINA LEAGUE

NORTHERN DIVISION

Frederick (MD) Keys, Harry Grover Stadium (5,400), Baltimore
Lynchburg (VA) Hill Cats, City Stadium (4,200), Pittsburgh
Prince William (Woodbridge, VA) Cannons, Prince William County Stadium (6,000), Chicago AL
Wilmington (DE) Blue Rocks, Legends Stadium (5,500), Kansas City

SOUTHERN DIVISION

Durham (NC) Bulls, Durham Athletic Park (9,033), Atlanta
Kinston (NC) Indians, Grainger Stadium (4,100), Cleveland
Salem (VA) Avalanche, Salem Baseball Stadium (6,000), Colorado
Winston-Salem (NC) Warthogs, Ernie Shore Field (6,280), Cincinnati

FLORIDA STATE LEAGUE

EASTERN DIVISION

Brevard County (Melbourne, FL) Manatees, Space Coast Stadium (7,200), Florida
Daytona (Daytona Beach, FL) Cubs, Jackie Robinson Ballpark (4,900), Chicago NL
Kissimmee (FL) Cobras, Osceola County Stadium (5,100), Houston
St. Lucie (Port St. Lucie, FL) Mets, St. Lucie County Sports Complex (7,400), New York NL
Vero Beach (FL) Dodgers, Holman Stadium (6,500), Los Angeles
West Palm Beach (FL) Expos, Municipal Stadium (4,400), Montreal

WESTERN DIVISION

Charlotte (Port Charlotte, FL) Rangers, Charlotte County Stadium (6,026), Texas
Clearwater (FL) Phillies, Jack Russell Stadium (7,385), Philadelphia
Dunedin (FL) Blue Jays, Grant Stadium (6,218), Toronto
Fort Myers (FL) Miracle, Lee County Sports Complex (7,500), Minnesota
Lakeland (FL) Tigers, Joker Marchant Stadium (7,000), Detroit
St. Petersburg (FL) Cardinals, Al Lang Stadium (7,004), St. Louis
Sarasota (FL) Red Sox, Ed Smith Stadium (7,500), Boston
Tampa (FL) Yankees, McEwen Field (3,000), New York AL

MIDWEST LEAGUE

EASTERN DIVISION

Fort Wayne (IN) Wizards, Memorial Stadium (6,000), Minnesota
Michigan (Battle Creek, MI) Battle Cats, C. O. Brown Stadium (6,200), Boston

South Bend (IN) Silver Hawks, Coveleski Stadium (5,000), Chicago AL

West Michigan (Comstock Park, MI) Whitecaps, Old Kent Park (5,500), Oakland

CENTRAL DIVISION

Beloit (WI) Snappers, Pohlman Field (3,500), Milwaukee

Kane County (Geneva, IL) Cougars, Elfstrom Stadium (4,800), Florida

Rockford (IL) Cubbies, Marinelli Field (4,300), Chicago NL

Wisconsin (Appleton, WI) Timber Rattlers, Fox Cities Stadium (3,200), Seattle

WESTERN DIVISION

Burlington (IA) Bees, Community Field (3,500), San Francisco

Cedar Rapids (IA) Kernels, Veterans Memorial Ballpark (6,000), California

Clinton (IA) Lumberkings, Riverview Stadium (3,400), San Diego

Peoria (IL) Chiefs, Pete Vonachen Stadium (6,200), St. Louis

Quad-City (Davenport, IA) River Bandits, John O'Donnell Stadium (5,500), Houston

Springfield (IL) Sultans, Lanphier Park (5,000), Kansas City

NEW YORK–PENN LEAGUE

McNAMARA DIVISION

Hudson Valley (Fishkill, NY) Renegades, Dutchess Stadium (4,000), Texas

New Jersey (Augusta, NJ) Cardinals, Skylands Park (4,331), St. Louis

Pittsfield (MA) Mets, Wahconah Park (5,200), New York NL

Vermont (Winooski, VT) Expos, Centennial Field (4,000), Montreal

PINCKNEY DIVISION

Auburn (NY) Astros, Falcon Park (2,500), Houston

Elmira (NY) Pioneers, Dunn Field (5,000), Florida

Oneonta (NY) Yankees, Damaschke Field (3,500), New York AL

Utica (NY) Blue Sox, Donovan Stadium (4,500), Boston

Watertown (NY) Indians, Alex T. Duffy Fairgrounds (3,500), Cleveland
Williamsport (PA) Cubs, Bowman Field (4,400), Chicago NL

STEDLER DIVISION

Batavia (NY) Clippers, Dwyer Stadium (3,000), Philadelphia
Erie (PA) Seawolves, Erie Ballpark (6,000), Pittsburgh
Jamestown (NY) Jammers, College Stadium (3,324), Detroit
St. Catharines (ONT, Canada) Stompers, Community Park (3,000), Toronto

NORTHWEST LEAGUE

NORTHERN DIVISION

Bellingham (WA) Giants, Joe Martin Stadium (2,200), San Francisco
Everett (WA) AquaSox, Everett Memorial Stadium (2,300), Seattle
Spokane (WA) Indians, Seafirst Stadium (8,314), Kansas City
Yakima (WA) Bears, Yakima County Stadium (4,485), Los Angeles

SOUTHERN DIVISION

Boise (ID) Hawks, Memorial Stadium (4,500), California
Eugene (OR) Emeralds, Civic Stadium (7,200), Atlanta
Portland (OR) Rockies, Civic Stadium (23,150), Colorado
Southern Oregon (Medford, OR) A's, Miles Field (2,900), Oakland

SOUTH ATLANTIC LEAGUE

NORTHERN DIVISION

Asheville (NC) Tourists, McCormick Field (4,000), Colorado
Charleston (WV) Alley Cats, Watt Powell Park (6,000), Cincinnati
Fayetteville (NC) Generals, J. P. Riddle Stadium (3,200), Detroit
Greensboro (NC) Bats, War Memorial Stadium (7,500), New York AL
Hagerstown (MD) Suns, Municipal Stadium (4,500), Toronto
Hickory (NC) Crawdads, L. P. Frans Stadium (4,500), Chicago AL
Piedmont (Kannapolis, NC) Phillies, Fieldcrest Cannon Stadium (4,700), Philadelphia

SOUTHERN DIVISION

Albany (GA) Polecats, Paul Eames Complex (4,200), Montreal
Augusta (GA) GreenJackets, Heaton Stadium (4,000), Pittsburgh

Capital City (Columbia, SC) Bombers, Capital City Stadium (6,100), New York NL
Charleston (SC) River Dogs, College Park Stadium (4,300), Texas
Columbus (GA) RedStixx, Golden Park (5,500), Cleveland
Macon (GA) Braves, Luther Williams Field (3,500), Atlanta
Savannah (GA) Cardinals, Grayson Stadium (8,000), St. Louis

ROOKIE

APPALACHIAN LEAGUE

NORTHERN DIVISION

Bluefield (WV) Orioles, Bowen Field (3,000), Baltimore
Burlington (NC) Indians, Burlington Athletic Stadium (3,500), Cleveland
Danville (VA) Braves, Dan Daniel Memorial Stadium (2,800), Atlanta
Martinsville (VA) Phillies, Hooker Field (3,200), Philadelphia
Princeton (WV) Reds, Hunnicutt Field (1,500), Cincinnati

SOUTHERN DIVISION

Bristol (VA) White Sox, DeVault Memorial Stadium (1,500), Chicago AL
Elizabethton (TN) Twins, Joe O'Brien Field (2,000), Minnesota
River City (Huntington, WV) Rumblers, St. Cloud Commons (3,200), MLB Co-Op
Johnson City (TN) Cardinals, Howard Johnson Field (3,250), St. Louis
Kingsport (TN) Mets, J. Fred Johnson Stadium (8,000), New York NL

ARIZONA LEAGUE

(This league does not charge admission, so no stadium capacities are available.)

Chandler (AZ) Brewers, Chandler Regional Park, Milwaukee
Mesa (AZ) Angels, Gene Autry Park, California
Mesa (AZ) Rockies, Fitch Park, Colorado
Peoria (AZ) Mariners, Peoria Sports Complex, Seattle

Peoria (AZ) Padres, Peoria Sports Complex, San Diego
Scottsdale (AZ) Athletics, Papago Park Complex, Oakland

GULF COAST LEAGUE

(This league does not charge admission, so no stadium capacities are available.)

NORTHERN DIVISION

Gulf Coast (Osceola, FL) Astros, Osceola County Stadium, Houston
Gulf Coast (Dunedin, FL) Blue Jays, Englebert Complex, Toronto
Gulf Coast (Lakeland, FL) Tigers, Joker Marchant Stadium, Detroit
Gulf Coast (Tampa, FL) Yankees, Yankee Complex, New York AL

EASTERN DIVISION

Gulf Coast (West Palm Beach, FL) Braves, Municipal Stadium, Atlanta
Gulf Coast (West Palm Beach, FL) Expos, Municipal Stadium, Montreal
Gulf Coast (Melbourne, FL) Marlins, Carl Barger Baseball Complex, Florida
Gulf Coast (Port St. Lucie, FL) Mets, Thomas J. White Stadium, New York NL

NORTHWEST DIVISION

Gulf Coast (Sarasota, FL) Orioles, Buck O'Neill Baseball Complex, Baltimore
Gulf Coast (Bradenton, FL) Pirates, Pirate City, Pittsburgh
Gulf Coast (Port Charlotte, FL) Rangers, Charlotte County Complex, Texas
Gulf Coast (Sarasota, FL) White Sox, Ed Smith Sports Complex, Chicago AL

SOUTHWEST DIVISION

Gulf Coast (Fort Myers, FL) Cubs, Red Sox Complex, Chicago NL
Gulf Coast (Fort Myers, FL) Red Sox, Red Sox Complex, Boston
Gulf Coast (Fort Myers, FL) Royals, Lee County Complex, Kansas City
Gulf Coast (Fort Myers, FL) Twins, Lee County Complex, Minnesota

PIONEER LEAGUE

NORTHERN DIVISION

Billings (MT) Mustangs, Cobb Field (4,500), Cincinnati
Great Falls (MT) Dodgers, Legion Park (3,834), Los Angeles
Lethbridge (ALTA, Canada) Mounties, Henderson Stadium (3,500), MLB Co-Op
Medicine Hat (ALTA, Canada) Blue Jays, Athletic Park (2,600), Toronto

SOUTHERN DIVISION

Butte (MT) Copper Kings, Alumni Coliseum (5,000), MLB Co-Op
Helena (MT) Brewers, Kindrick Legion Field (2,700), Milwaukee
Idaho Falls (ID) Braves, McDermott Field (3,800), San Diego
Ogden (UT) Raptors, Serge B. Simmons Field (5,000), Independent

Little League

The Little League is not the oldest program for young amateur ball players, but it certainly is the most famous. It was begun in 1939 by Carl E. Stotz of Williamsport, Pennsylvania, who decided that boys from about the ages of eight through 12 would benefit from more organized games of baseball. Only three teams in Williamsport played that year, and it cost only $35 to buy uniforms for the three clubs. The idea spread, and in 1940 another team was formed.

World War II put a slight damper on the program, but by 1946 there were 12 leagues in the system, all of them in Pennsylvania. When the war was over, Americans turned to baseball with renewed enthusiasm, and Little League began to take off. In 1947 the Hammonton, New Jersey, Little League became the first league established outside the state of

Pennsylvania. That same year, the first Little League World Series was played in Williamsport, and it was won by the Maynard Midgets of Williamsport.

WORLD SERIES SPURS GROWTH

The publicity from that first Series in 1947 greatly stimulated the growth of the Little League, and by 1948 there were 94 leagues with 416 teams. In 1949 the number almost doubled, and by 1950 there were 307 leagues. In 1951 there were 776, and the first Little League outside the United States was founded in British Columbia in Canada. By 1952 there were over 1,500 programs, and in 1953 the World Series was televised by CBS, with sportscaster Howard Cosell giving the play-by-play on radio.

The number of leagues rose to more than 3,000 in 1954, and by 1955, Little League baseball had spread to all of the states. In 1959, with the number of leagues up to over 5,000, President Dwight D. Eisenhower proclaimed the first National Little League Week in the second week in June. In 1960, Little League baseball had 5,500 leagues, the game had spread to Europe, and a team from Berlin in West Germany appeared in the World Series.

ORIGINAL IDEA EXPANDS

In 1961, Little League had proven so popular that it expanded to sponsor teams for boys aged 13 to 15. By this time the program had also spread to South America and the Far East. In 1968, Big League Baseball for players aged 16–18 was started, and there were more than 6,000 programs in the system. Girls were permitted to participate in Little League in 1974.

By 1978, Little League had grown to include over 6,500 Little Leagues for nine- to 12-year-olds, 2,850 Senior Leagues for 13- to 15-year-olds, and 1,300 Big League programs for 16- to 18-year-olds. Junior League Baseball was created for 13-year-olds in 1979.

By the 1980s, Little League could count over 14,000 leagues, with some 145,000 teams and 2.5 million youthful participants in over 30 countries (almost half of the teams and participants being in the United States). In 1989 the first graduate of the Little League program to be elected to the Baseball Hall of Fame in Cooperstown was inducted—outfielder Carl Yastrzemski of the Red Sox.

WORLD SERIES CHAMPIONS

Since the beginning of the Little League World Series, the finals have always been played in the city of its birth—Williamsport, Pennsylvania. Here are the winners:

1947—Maynard Midgets, Williamsport, Pennsylvania
1948—Lock Haven, Pennsylvania
1949—Hammonton, New Jersey
1950—Houston, Texas
1951—Stamford, Connecticut
1952—Norwalk, Connecticut
1953—Birmingham, Alabama
1954—Schenectady, New York
1955—Morrisville, Pennsylvania
1956—Roswell, New Mexico
1957—Monterrey, Mexico
1958—Monterrey, Mexico
1959—Hamtramck, Michigan
1960—Levittown, Pennsylvania
1961—El Cajon, California
1962—San Jose, California
1963—Granada Hills, California
1964—Mid Island, Staten Island, New York
1965—Windsor Locks, Connecticut
1966—Westbury American, Houston, Texas
1967—West Tokyo, Japan
1968—Osaka, Japan
1969—Taipei, Taiwan
1970—American, Wayne, New Jersey
1971—Tainan, Taiwan
1972—Taipei, Taiwan

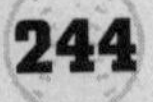

1973—Tainan City, Taiwan
1974—Kao Hsiung, Taiwan
1975—Lakewood, New Jersey
1976—Tokyo, Japan
1977—Kao Hsiung, Taiwan
1978—Pin-Tung, Taiwan
1979—Hsien, Taiwan
1980—Hua Lian, Taiwan
1981—Tai-Chung, Taiwan
1982—Kirkland National, Kirkland, Washington
1983—East Marietta National, Marietta, Georgia
1984—Seoul National, Seoul, South Korea
1985—Seoul National, Seoul, South Korea
1986—Tainan Park, Taiwan
1987—Hua Lian, Taiwan
1988—Tai-Chung, Taiwan
1989—Trumbull, Connecticut
1990—Taipei, Taiwan
1991—Tai-Chung, Taiwan
1992—Long Beach, California
1993—Long Beach, California
1994—Maracaibo, Venezuela
1995—Tainan, Taipei, Taiwan

In the Little League World Series of 1992, history was made on a number of fronts. The first was that the games were played in a round-robin format, which gave losers a second chance, since a team would have to be beaten twice in order to be knocked out of the competition. The second was that it was decided to have night games. The first Little League World Series night game was played on August 24, 1992, and the Hamilton Square, New Jersey, club beat Lake Charles, Louisiana, 5–0.

A most unusual thing happened after the 1992 World Series. Zamboanga City of the Philippines had beaten Long Beach, California, 15–4, in the championship game. But it was found that the Filipinos had used eight ineligible players, and the California team was awarded the championship by the 6–0 score of a forfeited Little League game.

FAMOUS LITTLE LEAGUERS

The list of people who went from Little League to success in sports and other fields is almost endless. Perhaps the most outstanding baseball example is Carl Yastrzemski, the Red Sox outfielder, who was the first Little Leaguer to go on to be elected to the Baseball Hall of Fame. Here are some of the others. (Teams listed are those the players are most associated with.)

Kareem Abdul-Jabbar (Los Angeles Lakers basketball player)
Bill Bradley (U.S. senator and New York Knicks basketball player)
George Brett (Royals third baseman)
Joseph Campanella (actor)
Gary Carter (Expos, Mets catcher)
Vince Coleman (Cardinals, Mariners outfielder)
Danny DeVito (actor)
Mike Ditka (Chicago Bears football coach)
Rollie Fingers (A's pitcher)
Doug Flutie (Calgary Stampeders quarterback)
Steve Garvey (Dodgers first baseman)
Mike Greenwell (Red Sox outfielder)
Tony Gwynn (Padres outfielder)
Orel Hershiser (Dodgers, Indians pitcher)
Tommy John (Yankees pitcher)
Davey Lopes (Dodgers second baseman)
Lee Mazzilli (Mets, Pirates outfielder)
Dale Murphy (Braves, Phillies outfielder)
Eddie Murray (Orioles, Indians first baseman)
Brent Musburger (TV sportscaster)
Jim Palmer (Orioles pitcher)
Dan Quayle (U.S. vice president)
Kurt Russell (actor)
Nolan Ryan (Angels, Astros, Rangers pitcher)
Ron Santo (Cubs third baseman)
Mike Schmidt (Phillies third baseman)
Don Schollander (Olympic gold medal swimmer)
Tom Seaver (Mets, Reds, White Sox pitcher)

Tom Selleck (actor)
Bruce Springsteen (rock singer)
Mel Stottlemyre (Yankees pitcher)
Don Sutton (Dodgers pitcher)
Al Trautwig (TV sportscaster)

American Legion

Although Little League has become almost synonymous with organized baseball for young Americans, it was not the first such program. The American Legion Junior League was founded in 1925 to sponsor teams for teenagers up to the age of 17. The first national competition was held in 1926, and by 1929 there was at least one team representing each of the then 48 states.

In 1950, 18-year-olds were admitted, and the word "Junior" was dropped from the official name. The program also later spread to the two newest states, Alaska and Hawaii, as well as to Puerto Rico and the Panama Canal Zone. The program depends on the sponsorship of American Legion posts, so it cannot spread as far as Little League can. By the 1970s, there were some 3,200 teams in American Legion baseball involving boys from 16 to 18 years of age.

Other Youth Leagues

Several other programs sponsor baseball teams for young amateurs. The largest organization in the United States that sponsors amateur baseball teams for players of all ages is the American Amateur Baseball Congress (AABC), founded in 1935 as the American Baseball Congress (the word "Amateur" was added in 1955), with its headquarters in Battle Creek, Michigan. Its program began with adult teams, but over the years it expanded to include five youth divisions: Pee Wee Reese (12 and under), Sandy Koufax (14 and under), Mickey Mantle (16 and under), Connie Mack (18 and under), and Stan Musial (19 and older). The AABC includes over 3,000 teams and has about 75,000 participants.

The Pony League (standing for Protect Our Nation's Youth) was founded in Washington, Pennsylvania, in 1950 for boys ages 13 and 14. A similar program, the Colt League, was founded in 1953 in

Martins Ferry, Ohio, for boys ages 15 and 16. The Colt League merged with similar programs, and in 1959 it joined with the Pony League to form Boys' Baseball, operating out of Washington, Pennsylvania. The organization later started a Junior League for boys ages eight to 12.

Another well-known program is the Babe Ruth League, which was originally called the Little Bigger League. It was founded in 1952 in Trenton, New Jersey, for boys ages 13 to 15.

In addition, some 15,000 U.S. junior high and high schools sponsor at least one baseball team, with perhaps 500,000 participating young people.

Colleges and Universities

When the minor leagues began to decline in the 1970s and 1980s, another source of baseball talent had to emerge. The major league clubs turned their attention to the college and university baseball teams. For a long time these teams were virtually ignored at schools where thousands turned out for football and basketball games, but they began to attract serious players and spectators, as well as scouts from the major league teams. Since 1963 organized baseball has supported summer leagues for promising undergraduates.

In 1947 the National Collegiate Athletic Association (NCAA) established a World Series for college baseball teams. The winners of this competition are as follows:

1947—University of California–Berkeley
1948—University of Southern California
1949—University of Texas
1950—University of Texas
1951—University of Oklahoma
1952—College of the Holy Cross
1953—University of Michigan
1954—University of Missouri
1955—Wake Forest University
1956—University of Minnesota
1957—University of California–Berkeley
1958—University of Southern California

1959—Oklahoma State University
1960—University of Minnesota
1961—University of Southern California
1962—University of Michigan
1963—University of Southern California
1964—University of Minnesota
1965—Arizona State University
1966—Ohio State University
1967—Arizona State University
1968—University of Southern California
1969—Arizona State University
1970—University of Southern California
1971—University of Southern California
1972—University of Southern California
1973—University of Southern California
1974—University of Southern California
1975—University of Texas
1976—University of Arizona
1977—Arizona State University
1978—University of Southern California
1979—California State University–Fullerton
1980—University of Arizona
1981—Arizona State University
1982—University of Miami–Florida
1983—University of Texas
1984—California State University–Fullerton
1985—University of Miami–Florida
1986—University of Arizona
1987—Stanford University
1988—Stanford University
1989—Wichita State University
1990—University of Georgia
1991—Louisiana State University
1992—Pepperdine University
1993—Louisiana State University
1994—University of Oklahoma
1995—California State University–Fullerton

Women's Baseball

On November 5, 1988, the Baseball Hall of Fame in Cooperstown, New York, finally recognized the fact that there have been women baseball players too (over 550 of them) by opening a permanent exhibition called "Women in Baseball." It is a celebration of the All-American Girls Professional Baseball League, which featured women's teams from 1943 to 1954.

The AAGPBL was founded late in 1942 by Philip K. Wrigley, the owner of the Chicago Cubs, who feared that major league play might be suspended during World War II. Of course, the major leagues never shut down, but the women's league provided good, hard-nosed baseball that at its peak of popularity drew a million paying fans in 1948. A series of basesball cards was printed for the women.

And despite the hullabaloo in 1988 when the Cubs finally installed lights for night games at Wrigley Field, history tells us that at least two AAGPBL games were played there in the mid-1940s at night, under temporary lights.

The players, wearing short-skirted uniforms, played real baseball, not softball—hardball, overhand, stealing, sliding—for the following teams in the Midwest:

Battle Creek (Michigan) Belles
Chicago (Illinois) Colleens
Fort Wayne (Indiana) Daisies
Grand Rapids (Michigan) Chicks
Kalamazoo (Michigan) Lassies
Kenosha (Wisconsin) Comets
Milwaukee (Wisconsin) Chicks
Minneapolis (Minnesota) Millerettes
Muskegon (Michigan) Belles
Muskegon (Michigan) Lassies
Peoria (Illinois) Redwings
Racine (Wisconsin) Belles
Rockford (Illinois) Peaches
South Bend (Indiana) Blue Sox
Springfield (Illinois) Sallies

The regimen was strict, which was appropriate for those more innocent days. The women could not drink or smoke. They had to wear makeup on the field. They could not wear pants on or off the field. They were given grooming and deportment lessons. And their chaperone (every team had one) had to approve of any man who took a player out on a date.

The seasons were tough. The 15-team league played 115 to 127 games a season—often seven days a week with a doubleheader on Sundays. The players had to play hurt, since each team had a maximum of 15 players, with no minor league to furnish relief. No wonder Alice "Lefty" Holmayer McNaughton, a former Kenosha Comets pitcher and first baseman, recently put down modern male major leaguers with: "Boys today, they get a hangnail and they can't play."

For all this, the women were paid a small amount. In the beginning years they earned as little as $50 a week. Toward the end, they got as much as $125 per week.

Eventually, the league disappeared for lack of sponsorship. Then, too, the major league men returned from the armed forces, and wartime gas rationing ended and people could travel to see men play in the larger cities.

Only in 1992 were people reminded of the AAGPBL. The film *A League of Their Own* told a tiny bit of the story. And a book was published that chronicled the women of the diamond—*Girls of Summer: In Their Own League*, by Lois Browne.

There have been more than 125 father-son baseball-playing duos. But there has been only one example of a major league ball player who had a major league mother. Helen Callaghan St. Aubin, an outfielder for the Fort Wayne Daisies, was once compared to Ted Williams for her hitting ability. Her son, Casey Candaele, played second base for the Montreal Expos and Houston Astros.

A judge's decision in the early 1970s that girls should be permitted play Little League baseball began to turn things around again for women in the overall sport. Women's teams began to appear, and even women's leagues were born. One of them, the American Women's Baseball Association in suburban Chicago, dates back to 1988. Today, women's leagues can be found all over the country.

The most unique single team, however, is the Colorado Silver Bullets—a group of women who play exhibition games against minor league, semi-pro, and over-30 teams of men. Formed in 1994, it is a truly professional team inasmuch as the players are paid $20,000 for the season—three times more than many male minor leaguers are paid. So much attention did the Bullets attract that the great tennis star Martina Navratilova asked for a tryout in 1995, claiming that she had been getting instruction and had been working out in the batting cages—hoping to be picked to play either first base or outfield.

Pure Nostalgia

Without doubt, the strangest baseball league ever devised was the Senior Professional Baseball Association. It played one whole season, from November 1, 1989, to February 4, 1990. In the middle of its second season, it collapsed because of weak financial management.

The league was set up to feature former major league players ages 35 and over (catchers could play at age 32). The teams were located in Florida, where it was figured that retired people would be big fans. They weren't.

There were eight teams, and Curt Flood, the former star outfielder of the Cardinals, was named commissioner of the league. Among the managers were Earl Weaver (former Orioles manager) of the Gold Coast Suns, Dick Williams (former manager of the Red Sox, A's, Angels, Expos, Padres, and Mariners) of the Palm Beach Tropics, Bill "The Spaceman" Lee (former pitcher for the Red Sox and Expos) of the Winter Haven Super Sox, and Bobby Tolan (former outfielder for the Cardinals, Reds, Padres, and other teams) of the St. Petersburg Pelicans.

A number of former major league stars signed aboard—who can say whether it was for the purpose of reliving old glories, making money, or even of getting another chance at the big leagues? Among them were Vida Blue (former pitcher for the A's, Giants, and Royals); Graig Nettles (former outfielder/third baseman for the Indians,

Yankees, and other teams); Dock Ellis (former pitcher for the Pirates and other teams); Luis Tiant (former pitcher for the Indians, Red Sox, and other teams); Dave Kingman (former first baseman/third baseman/outfielder/DH for the Giants, Mets, Yankees, and other teams); and Joaquin Andujar (former pitcher for the Astros, Cardinals, and A's).

For what it's worth, the first and only championship was won by the St. Petersburg Pelicans.

Foreign Leagues

Baseball was born in the United States, but it has become popular in other countries over the years. Part of this popularity stems from the fact that Americans have carried the game with them wherever they have gone, both in peace and in war. American servicemen, for example, have been playing the game among themselves for many years now, and in so doing have introduced the game to many people around the world. The American-based Little League has also spread the game among young people in many countries.

It seems natural that baseball would be played widely and well in neighboring countries of the United States—Canada and Mexico. After all, their minor league teams have long fed players to the major leagues. There was even an attempt in 1946 by wealthy Mexicans to start a third major league, but it was quickly squelched by U.S. organized baseball.

THE LATIN AMERICAN CONNECTION

Baseball has been extremely popular throughout Latin America and the Caribbean Islands, and not only in places where the United States has had direct contacts, such as Puerto Rico, Panama, and the Virgin Islands. Baseball is popular in Venezuela, Nicaragua, and the Dominican Republic, and there is a lengthening list of players from those countries who have moved up to become prominent players in the major leagues. And during the winter in North America, it has long been the custom of many players in the major leagues to play with various Latin American teams, which, since 1947, have had their own Latin American championship series.

Cuba is a special case. Baseball was played there as early as 1878, and eventually Cuba supported a team, the Havana Cubans, which belonged to the Triple A International League. After Fidel Castro (who was good enough to have had a minor league contract offer to play baseball in the United States) took over as leader, the United

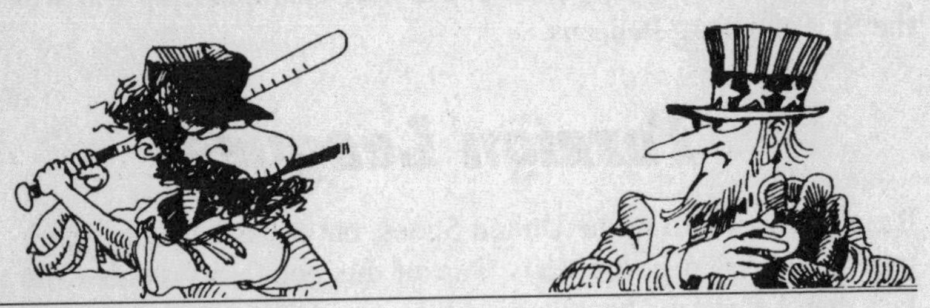

States severed diplomatic relations with Cuba in 1961, thus cutting off movement between the two countries. *Béisbol* has become the Cuban national game, and the Cubans are good enough to win more than their fair share of gold medals in the Olympics and the Pan American Games. Actually, Cuban baseball has been rated as being at least at the AA or AAA level—and they are amateurs.

Mexico is another hotbed of *béisbol*. The Mexican League, with its 116-game schedule, is a member of the St. Petersburg, Florida–based National Association of Professional Baseball Leagues and is classified as a Triple A organization. In 1994 the league drew more than 3 million spectators. Here are the 16 teams in the Mexican League.

NORTHERN DIVISION

Aguascalientes (Aguascalientes) Rioleros
Jalisco (Guadalajara, Jalisco) Cowboys
Laredo (Nuevo Laredo, Tamaulipas) Owls
Monclova (Coahuila) Acereros
Monterrey (Nuevo León) Sultanes
Reynosa (Tamaulipas) Broncos
Saltillo (Coahuila) Saraperos
Union Laguna (Torreón, Coahuila) Algondoneros

SOUTHERN DIVISION

Campeche (Campeche) Pirates
Mexico City (Federal District) Rojos Diablos
Mexico City (Federal District) Tigers
Minatitlan (Veracruz) Petroleros
Puebla (Puebla) Pericos
Tabasco (Villahermosa, Tabasco) Olmecas
Veracruz (Boca del Rio, Veracruz) Aguilas
Yucatan (Mérida, Yucatan) Leones

The Dominican Republic is also *béisbol* country. The Dominican League plays a winter schedule at about the AAA level and provides a home for many major leaguers. The Dominican Summer League, with its 22 teams in four divisions, is rated at the Rookie level. All but one of the teams is an affiliate of one, or sometimes two, major league teams.

Venezuela's Venezuelan League plays a 60-game October-December season of *béisbol.* Experts rate it at the AA level.

Puerto Rico has the Puerto Rican *Béisbol* League. Its 54-game season runs from November to January. This league is also rated at the AAA level.

ACROSS THE PACIFIC

Besuboru was introduced to Japan by Horace Wilson, an American teacher in Tokyo, in 1873. The sport caught on quickly and was supported by schools and universities, spurred on by occasional tours by American collegiate teams. Until the 1930s, baseball in Japan was an amateur sport, with the strongest teams coming out of the Japanese universities.

Then came the visits of All-Star teams of American professionals in 1931 and—with Babe Ruth—1934. Since then, the Japanese have embraced baseball. They now support two major leagues, the Pacific and the Central, each with six clubs that play 130-game seasons and their own Japan Series. The games draw huge crowds. One difference, however, is that the teams in Japan are owned by big industrial companies, unlike the U.S. teams. To this day, the Japanese university teams remain the "farm teams" for the professional leagues, which played at a high AAA level.

In Australia, there is the Australian Baseball League, which plays a 64-game season from October to February. Their game has been characterized as low-level A.

In Taiwan, the Chinese Professional Baseball League plays a 100-game *pang ch'iu* season from March to November. The Taiwan game is about at A level.

South Korea's Korea Baseball Organization plays its 63-game season from April to September. Their level of *va-goo* is about at the A level, but lower level, to be sure.

ACROSS THE ATLANTIC

Ever since World War II, when Italian youngsters saw American soldiers playing baseball during their brief recreational times, America's national game has been popular in Italy. Today, this country is regarded as Europe's leading power in the game. The Italian Baseball Federation has a 54-game season from April to September, and the players are at the good Rookie League level.

But the Italians are not alone. In France, La Fédération Françoise de Baseball, de Softball et de Criket boasts a 28-game baseball season. The games are played from March to October. But the organization is rated at below the Rookie League level.

In the Netherlands, the Royal Dutch Baseball Federation has a 35-game baseball season. This *honkbal* league rates at about the Rookie League level.

While soccer and cricket are still the favorite team sports in England, there is a group called the London Baseball Association. The teams have been playing in Hampstead Heath, a huge park in London, for almost 20 years.

Baseball has yet to catch on elsewhere around the world as it has in Japan and in Latin America, but it has truly become international.

Science at the Ball Game

Most baseball players don't realize it, but they are constantly being influenced by science and technology. Here are some explanations of how science and technology have shaped the game of baseball.

HOW DOES A RUNNER ATTEMPT TO STEAL SECOND?

A runner on first base trying to steal second must get to second base during the time that it takes the pitcher to deliver the pitch and the catcher to catch the ball and throw it back to the second baseman or shortstop, who will attempt to tag out the runner.

Of course, the runner has taken a lead off first base. That means that the distance to be run has been cut down, which will shorten the runner's time in running from first to second base. And the runner will probably slide into second base.

WHAT'S THE PURPOSE OF A SLIDE?

Does sliding help a runner to get to second base any faster? Of course not. It does help him or her come in under the throw, but the opposing infielder is expecting that and will try to tag the runner low down. Actually, the runner is using the slide to slow down. Running flat out might cause him or her to run across second base, and the runner must stop there or he or she can be tagged out for not being on the base. The runner is really using the friction between the body and the ground to decrease acceleration and stop in a hurry.

WHY DOES A RUNNER ROUND THE BASES?

Inertia has been defined as the characteristic of all bodies that causes them either to stay at rest or to stay in constant motion—that is, unless an outside force acts upon the bodies. We have all experienced this when an automobile goes around a turn. Remember that objects tend to go in a straight line. If a turn is taken too fast without seat belts being fastened, we tend to slide right across the seat.

Now suppose a batter is trying to score an inside-the-park home run. The batter must run as fast as possible, so he or she does not run straight to first base, turn left, run straight to second base, turn left, etc. What must be done is called rounding the bases.

If the player were to make a sharp turn at each base, it would be necessary to stop, then turn, and then head to the next base. There is no time for that, so the runner must follow a curved path around the infield, fighting inertia while keeping most of his or her speed. Running in a curved path is easier than stopping at each base and making a 90-degree turn toward the next base.

Think of how a runner tries to beat out an infield hit. He or she runs straight toward first base, trying to beat the throw. This is covering the shortest distance between home and first. But if the player thinks there is a chance to stretch the hit into a double, he or she will follow a curved path toward first, therefore being in a position to make the turn toward second more effectively.

HOW DOES A PLAYER CATCH A HARD-HIT LINE DRIVE?

Newton's second law of motion says that the net force on a mass is directly proportional to, and in the same direction as, the acceleration of that mass. In other words, force = mass times acceleration, or F = ma. The mass stays the same, of course, so if the force increases or decreases, so will the acceleration. And if the acceleration increases or decreases, so will the force.

When an infielder catches a hard-hit line drive, he or she does it automatically. The ball is still traveling along an almost straight line, and it may even still be accelerating. What does the player do? Stand like a statue, holding the glove where he or she knows the ball will hit it? No. That would hurt.

Instead, just as the ball hits the glove, the player moves his or her arm and hand back with the ball in the glove. And if the ball is a real screamer, the player's whole body may move backward. This is not because he or she is knocked back by the force of the ball. What is happening is that the arm, hand, and body "give" a little bit, and this spreads the force of the ball hitting the glove over a greater span of time. The point is that when a ball is caught, its speed must be reduced to zero almost immediately. By having the hand give on impact, the player is increasing, by a fraction of a second, the time of reducing the speed to zero. The result is that the hand feels less shock and does not sting as much.

HOW DOES A PLAYER THROW A BALL TO MAKE IT GO FARTHER?

Everyone knows that the acceleration due to gravity is with us all the time. Drop a glass, and it will fall to the floor. Gravity acts on any thrown object, too. You know that your throw is eventually going to hit the ground, so if you want the ball to go farther, you have to keep it in the air longer, before gravity forces it to earth.

To do this a player must increase the angle of the throw when he or she wants it to carry a longer distance. Throwing to the plate from center field requires an arched throw, which will keep the ball in the air. If it is thrown flat, even with the same amount of force, it will hit the ground sooner.

But that doesn't mean that the pitcher, when throwing a fastball the short distance to the catcher's mitt, can throw a flat ball. He or she, too, must put some arch in it, although not as much as the center fielder.

As soon as the ball leaves the pitcher's hand, gravity begins pulling it downward. Even the fastest pitcher's smokeball may drop as much as 2½ feet by the time it reaches the catcher. That's why there is such a thing as a pitcher's mound. Even so, the pitcher must always aim a little higher than the point where he or she wants the ball to go.

The pitcher knows that the ball will reach a point where its upward acceleration will be zero and the ball will start to drop.

CAN PITCHING BE LEARNED?

Two researchers—Dr. Joe P. Bramhall, a team physician at Texas A&M University, and Dr. Charles Dillman, of the American Sports Medicine Institute—videotaped the deliveries of 48 major league pitchers, including Dwight Gooden, Nolan Ryan, Roger Clemens, and Dave Stewart. They found out that, although these men have different styles, from a scientific point of view they still pitch in the same way. As far as the arm angle, elbow angle, shoulder angles, and balance were concerned, these men do the same things.

The purpose of the study was to teach young players the correct way to pitch and thus prevent them from making mistakes that might lead to injuries of the pitching arm. The researchers came up with some rules:

1. In the windup, the pitcher should be balanced at the top of the leg kick, coiled, and ready to spring forward.
2. The length of the stride should be slightly less than the body height. The left foot of a right-hander (or the right foot of a left-hander) should step directly toward home plate, moving to the side six inches or less.
3. In the delivery, the back rotation of the shoulder should not be greater than 165 to 180 degrees. The elbow should be flexed between 70 and 115 degrees.
4. In the follow-through, a smooth, extended motion should slow down the pitching arm gradually. The throwing shoulder should be aligned over the opposite knee after the release of the ball. The upper body should be slightly flexed.

HOW IS THE CURVEBALL THROWN?

The most common effect of spin in sports is something that some people do not believe exists—the curveball in baseball. You can still find some people who think that the curveball is just an optical illusion.

The argument of whether a baseball can curve went on for so many years that scientists finally got into the act. A long strip of lightweight tape was attached to a baseball. Then a major league pitcher was asked to throw a curveball. This is usually done by gripping the ball with the thumb and first two fingers only, with the inside of the thumb pressed against one of the seams of the ball. The ball is then released with a sharp outward snap of the wrist. And the friction between the ball and the thumb and fingers starts it spinning as it heads toward the plate.

After the pitcher threw the ball, the scientists counted the number of twists in the tape. This gave them the number of complete spins the ball had made. Then the ball was placed in a wind tunnel and spun at the same rate. The results indicated that it is possible to make a ball curve as much as 18 inches away from a straight line within a distance of 60 feet, six inches—the official distance from the pitcher's mound to the plate. But the ball must be traveling about 100 feet per second and spinning at a rate of 1,800 revolutions per minute.

Here is what happens: Any thrown object meets air resistance, almost as if there were a wall of air rushing to resist it. But the spinning ball changes this solid wall of air. Suppose that it is thrown by a right-handed, sidearm pitcher. The spinning ball pulls air around it, but the pressure is increased on the right side (toward third base) and decreased on the left (toward first base). It is spinning counterclockwise, in the same direction that a base runner runs around the bases.

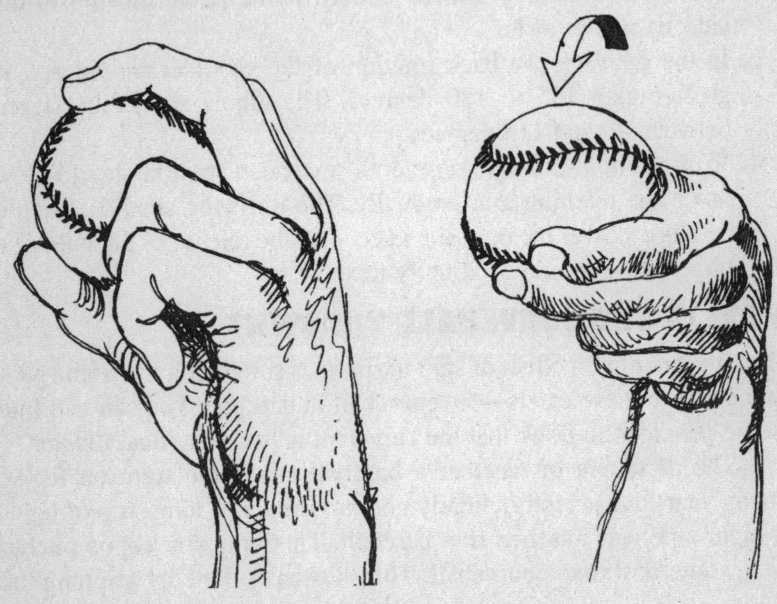

The increased pressure on the right side runs into the wall of air that has piled up in front of the ball and causes the ball to veer to the left. The ball is following the path of least resistance, as the air pressure is lower on the left side. By the way, a curveball thrown by a sidearm left-hander would curve in the opposite direction, since the ball is spinning clockwise.

HOW IS THE KNUCKLEBALL THROWN?

The knuckleball, too, depends on air resistance. It is a tricky pitch, and most catchers hate to be part of the battery with a knuckleball pitcher. You never know where it is going—toward the dugout, toward the batter—moving erratically up, down, or sideways as much as 11 inches. The reasons for this are the seams on the baseball and the pitch's slow rotation of as little as a half-spin between the mound and the plate. That's against the typical fastball's eight-time rotation.

The ball is held with the index and middle fingers (and the nails) digging into the ball just behind the seam's loop, with the other two fingers on the side of the ball and the thumb along the side of the underseam. The drag is greater on the smooth, unstitched part of the ball, and the ball gets a deflecting push from the smooth side toward the stitched side. As the stitches rotate, the force changes direction. The less spin, the more deflection.

HOW DOES A BAT WORK?

One of the common simple machines used in baseball is really a lever—it's the bat. A lever is only a stiff bar arranged to turn around some fixed point. The bar does not even have to be straight. The fixed point is called the "fulcrum." The function of the lever is to change the position of a load by applying a force. In the case of the baseball bat, the fulcrum is at the small end, the force is at the point where you grip the bat, and the load is where the ball strikes the bat.

A lot of people argue about what is the best bat. There are those who stick with the old-fashioned wooden bat (including the professional leagues) and those who opt for the aluminum type. And others think the only difference is the sound the bat makes when it hits the ball.

But mechanical engineering students at Tufts University in Medford, Massachusetts, decided to do some investigating in 1991.

They used a bat that weighed 32 ounces, had a diameter of 2¾ inches (a quarter-inch thicker than standard wood and aluminum bats), and was made of materials that included wood, glass-fiber composites, resins, and fabrics. It supposedly responded like a hardwood bat and had the durability of an aluminum bat.

Developed by Steven Baum of Traverse City, Michigan, it was tested on the Tufts campus by the baseball team (only in practice), and the Boston Red Sox and Detroit Tigers used it in spring training. The idea was to market the bat first to minor league teams, since wood bats have such a long tradition in the major leagues.

One of the Tufts players claimed that the experimental bat had a bigger "sweet spot" than the usual bat. But he pointed out that it stung more than an aluminum bat if he didn't hit the ball on that sweet spot.

WHAT MAKES A PLAYER A GOOD HOME RUN HITTER?

Everyone loves a home run hitter, and some years ago a study was made on several home run hitters. You might guess that they had more going for them than mere strength. James L. Breen, the head of the Department of Physical Education at Tulane University in New Orleans, found that there were mechanical traits that great home run hitters had in common. He came up with his list by studying hundreds of major league batters and thousands of feet of film. Finally, he concentrated on six of the leading home run hitters of the 1950s and 1960s: Stan Musial (Cardinals), Ernie Banks (Cubs), Hank Aaron (Braves), Willie Mays (Giants), Ted Williams (Red Sox), and Mickey Mantle (Yankees).

Breen's list of mechanical traits was made up of four items.

1. The center of gravity of the player followed a level plane throughout the swing. (The center of gravity of a body is that point in the object at which the mass is evenly distributed in all directions.)
2. From his stance, the batter was able to adjust his head from pitch to pitch.
3. The length of stride was the same on all pitches.
4. After contact with the ball, the upper body position was in the same general direction as the flight of the ball.

Breen also found that if the body is kept level at the center of gravity, the bat will be swung in a level path. This is the most effective kind of swing. Having the proper head position lets the batter watch the pitch for the longest amount of time. This is especially important when the pitch is a breaking ball, such as a curve or a sinking fastball. The longer the batter follows the pitch with his eyes, the better he will be able to see the point at which the pitch breaks. Also, by holding his head properly, the batter can reduce the angle at which he sees the ball—which means he will see it more clearly.

If the batter keeps his arms straight when he is swinging, he can bring the bat around much faster than if his arms are bent. Hitters who bend their arms tend to pull the handle of the bat around as they swing. That messes up the lever action of the bat.

Quicker bat speed, along with the ability to watch the ball for the longest period of time, helps the batter to judge more accurately where the ball will be when it is hit. The average batter, looking at a pitch that is traveling 80 miles per hour, has to start his swing when the ball is about 33 feet from the plate. The home run hitters in this study were able to wait until the ball was only 24 feet from the plate.

The speed of the swing from the time the bat was swung until contact was made varied in this group of hitters. Musial's time was 0.19 seconds, and Williams's time was 0.23 seconds. An average hitter's speed would be about 0.28 seconds.

Each of these hitters, although their batting stances were different, took the same straightforward stride as he swung. And each had a similar follow-through motion. As the bat was swung, they pushed off on the back foot, putting all of their force in one direction. Their weight was taken off the back foot when contact was made with the ball, which shifted the center of gravity of their bodies in the direction of the ball. Poorer hitters often shift their centers of gravity backward by putting their weight on the back foot. This results in a loss of power. Gravity, stride, straight arms, head position—whatever these men were doing, they obviously were doing it right.

MORE ON THE SCIENCE OF HITTING

You can forget your thinking caps. Baseball, with its many strategies, is often thought of as being a thinking person's game. But it may be that the smartest hitters leave their brains in the dugout. Yogi Berra's statement that he couldn't think while he hit might have been one of the smartest things that that baseball analyst ever said.

Tom Hanson, a baseball coach at Skidmore College in Saratoga Springs, New York, wrote his doctoral dissertation on the thinking hitter. He claimed that batters simply have no time to think during the four-tenths of a second it takes a good fastball to go from the pitcher's hand to the catcher's mitt. Hanson contended: "If you are thinking, you are in trouble. Information should go from your eyes to your hands and bypass the brain." The best hitters, he found, are the most relaxed hitters. "The key is not to get tense and anxious. That tightens the muscles and a tight muscle is a slow muscle."

And Judson Berkey, a senior at Thomas Jefferson High School for Science and Technology, designed a computer model in 1991 to simulate the flight of a baseball. He had come across a study by scientists at Tulane University that assumed that the spin of the ball does not decrease as it travels through the air. That didn't make sense to Berkey, who pointed out that "the ball doesn't come down whizzing through the air. It's coming down pretty soft."

From his computer work, he theorized that to launch a ball the farthest, a batter should connect with the ball at an angle between 32 and 40 degrees from the horizontal and apply as much backspin as possible.

As he said, and you might have to go to a physics teacher to get this translated: “Previous research stated that the vertical launch angle of the baseball from a baseball bat that maximizes the distance the ball travels decreases considerably as the magnitude of the spin increases. These results, however, neglected two aspects of a baseball in flight. They neglected to consider the variation of the coefficient of drag with the velocity of the baseball and the spin reduction due to the torque that is produced by the spin of the baseball.”

Finally, Dr. Paul Lagace of the Massachusetts Institute of Technology noticed something after the roof behind home plate in Boston’s Fenway Park was torn down following the 1988 season and replaced with a higher one. Balls that once soared into the stands were falling short.

He had students in his aeronautics and astronautics courses build a wooden model of the ballpark. The model was then put in a wind tunnel for tests. He found that the higher stands created a vortex, or backwind, that could cause a fly ball hit to center field to travel about ten feet less.

Index